What are the Questions ?

AND OTHER ESSAYS

BY JOAN ROBINSON

What are the Questions ?

AND OTHER ESSAYS

Further Contributions to Modern Economics

M. E. SHARPE, INC., ARMONK, NEW YORK

This edition published in 1981 by M. E. Sharpe, Inc., 80 Business Park Drive, Armonk, New York 10504

Library of Congress Cataloging in Publication Data

Robinson, Joan, 1903-
    What are the questions?
    1. Economics—Addresses, essays, lectures.
I. Title.
HB171.R6443   330   80-28062
ISBN 0-87332-199-5
ISBN 0-87332-200-2 (pbk.)

Published in the United States of America

TO MY CRITICS

CONTENTS

ASPECTS OF MARXISM

INTRODUCTION

MY first volume of collected papers (1951) was dedicated to my pupils because of the incentive that they gave me to try to express what I had to say as comprehensibly as possible. The present volume is dedicated to my critics because of the incentive that they have given me to try to think out what I had to say as coherently as possible.

The previous collection of *Contributions to Modern Economics* (1978) covered a span of fifty years. The present one is mainly concentrated on the dismal 1970s.

The first group of papers — Analysis — contains some discussions of methodological principles and a few examples of their application. The methodology is self-conscious. I hold very strongly that the purpose of economic theory should be to try to throw some light on the world that we are living in. (The history of economic doctrines is a separate study.) It should proceed by advancing hypotheses which are in principle refutable. But to sort out the questions to be discussed it is often necessary to pass through a phase of purely logical, *a priori* argument — intellectual experiment — before hypotheses can be formulated. There are many interacting elements in any economic situation; we cannot control our experiments so as to observe the effect of a single change *other things remaining the same*, still less the concomitants of a difference in a single element in the complex, since one variable cannot display two values at one point in time and space.

Unfortunately, it is often necessary to begin by clearing out of the way unsatisfactory thought experiments which are already established in the field.

1

After the Keynesian revolution, what used to be the central topic of textbook economics — the normal long-run prices of particular commodities – appeared to fall into decay. It was treated in scraps of incompatible models – a Walrasian market where individuals exchange items from their 'endowments' of ready-made goods; specifications of Pigovian supply curves which remain, as ever, empty economic boxes, and a treatment of 'factors of production' which is crippled by reluctance to define a 'quantity of capital'.

Piero Sraffa's rediscovery of Ricardo's theory of profits provided the basis for clearing all this up. First, he disinterred a lost thought experiment – the corn model. For labour-intensive agriculture with a single annual crop, the major part of the stock of inputs necessary for cultivation, besides seed, is a supply of corn to feed the workers from one harvest to the next. Suppose that there is literally no other stock required except a quantity of corn. Then profit per annum is the excess of the harvest over the stock consumed during the year and the rate of profit on capital per annum is the ratio between them.

The stock is capital because it is owned and managed by employers, not by the cultivators themselves. (Ricardo, of course, was interested in the relation between the capitalist farmers and the landlords to whom they paid rent. For our purpose the argument can be confined to the least productive land in use, which is paying no rent.)

The point of the argument is that the rate of profit depends upon two separate sets of factors – first, on technical conditions, which include the skill and discipline of workers as well as the fertility of the soil, the weather and so forth, and second, on the level of real wages, which cannot be reduced entirely to mechanical terms – the needs of subsistence – but is necessarily subject to social and political influences.

Production of Commodities by Means of Commodities elaborates the model to fit industrial conditions. First comes the specification of the technology for producing a particular flow of output, with a given labour force, as an input-output table in physical terms – there are no separate 'supply curves'; the whole labour force produces the whole flow of net output while replacing the inputs used up in the process.

Then, turn to the share of wages in the flow of net output. Corresponding to a given share of wages, there is a pattern of prices and of gross margins that establishes a uniform rate of profit on the value of the stock at those prices. Here, all the beauty and ingenuity of the model is displayed.

Looking at the rate of profit and the value of capital in this light suggests that elements in the textbook model have been hitched together the wrong way round. It is usually suggested that technology (marginal products) determines the distribution of income and that 'factor prices' (sometimes 'the rate of interest') determines the choice of technique,[1] but the choice of a technique involves the accumulation of the stock of inputs required to implement it. We must allow the heavy elements, that is the stock of productive capacity in existence, to be settled first and the lighter elements — distribution between wages and profits and the level of effective demand — to play over it afterwards.

In the article written with Amit Bhaduri, the thought experiment is elaborated to bring out the meaning of a self-reproducing stock, to exhibit the relationship between the technical generation of a surplus and its realization as profit and to show the role of 'animal spirits' even in a stationary state.

The simplest way of setting out the model is to postulate an arbitrarily given annual wage bill in money terms. The distribution of income between wages and profits then appears in the price level. (The remuneration of the highest levels of management in capitalist business may be regarded as a border line case between earnings and a distribution of profits.) We can later examine the hierarchy of earned incomes within the total as a separate topic, though very little is said about that in the textbook system.

All this is at the level of a thought experiment. There is no causation in the model. The prices corresponding to a given share of wages in net output yield a uniform rate of profit on capital only because Sraffa says that they shall. There is no mechanism in the system to make them do so.

It is sometimes said that the aim of a business is to maximize its rate of profits and that competition between businesses will *tend* to establish a uniform rate, but this is an error. The *rate* of profit is reckoned after the allowance for depreciation has been calculated. The exact physical replacement of inputs used up which permits Sraffa to represent the flow of net output in physical terms does not occur in reality. The rate of profit is always ex post while the search for profit is ex ante. Price policy and investment plans are guided by the *rate of return* to be expected on a given outlay of finance. It is true that high current profits attract investment but then it is liable to overshoot so that continual fluctuation in profit rates ex post, rather than a gradual approach to a dead level, is the normal rule.

By the same token, the stock of inputs appropriate to a pure single technique — Sraffa's system of equations — is never found in reality. As

---

[1] There is some ambiguity in Sraffa's own argument here. I am neglecting Part III of *Production of Commodities by Means of Commodities*.

accumulation goes on, the composition of output changes and new methods of production are introduced. Each type of input continues to be used for some time after it has ceased to be the most eligible so that the stock in existence at any moment is a 'job lot' reflecting the evolution of industry in the recent and more distant past.

Sraffa's model is too pure to make a direct contribution to formulating answerable questions about reality but it makes a very great contribution to saving us from formulating unanswerable questions.

2

When we have disentangled inappropriate theory, we can take stock of what we know and what we need to find out.

Sraffa's model is not equipped to take us any further. For him, the share of wages in net product is simply a number; it is not identified with a supply of commodities for workers to consume. Where should we look for a theory of distribution?

First and foremost to demography. When the great population explosion of nineteenth century Europe was going on there were empty lands to bag. Now that numbers are increasing violently in the Third World, the whole map is already occupied by national states. The Marxian concept of the reserve army of labour was an invaluable clue to the level of wages but it was not followed up. Marx himself evidently had a blind spot on the question of birth control and until recently his dogmatic followers joined with the Pope in decrying it as pernicious. In some parts of the Third World development of modern industry has been going on briskly, but it continues to be surrounded by a swamp of misery.

When the growth of numbers tapers off while capital accumulation continues, a rise in the standard of consumption for the masses of the population becomes possible. Then organized labour can succeed in demanding a share through raising real-wage rates. In Western-style democracies, this has been helped by social legislation — free eduction, health insurance and so forth. (The deliberate and systematic policy of increasing inequality initiated by the Conservative government of UK in 1979 is so far unique.)

A rising share of real wages in net output tends to reduce the overall ex post rate of profit on capital. Above we rejected the textbook theory that this causes more labour-saving techniques to be selected from a pre-existing 'book of blueprints' but it may well encourage a tilt of new technology in that direction. New technology that is labour saving is not necessarily capital using. It may bring about a sharp increase in output per man employed in some important lines of production without requiring an increase in investment per man. Unless effective demand is rising sufficiently, long-period unemployment emerges.

Short-period theory, showing how the utilization of given productive capacity varies with effective demand, is already well developed (in the Cambridge tradition). This can be grafted onto the analysis of development once we have thrown off the incubus of equilibrium and can treat economic theory as an adjunct to the study of history as it unfolds.

In the old doctrine of 'consumers' sovereignty', the analysis of supply and demand, also, was hitched together the wrong way round. The initiative in designing and advertising commodities comes from the side of supply; changes in the way of life of the community – the motor car, television – are brought about by producers exploiting opportunities for making profits not by consumers formulating their needs and desires.

There is a great emphasis upon tastes in the textbook theory rather than on the major influence upon the pattern of consumption – the distribution of purchasing power among households according to ownership of property and the hierarchy of earnings from different occupations. Presumably, this is played down because it is admittedly difficult to present the existing degree of inequality as maximizing the welfare obtainable from a given flow of resources.

The old-fashioned habit of praising the 'free play of market forces' and the 'presumption in favour of laisser faire' leads to treating pollution and the destruction of free goods as being mere 'externalities' that could be corrected by attaching prices to them in the form of fines. Arguments such as *Small is Beautiful* are often dismissed as being somehow soft-headed without a fair examination of the evidence. This is regrettable, for the profit motive can always rely on specious defences. Independent economists ought to be speaking up on the side of humanity.

3

The section of Controversy is mainly concerned with attacking equilibrium theory and withdrawing from the blind alley of the pseudo-production function. The Surveys on the 1950s and 1960s are drawn from the respective Introductions to the second editions of *Collected Economic*

Papers, Volumes II and III, published in 1975. Debate: 1970s and Retrospect: 1980 complete the discussion.

Some readers may find my style of criticism excessively sharp. To compensate, I include three Tributes to writers from whom I have learned a great deal. (There is a corresponding tribute to Michal Kalecki in my first volume of *Contributions to Modern Economics*.)

The last group of papers constitute an appeal to contemporary Marxists to eschew dogmatism and join in the project of getting economic theory out of the desert of equilibrium into fruitful fields.

ANALYSIS

1

WHAT ARE THE QUESTIONS?

1

INTRODUCTION

THE 1930s have been described as the years of high theory, but all the great mass of work that has been done since and the proliferation of academic economic teaching has been very little illuminated by the ideas that emerged at that time, and there are no consistent and accepted answers to the questions that were then raised.

One reason for this lack of progress is connected with the origin of the new ideas themselves. George Shackle[1] treated 'high theory' as a purely intellectual movement, but in fact it arose out of the actual situation of the thirties − the breakdown of the world market economy in the great slump. Kalecki, Keynes, and Myrdal were trying to find an explanation for unemployment; the exploration of imperfect and monopolistic competition set afoot by the challenge, from opposite directions, of Piero Sraffa[2] and Allyn Young[3] to the orthodox theory of value, though it proved to be a blind alley, arose from the observation that, in a general buyers' market, it could not be true that prices are equal to marginal costs. The movement of the thirties was an attempt to bring analysis to bear on actual problems. Discussion of an actual problem cannot avoid the question of what should be done about it; questions of policy involve politics (laisser faire is just as much a policy as any other). Politics involve ideology; there is no such thing as a 'purely economic' problem that can

---

[1] *The Years of High Theory*, Cambridge, 1967.

[2] 'The Laws of Returns under Competitive Conditions', *Economic Journal*, December 1926, pp. 535–50.

[3] 'Increasing Returns and Economic Progress', *Economic Journal*, December 1928, pp. 527–42.

Journal of Economic Literature, December 1977.

be settled by purely economic logic; political interests and political prejudice are involved in every discussion of actual questions. The participants in every controversy divide into schools – conservative or radical – and ideology is apt to seep into logic. In economics, arguments are largely devoted, as in theology, to supporting doctrines rather than testing hypotheses.

Here, the radicals have the easier case to make. They have only to point to the discrepancy between the operation of a modern economy and the ideals by which it is supposed to be judged, while the conservatives have the well-nigh impossible task of demonstrating that this is the best of all *possible* worlds. For the same reason, however, the conservatives are compensated by occupying positions of power, which they can use to keep criticism in check.

Benjamin Ward observes:

> The power inherent in this system of quality control within the economics profession is obviously very great. The discipline's censors occupy leading posts in economics departments at the major institutions. . . . The lion's share of appointment and dismissal power has been vested in the departments themselves at these institutions. Any economist with serious hopes of obtaining a tenured position in one of these departments will soon be made aware of the criteria by which he is to be judged . . . the entire academic program, beginning usually at the undergraduate level but certainly at the graduate, consists of indoctrination in the ideas and techniques of the science. . . .[4]
>
> These inside instruments of control are accompanied by outside instruments exercised by members of the larger society. Probably the most important of these is control of funds for research and, to a lesser extent, teaching. Consciences are not much troubled by such practices because economics has mixed its ideology into the subject so well that the ideologically unconventional usually appear to appointment committees to be scientifically incompetent.[5]

For this reason, the conservatives do not feel obliged to answer radical criticisms on their merits and the argument is never fairly joined.

Moreover, with the best will in the world, it is excessively difficult to find an agreed answer to any question concerned with reality. Economists cannot make use of controlled experiments to settle their differences; they

[4] *What's Wrong with Economics?* New York, Basic Books, 1972, pp. 29–30.
[5] Ibid., p. 250.

have to appeal to historical evidence, and evidence can always be read both ways.

The laboratory sciences proceed by isolating a question and testing hypotheses about possible answers to it, one by one. In economics, questions cannot be isolated because every aspect of human society interacts with every other; hypotheses can be put forward only in the form of a 'model' of the whole economy. Before a model can be confronted with empirical tests, it has to be examined for internal consistency and for the *a priori* plausibility of its assumptions. There is a whole branch of the subject – that which carries the highest prestige – which is concerned simply with criticizing and defending hypotheses. The 'high theory' of the thirties consisted of advancing alternative hypotheses to replace those, derived from the theory of supply and demand for labour, which had been too much discredited in the slump.

Even when it is possible to mark off some element in such a way that it can be confronted with evidence, the collection of evidence from available statistics is enormously laborious. To establish the simplest of statistical 'facts' requires years of patient toil. Since it is so laborious, there is a powerful temptation to take short cuts, to overlook awkward details and favour evidence that supports an attractive theory. No doubt natural scientists are also subject to such temptations, but the experimental method provides a sieve to keep out error which has a much finer mesh than any that can be produced by an appeal to history.

There is a still more baffling difficulty in applying an economic model to statistical evidence. It may be possible to find evidence of the relationships within the model over a certain period of time and then to predict what they will be, say over the following years; but when it is found that the relationships turned out to be different, there is no way of telling whether it is because there was a mistake in specifying the model in the first place or because circumstances have changed meanwhile. And when they turn out the same, it is possibly by accident.[6]

> Difficult as it is to collect good physical data, it is far more difficult to collect long runs of economic or social data so that the whole of the run shall have a uniform significance. The data of the production of steel, for instance, change their significance not only with every invention that changes the technique of the steelmaker but with every

[6] For instance, it has been found that a 'Cobb–Douglas production function' will fit any time-series of outputs, whatever the technology, provided that the share of wages in value added was fairly constant over the period.

social and economic change affecting business and industry at large, and in particular, with every technique changing the demand for steel or the supply and nature of the competing materials. For example, even the first skyscraper made of aluminium instead of steel will turn out to affect the whole future demand for structural steel, as the first diesel ship did the unquestioned dominance of the steamship.

Thus the economic game is a game where the rules are subject to important revisions, say, every ten years, and bears an uncomfortable resemblance to the Queen's croquet game in *Alice in Wonderland*. . . . Under the circumstances, it is hopeless to give too precise a measurement to the quantities occurring in it. To assign what purports to be precise values to such essentially vague quantities is neither useful nor honest, and any pretense of applying precise formulae to these loosely defined quantities is a sham and a waste of time.[7]

Evading these difficulties, a great part of current teaching is conducted in terms of models that are evidently not intended to be taken seriously as hypotheses about reality but are used rather to inculcate an orthodox ideology. For a model to be taken seriously, the assumptions must be carefully specified, while a doctrine can appeal to a general body of received ideas. This distinction is illustrated below in terms of the contention that market prices provide an efficient mechanism for allocating scarce means between alternative uses, expressed in the proposition that 'a competitive equilibrium is a Pareto optimum'.

2

MARKET EQUILIBRIUM

In current teaching, a sharp distinction is usually made between micro- and macroeconomic problems, each being treated in terms of quite different concepts. It is necessary, of course, as the subject grows more complex, to focus upon particular questions one at a time, but a *general* theory cannot be split into these two parts. Micro questions – concerning the relative prices of commodities and the behaviour of individuals, firms, and households – cannot be discussed in the air without any reference to

[7] Norbert Wiener, *God and Golem, Inc.: A comment on certain points where cybernetics impinges on religion*, Cambridge, Mass., MIT Press; London, Chapman and Hall, 1964, pp. 90–1.

the structure of the economy in which they exist, and to the processes of cyclical and secular change. Equally, macro theories of accumulation and effective demand are generalizations about micro behaviour: the relation of income to expenditure for consumption, of investment to the pursuit of profit, of the management of placements in which financial wealth is held to rates of interest, and of wages to the level of prices result from the reactions of individuals and social groups to the situations in which they find themselves. Even the artificial conception of a stationary state has to be specified in terms of the behaviour of its inhabitants. Supposing all natural and technical conditions are constant, we still have to describe the individual and social behaviour which is conceived to make total consumption exactly equal to net output, neither more nor less, so that net saving and net investment are exactly zero. If there is no micro theory, there cannot be any macro theory either.

The analysis of markets is treated under the heading of micro theory, but it cannot be understood without some indication of the macro setting in which it operates. A prisoner-of-war camp, a village fair, and the shopping centre of a modern city cannot all be treated in exactly the same terms.

The macro setting of the analysis of 'scarce means with alternative uses' is very vaguely sketched. It appears to rely upon Say's Law, for the scarce means are always fully utilized.[8] The central concept is the production-possibility surface showing the combinations of quantities of a list of specified commodities that could be produced by various combinations of the given resources.

Nothing much is usually said about the inhabitants of the model. The ancestry of Adam Smith is often claimed for it, but his world was inhabited by workers, employers, and gentlemen. Here there are only 'transactors' or 'economic subjects.' To borrow Michio Morishima's trope, the people in this model are like the conventionally invisible property men of the Kabuki theatre, and only the commodities have speaking parts.

The 'scarce means' consist of 'labour', that is, workers who can be employed in various occupations, privately-owned land providing various kinds of natural resources, and the produced means of production (buildings and industrial equipment) that have already been accumulated. Thus, it purports to deal with a capitalist economy that has a future and a past,

---

[8] Strictly speaking, the rule is that any resource that is under-utilized has a zero price. When this applies to labour, presumably the workers must have died long ago.

but the analysis applies rather to a once-over meeting of independent peasants at a rural market or to the prisoner-of-war camp where parcels were occasionally received from the Red Cross.

As Nikolay Bukharin observed when he was in exile in the West, there is almost no discussion of how scarce means are organized to yield outputs; the whole emphasis is on exchanges of ready-made goods.[9]

Robert Clower subsumes production under exchange:

> An ongoing exchange economy with specialist traders *is* a production economy since there is no bar to any merchant capitalist acquiring labour services and other resources as a 'buyer' and transforming them (repackaging, processing into new forms, etc.) into outputs that are unlike the original inputs and are 'sold' accordingly as are commodities that undergo no such transformation. In short, a production unit *is* a particular type of middleman or trading specialist.[10]

And he supports the view 'that "capitalists" are just individuals who have the wit and forethought to exploit profit opportunities by accumulating trade capital and engaging in the "production" of both trading services and new types of commodities.'

It is true, of course, that industrial capitalism developed out of commercial capitalism, but the process of exchange does not explain why there are so many (presumably dull-witted) individuals who are available to sell labour services.

There are various brands of micro theory; Clower has been critical of others, but all share the characteristic of stressing exchange and neglecting production.

Even the process of marketing commodities is not much discussed. Since the tastes of individuals are hard and fast, there is no scope for advertisement and salesmanship to affect them. Indeed there is no scope for competition at all. To quote Oskar Morgenstern:

> Competition means struggle, fight, maneuvering, bluff, hiding of information – and precisely *that* word is used to describe a situation in which no one has any influence on anything, where there is *ni gain, ni perte* where everyone faces *fixed conditions, given prices*, and has only to adapt himself to them so as to attain an individual maximum. . . .[11]

---

[9] *Economic Theory of the Leisure Class*, English translation, London, Martin Lawrence, 1957. (In Russian, 1919.)

[10] Private communication, quoted with permission, 1976.

[11] 'Thirteen Critical Points in Contemporary Economic Theory: An Interpretation', *Journal of Economic Literature*, December 1972, Vol. 10, No. 4, pp. 1163–89.

There is a large number of sellers of each kind of commodity, and though they are all assumed to be 'maximizing profits', none of then ever forms a group which could increase proceeds for each member above what they could get individually.[12] On the demand side, the market is made up of transactors each with a certain amount of purchasing power, in terms of some numeraire, which he spends on a selection from among the commodities offered, according to his tastes and their prices. Here the argument does correspond to Adam Smith's treatment of the subject, for when he speaks of appealing to the self interest of the butcher, the brewer, and the baker to get us our dinner, he is evidently thinking of a gentleman with independent means spending money on the tradesmen, rather than of their competitive struggle to make a living.

At an equilibrium position on the production-possibility surface, the prices and flows of sales of the various commodities determine the earnings of various types of resources so that the income of each transactor depends upon the specific resources that he commands. An observing economist may make use of a single numeraire but, for each inhabitant of the model, the numeraire is a unit of whatever he has to sell.

The situation is described as an optimum when it is impossible to improve the position of one individual without doing harm to any other, but in Pareto's formulation individuals are not depicted in human terms. No aspect of economic life is considered but the individual's choice of how to spend given purchasing power, at a given moment, among a given assortment of goods. Pareto's optimum only repeats the definition of the production-possibility surface on which the output of one commodity cannot be increased without reducing the output of any other. (Only the commodities have speaking parts.)

The principle of measuring the cost of any benefit in terms of the alternative opportunities that must be foregone in order to get it can be applied in a general way to any decision-making unit, such as a family with limited income, a farm with limited space, a business with limited finance, or a planning commission with the limited investable resources of a particular socialist nation. But the choices that any such unit makes must depend upon the information at its disposal, both about technical conditions and market possibilities. In a perfectly static society, relevant knowledge might be handed down to everyone by tradition, but their behaviour also would be governed by tradition and no one would be conscious of ever making choices at all. In the world where we are living,

---

[12] It has been found by mathematical analysis that to ensure that combinations do not pay, the number of sellers must be indefinitely great.

choices have to be made in the light of more or less inadequate information. The full information required to make a correct choice can never be available because of the inescapable fact that:

> the basic data simply do not exist, and cannot exist, no matter what information is devised. There is no certain knowledge about the future, not even certain knowledge of probability distributions. There are expectations (or guesses) formulated with greater or less care; and unfortunately those formulated with the greatest care are by no means always the most accurate. The New York State legislature has deliberated on these difficulties, and enacted in Section 899 of the Code of Criminal Procedure that persons 'Pretending to forecast the future' shall be considered disorderly under subdivision 3, Section 901 of the Code and liable to a fine of $250 and/or six months in prison.[13]

John Hicks, having repudiated the works of his former incarnation, J. R. Hicks,[14] has observed that the very concept of equilibrium arose from a misleading analogy with movements in space, which cannot be applied to movements in time.[15] In space, it is possible to go to and fro, but times goes only one way; there is no going back to correct a mistake; an equilibrium cannot be reached by a process of trial and error. Since all individual choices are based upon more or less independent and inaccurate judgments about what outcomes will be, it is impossible that they should be consistent with each other. The assumption of 'perfect foresight' carries the argument out of this world into a system of mathematical abstraction, which, although the symbols may be given economic names, has no point of contact with empirical reality.

The question of scarce means with alternative uses becomes self contradictory when it is set in historical time, where today is an ever-moving break between the irrevocable past and the unknown future. At any moment, certainly, resources are scarce, but they have hardly any range of alternative uses. The workers available to be employed are not a supply of

---

[13] B. J. Loasby, *Imperfections and Adjustment*, University of Stirling Discussion Papers No. 50, 1977.

[14] 'Revival of Political Economy, the Old and the New', *Economic Record*, September 1975, Vol. 51, No. 4, pp. 365–7.

[15] John Hicks, 'Some Questions of Time in Economics', in *Evolution, Welfare and Time in Economics: Essays in honor of Nicholas Georgescu-Roegen*, edited by Anthony M. Tang, Fred M. Westfield, and James S. Worley, Lexington, Mass., Heath, Lexington Books, 1976, pp. 135–57.

'labour', but a number of carpenters or coal miners. The uses of land depend largely on transport; industrial equipment was created to assist the output of particular products. To change the use of resources requires investment and training, which alters the resources themselves. As for choice among investment projects, this involves the whole analysis of the nature of capitalism and of its evolution through time. Something like a production-possibility surface might appear in the calcualtions made for investment plans in a fully socialist economy, but in the world of private enterprise it cannot exist.

A completely different approach to the analysis of markets was proposed in *The Theory of Games and Economic Behaviour*.[16] This provides a powerful criticism of orthodox doctrine, but it is itself open to the objection that the type of games susceptible to mathematical analysis, such as noughts and crosses or go, are subject to set rules that all players accept and to the condition that each play has an agreed time limit. The scope of economic life, even that part of it which is concerned with markets, cannot be so narrowly confined.

The most basic objection to orthodox doctrine is raised by Kenneth Arrow, for he rejects the principle of individualism. The conduct of economic life requires the authority of institutions, such as corporations or national governments:

> There are many other organizations beside the government and the firm. But all of them, whether political party or revolutionary movement, university or church, share the common characteristics of the need for collective action and the allocation of resources through non-market methods. . . .
>
> There is still another set of institutions, if that is the right word, I want to call to your attention and make much of. These are invisible institutions: the principles of ethics and morality.[17]

The familiar story of the prisoners' dilemma illustrates this point. If each man acts selfishly, both will be worse off than if they follow the moral rule of refusing to betray a chum. But this rule cannot be introduced *ad hoc*. If it is followed at all it must be followed for its own sake, equally in circumstances where the individual will suffer for it.

With this objection, the whole structure of the model collapses.

[16] John von Neumann and Oskar Morgenstern, Princeton, 1944.
[17] *The Limits of Organization*, New York, Norton, 1974.

3

Theory of the Firm

Keynes described the orthodox equilibrium theory as a pretty, polite technique 'which tries to deal with the present by abstracting from the fact that we know very little about the future.'[18] Alan Coddington observes:

> To stress the basis of all economic activity in more or less uncertain expectations is precisely to emphasize the openness and incompleteness of economic theorizing and explanation.[19]

Certainly it is true that a mechanical model cannot survive when it is set afloat in historical time. (It was recognizing the difference between the future and the past that caused Hicks to become disillusioned with the *IS/LM* model with which generations of students have been taught to misinterpret the *General Theory*.) But this does not mean that economic theory is useless. We cannot help trying to understand the world we are living in, and we need to construct some kind of picture of an economy from which to draw hypotheses about its mode of operation. We cannot hope ever to get neat and precise answers to the questions that hypotheses raise, but we can discriminate among the pictures of reality that are offered and choose the least implausible ones to elaborate and to confront with whatever evidence we can find. This is one function of economic models. The other is to satisfy the requirements of ideology.

Hypotheses are invented and die every day. The criteria by which some are chosen to survive and enter into the corpus of economic teaching are of two kinds. One is that a hypothesis seems life-like and offers some explanation that appears sufficiently promising to be worth exploring, and the other is that it fits into and supports received doctrine. Clearly the model of competitive equilibrium has a low score on the first criterion and owes its support to the second.

There is another approach to the analysis of competition in which the relations between observation and doctrine are more subtle, that is, the problem known as Marshall's dilemma.

---

[18] 'The General Theory of Employment', *Quarterly Journal of Economics*, February 1937, *Collected Writings of John Maynard Keynes* (JMK, London, Macmillan), Vol. XIV, 1973.

[19] 'Keynesian Economics: The Search for First Principles', *Journal of Economic Literature*, December 1976, Vol. 14, No. 4, pp. 1258–73.

Marshall's model was concerned not only with exchange but also stressed manufacture. The most basic micro-macro question for an industrial economy concerns the way production is organized in firms. Marshall had a picture, based on observation, of the family business in British manufacturing industry. He found it plausible to argue that as a firm's business expands, its costs of production fall because of 'internal and external economies of scale.' He observed, moreover, that in many cases the fortunes of a business are bound up with the life of a family. An individual sets it going and it prospers, but by the third generation its vigour is lost.

Now, on the plane of doctrine, Marshall held that in competitive conditions, prices are determined by costs, so that the benefit of economies of scale are passed on to the public. But how can competition be maintained if any firm that gets a start undersells its competitors, gains more economies, and therefore cuts prices further until it establishes a monopoly for itself?

To get out of the difficulty, Marshall fell back on the observation, which was quite correct in many instances, that family firms lose competitive power as they grow. He made this into a general rule (allowing for monopoly as an occasional exception) and described industry as a forest in which each individual tree grows only to a certain height.

This raised the obvious difficulty that when the grandsons of its founder lose their grip on a business, it can go public and become immortal as a joint-stock company. Marshall recognized this possibility, but he did not allow it to spoil his doctrine. The joint-stock company loses 'its elasticity and progressive force', so that it is unlikely to be able to continue to grow in competition 'with younger and smaller rivals'.[20]

A. C. Pigou[21] was a loyal disciple of Marshall and quite innocent of any knowledge of industry. He therefore constructed a U-shaped average cost curve for a firm, showing economies of scale up to a certain size and rising costs beyond it. Pigou's firm, in a perfectly competitive market, is always selling the output that maximizes profits, that is, at which a small increase in production would cause marginal cost to exceed the price; when price exceeds average cost, the firm is making a super-normal profit, which will attract in new competition; when price is below average costs, some firms are dropping out. Equilibrium requires that both marginal and average costs are equal to price, that is, that the size of the firm is such that

---

[20] *Principles of Economics*, Seventh edition, London, Macmillan, 1916.
[21] *Economics of Welfare*, Fourth edition, London, Macmillan, 1934, Appendix III.

it is producing at minimum cost. In the ultimate equilibrium of a stationary state, the flow of profits obtained by each firm is just sufficient to cover interest at the ruling rate on the value of the capital that it operates, leaving nothing over as the 'reward of enterprise'.

In Marshall's world, however, profits accrue to 'business ability in command of capital'; successful firms retain part of their profits to invest in expanding their activities, and the more capital they own the easier it is to borrow outside finance. The conception is absurd that a firm when it is making more than normal profits sits around waiting for competition to invade its market and drive it back towards its optimum size. It would be the height of imprudence for a business to distribute the whole of its net profit to the family or to shareholders, and no business could borrow if prospective profits did not exceed its interest bill.

If Marshall's theory had been taken on its merits as a hypothesis, it would have soon appeared that the way out of his dilemma was the opposite to that proposed by Pigou. Successful firms accumulate finance and devour the unsuccessful ones. Most joint-stock companies continue to grow, and many competitive industries tend towards a condition of dominance by one or a few firms. But the great corporations do not behave monopolistically in the sense of restricting output in order to raise prices. They continue to compete with each other, invading new markets, introducing new products, and evolving new techniques, while at the same time throwing up opportunities for new small businesses to make a start.

Marshall's analysis was half in historical time and half in equilibrium doctrine. It is the first half that can pass the test of *a priori* plausibility and provide a starting point for a 'theory of the firm' appropriate to an economy of private enterprise.

Keynes developed his analysis in the setting of a short-period situation with given productive capacity and training of labour. This was appropriate to his problem: the influence of the level of effective demand on the utilization of resources already in existence. He had to concentrate upon forcing his readers to admit that there was such a problem. He was concerned with investment primarily as the source of instability and, apart from some quite conventional remarks, he did not have much to say about the process of accumulation either for firms or for nations.

Hicks[22] complains that Keynes' argument is not set wholly in historical time because the multiplier theory (and the theory of production that goes

---

[22] Hicks, op. cit., 1976, p. 140.

with it) is couched in terms of equilibrium. This is quite untrue. The original purpose of the multiplier was to work out what increase in income could be expected over the immediate future if the level of home investment were to be stepped up, beginning from a particular date. Admittedly the time-scheme was not very clearly worked out (Dennis Robertson complained a lot about this), but the main topic of the *General Theory* was the consequences of a *change* in the level of effective demand within a short-period situation with given plant and available labour.[23] The consequences of changing the stock of plant as investment matures hardly came into the story.

It is paradoxical that during the great Age of Growth – the twenty-five years that followed World War II – so-called macro theory was taught in 'Keynesian' terms, though Keynes himself had almost nothing to say about growth. Once he had thrown off the incubus of Say's Law, the whole field of the long-period theory of accumulation remained to be explored.

Side by side with the timeless equilibrium model, there have grown up a number of treatments of the behaviour of firms in a growing industrial economy, but no plausible simple general hypothesis has so far been found.[24]

The doctrine that firms 'maximize profits' collapses as soon as it is taken out of the equilibrium world and set in historical time. For a firm which is growing from year to year by investing retained profits, the maximum flow of profits will be reached when it commands an indefinitely large value of capital. Certainly, it is true that firms pursue profit, for without profits they would perish, but to 'maximize' profits over the long run is a meaningless phrase.

A less vapid statement would be that, in respect to each particular choice, say, of an investment programme, the firm will prefer the most profitable alternative. But, as Loasby has observed,[25] the firm does not know which would in fact be the most profitable alternative. The observing economist can only advance the hypothesis that the alternative actually chosen was that which was expected to be the most profitable.

[23] It must be admitted that there are many Marshallian remnants in the General Theory, which obscure exposition, but in the reply to Jacob Viner the point is made clearly (see Keynes, 'The General Theory of Employment', JMK, Vol. XIV).

[24] The question was opened by Edith Penrose (*The Theory of the Growth of the Firm*) in 1959. A recent contribution is *The Megacorp and Oligopoly*, Alfred S. Eichner, Cambridge University Press, 1976.

[25] See p. 8 above.

Furthermore, any plan a firm makes is multidimensional — it involves the selection of products; the choice of technique, including the choice of workers to employ; it involves pricing policy and salesmanship; and it involves the availability of finance. In a small business, all these considerations revolve in the mind of the boss, who acts on business instinct and does not explain, even to himself, exactly what his motives are. In a large corporation, any decision involves the personnel of many departments in the technostructure — salesmen, accountants, engineers — each of which has its characteristic beliefs and interests, and which have to be coordinated by bureaucratic rules.

The stress that John Kenneth Galbraith[26] lays on the dependence of large corporations on their technostructures has been taken to suggest that they are not governed by the profit motive. This is a misunderstanding. The specialists who serve a particular corporation depend upon it for their incomes and careers and generally develop a kind of patriotism for it. They have just as much motive to promote its profitability as an old-fashioned capitalist. But the complexity of multidimensional choice in conditions of uncertainty means that maximizing profits, even in the limited sense of preferring more to less profitable policies, is by no means a simple matter.

An alternative hypothesis is that the motive of firms is to maximize their rate of growth. But this does not take us much further than the observation that firms that are not profitable do not survive, and those that are, grow.

Another approach is to start from the growth of the market for a range of products and suggest that each of a group of competing firms keeps its productive capacity growing so as to maintain its share. But fast-growing firms expand into diversified markets.

One view is that the growth of the productive capacity of an industrial firm is a function of its flow of profits — as fast as its cash flow comes in, it looks around for opportunities to invest. Another view is that when an investment opportunity offers, the firm adjusts the prices of its existing output in such a way as to get the profit that it needs to finance the investment.

All these hypotheses have turned up many interesting and plausible concepts, but it seems to me that the search for a single generalization is a hangover from the equilibrium model. There is no simple theory to cover the multifarious evolution of a private enterprise economy. The methods

---

[26] *The New Industrial State*, London, Hamilton, 1967.

of ethology are more appropriate than mathematics to the study of industry, and, indeed, we do know a great deal about the natural history of business life from studies of the economics of industry, of finance, and of conditions of labour. But this knowledge cannot be well organized if it has to be squeezed into formulae that smooth over the distinction between the future and the past.

Galbraith sets out to substitute for Marshall a picture, based on general observation, of the New Industrial State. His account of the behaviour of giant firms appears plausible or, at the very least, worth discussing, but it has had no success as an ideological doctrine. As he points out, a very large proportion of the educated and professional class in industrial nations is employed directly or indirectly by great corporations, and the educational system is largely at their service. For this reason, the power that Ward refers to,[27] prevents critical views from penetrating into orthodoxy.

4

PRICES

Keynes complained of the theory in which he was brought up:

> So long as economists are concerned with what is called the theory of value, they have been accustomed to teach that prices are governed by the conditions of supply and demand; and, in particular, changes in marginal cost and the elasticity of short-period supply have played a prominent part. But when they pass in volume II, or more often in a separate treatise, to the theory of money and prices, we hear no more of these homely but intelligible concepts and move into a world where prices are governed by the quantity of money, by its income-velocity, by the velocity of circulation relatively to the volume of transactions, by hoarding, by forced saving, by inflation and deflation *et hoc genus omne*; and little or no attempt is made to relate these vaguer phrases to our former notions of the elasticities of supply and demand.[28]

He proposed a micro-macro theory in which the prices of commodities

---

[27] See p. 2 above.
[28] *General Theory of Employment, Interest and Money*, 1936, JMK, Vol. VII, p. 174.

are primarily governed by the cost of production, and he observed that the main element in the general level of costs (internal to one country) which can change in the short period, is the level of money wage rates. He was concerned to argue that cutting wage rates would lower prices. We now have to adapt the argument to the case where raising money-wage rates (relatively to the growth of productivity) causes prices to rise. Keynes' 'homely but intelligible' concepts now appear old-fashioned. A great deal of work remains to be done to establish a macro-micro analysis of prices appropraite to the modern world. Moreover, during the Age of Growth the industrial economies have gone through a mutation so that unemployment no longer prevents wage rates from rising.

Meanwhile the 'vague phrases' that Keynes complained of have come back into fashion. 'Monetarism' is now a powerful doctrine, but it is not easy to confront it with the post-Keynesian system, to discuss which is the more plausible, for the hypotheses on which the quantity theory is based have never been clearly stated.

The post-Keynesian system dwells in historical time; it is designed to analyse the consequences that may be expected to follow a change taking place at a particular date in particular circumstances. The system is set up like an artist's mobile. A flick on any point sets everything in motion, but it is possible to see which are the principal interactions and which way causation runs from one to another.

The old-fashioned formula, $MV = PT$, can be interpreted in terms of this mobile. Suppose that, since this time last year, there has been an all-round rise in money-wage rates and also some increase in employment. Both the flow of transactions (T) and the level of prices (P) are now higher. This has led to an increase in bank deposits, with a corresponding increase in currency in circulation because the value of working capital having gone up, many businesses have taken larger advances from banks or drawn upon overdraft facilities. At the same time, average velocity of circulation may have risen, as liquid reserves have been drawn upon so that a larger proportion of the total stock of money is now in accounts that are more frequently turned over. (It is in general more true to say that an increase in prices causes the quantity of money to increase than the other way round.)

However, if a spontaneous rise in M and V was not sufficient to provide for the higher PT, then interest rates must have risen, and a smaller proportion of the stock of money is now held by bearish owners who prefer cash to securities (in existing circumstances) as a placement for their wealth.

When the monetary authorities are endeavouring to prevent M from increasing, interest rates are raised all the more, and a credit squeeze checks the growth of activity or even precipitates a slump. But this, unfortunately, is not guaranteed to reduce prices.

The monetarist theory is not so easily described. The modern version of the quantity theory connects M, not to the flow of transactions, but to PQ, the value of gross output, so that V simply means GNP divided by some figure representing the quantity of money; all the interactions in the mobile are collapsed into one opaque relationship.

There seems to be a chronic confusion, in latter-day expositions of monetarism, between changes in the stock of money deliberately brought about by the authorities and the effects of changes in the flow of government expenditure. The story of currency notes dropped from helicopters is presumably intended to illustrate the case of a budget deficit financed by 'using the printing press'.[29] A shower of notes, picked up by passers-by, might be expected to produce a burst of expenditure that would peter out over a short time; a budget deficit continued from year to year tends to support a flow of expenditure as long as it continues. An *increase* in the deficit from one month to the next tends to increase expenditure over the following months in much the same way as a commensurate rise in investment or reduction in thriftiness. This is not a *monetary* phenomenon, though it is likely to be accompanied by an increase in MV. There is no way to distinguish between a rise in activity that is 'inflationary' in the monetarist sense from one that is not.

Monetary influences on the behaviour of the economy, in the proper sense, arise from changes in the stock of placements (including currency) available to the public relative to the demand for them. A shower of notes would leave behind (after the increase in expenditure with its multiplier effect was exhausted) an addition to wealth equal to the savings made out of the extra income generated by the expenditure and an equal addition to the stock of currency notes. Assuming that the demand for currency has been increased less than the supply, credit will be somewhat easier in the final position than it would otherwise have been. This is the only *monetary* element in the story of the helicopters.

A budget deficit may be financed by borrowing through the banking system and so increasing the quantity of money, but it need not be. A modern government has a large national debt to operate upon, not only

[29] M. Friedman, *The Optimum Quantity of Money*, London, Macmillan; Chicago, Aldine, 1969.

what it borrowed last week. If it thinks right, it can sell long-term bonds and generate a credit squeeze whatever its budgetary balance may be. The trouble is that when money-wage rates and prices are rising, increasing values of working capital have to be financed and the authorities can prevent the quantity of money from increasing only by bankrupting business and bringing production to a halt.

Keynes, looking forward to a period of continuous high employment, expected money-wage rates to rise faster than productivity. He regarded this as an essentially political problem and did not suggest any remedy.[30] Michal Kalecki observed: 'If capitalism can adjust itself to full employment a fundamental reform will have been incorporated in it'.[31] The revival of monetary theory is a device for avoiding discussion of political problems. This makes it very attractive as a doctrine, but fails to provide any plausible hypotheses for interpreting experience.

Keynes intended to bring the theory of prices back from Volume II, Money, to Volume I, the Principles of Economics, but Michal Kalecki[32] made a greater contribution than Keynes himself to carrying this programme forward.

Kalecki drew attention to the fact that there are two distinct systems of price formation in the modern world, one dominated by supply and demand and one by costs plus profits. This distinction has recently been rediscovered by Hicks.[33] The market for some commodities is created by specialist merchants who buy to sell again, and make their profits out of price differences. They carry stocks; when the outflow of sales exceeds the inflow of purchases so that stocks are falling, they raise prices, and conversely. A large part of the produce of agriculture and extractive industries is handled in this way. For manufactures, in modern times, the producers have taken over the merchanting function. They offer their commodities at an advertised price and produce for sale what the market will take. There are various intermediate forms and overlapping conditions, but the main distinction is between these two types.

Kalecki analysed industrial prices in terms of gross profit margins expressed as a mark-up on average prime cost. As his theory evolved, he rejected the view that Keynes had taken over from Marshall, that an increase in output requires a rise of prices because of rising marginal costs.

[30] See Richard Kahn, On Re-reading Keynes, London, British Academy, 1974.
[31] 'Political Aspects of Full Employment', Political Quarterly, Vol. 14, No. 4, 1943, pp. 322–31.
[32] Essays in the Theory of Economic Fluctuations, London, Allen and Unwin, 1939.
[33] Op. cit., 1976, p. 149.

On this, his opinion now generally prevails. In general, it seems that average prime costs fall rather than rise with rising utilization of plant. A sellers' market, in which the flow of outputs is limited by capacity, is rather rare because it quickly leads to investment to expand capacity for production of the commodities concerned; if it is expected to last, it will not. Even while it prevails, firms generally prefer to lengthen delivery dates rather than to choke back demand by raising prices.

Kalecki observed that prime costs are made up of two independent elements, the wage bill and the cost of materials and power. Here there is an interconnection between the two types of price formation, for costs of materials are strongly influenced by supply and demand. Bargaining for money-wage rates depends upon the balance of forces in the labour market. Assuming a stable pattern of gross profit margins, we can deduce the behaviour of prices to be expected in the short period. A rise in the overall level of activity entails an increase in demand for materials, which raises their prices. The rise in prime costs that this entails leads to a more or less proportional rise in prices. Now real wage rates have been reduced, while profits in money terms have risen. This sets the stage for a rise in money-wage rates. On the other tack, a decline in general industrial activity tends to lower material prices, but the resistance of organized labour is generally strong enough to prevent money-wage rates from being cut (though unemployment and short-time reduce earnings).

Kalecki's analysis reinforces Keynes' view that inflation is essentially a political problem by stressing the relationship between the formation of prices and the share of wages in the proceeds of industry, although the treatment of profit margins, which Kalecki derived from 'imperfect competition', was not thoroughly worked out.

Some evidence has been found to support the assumption that the ratio of gross margins to prime costs is fairly stable in respect to changes in the general level of demand.[34] But the hypothesis that the pattern of gross margins for various commodities can be explained solely by the 'degree of monopoly' was in the nature of a shot in the dark. A high degree of monopoly, in Kalecki's sense, means a weak state of price competition. It is true that the great oligopolistic corporations can set higher margins on their products than small competitive firms, but they may be using them

---

[34] R. R. Nield, *Pricing and Employment in the Trade Cycle: A study of British manufacturing industry,* 1950–61, Cambridge University Press, 1963. See also Wynne A. H. Godley and William D. Nordhaus, 'Pricing in the Trade Cycle', *Economic Journal,* Vol. 82, No. 327, September 1975, pp. 365–7.

partly to cover the expenses of nonprice competition among themselves. Moreover, the degree of monopoly is itself partly a function of the level of margins required to cover overhead costs of production. Risky investments requiring a heavy initial capital cost are made only by powerful corporations which have sufficient command over their markets to expect to be able to recover adequate gross profits.

Here we come to the border-line between long- and short-period theory of prices, which has been very inadequately explored.

5

LONG-RUN GROWTH

Hicks in the course of his 'long struggle to escape' from *Value and Capital*, came to the conclusion that models of steady growth are futile.[35] Certainly, if steady growth is proposed as a hypothesis, it sinks at the first step, but, as Hicks himself found, it is useful in what János Kornai describes as intellectual experiments, which are necessary to sort out the questions involved in analysing complicated processes.

Hicks describes his attempt to analyse disequilibrium growth in *Capital and Time*:

> I had to start very slowly. If I had started with a fine set of plausible assumptions, drawn from the real world, I am sure I should have got nowhere. I had to build up my model bit by bit. I began from a steady state (but that was simply because I had to have something firm, which I thought I understood, from which to start), but the point of the steady state . . . is that it is to be *disturbed*.[36]

I intended my golden age (which has often been mistaken for a hypothesis) to be used in this way, as I suggested in *Exercises in Economic Analysis* in 1960:

> Most economic questions lead up to a discussion of what consequences may be expected to follow a certain event. We cannot isolate a particular causal element from its surrounding circumstances by a controlled experiment. . . . We have to proceed by breaking the

[35] Op. cit., 1976, p. 143.
[36] Ibid., p. 145.

question up into parts, and after discussing each separately, reassemble the pieces as best we may.

First, compare two economies which are alike in all relevant respects except the one which we wish to isolate. . . . Each has its own past and its own expectations about its own future. They need not be in stationary conditions provided that any change that has been taking place or is expected is smooth and regular so that we know where we are with it.

Next consider a single economy, following a regular predictable path, and consider how its subsequent course is altered by an event happening at a particular moment. . . .

Then consider an economy which is not following a smooth path, but is caught for examination, so to speak, at particular moment in a more or less turbulent history. We have to try to work out what future development is inherent in the situation as it exists to-day. . . .

Finally, we have to try to see what effect upon this in any case turbulent path would be introduced by a particular event.[37]

This is what makes serious economics difficult.

A discussion of growth immediately raises the question of technical change. This was for a long time held up by the conception of a production function in labour and 'capital.' The concept of 'malleable machines'[38] was introduced precisely to abolish the difference between the future and the past so that a growing economy could be always in equilibrium. A pseudo-production function or 'book of blueprints' was a half-way house between history and a timeless production function. The pseudo-production function consists of the specification of a set of mutually non-inferior techniques, each requiring a particular stock of means of production per man employed. Each is eligible for at least one rate of profit, and none is superior to the rest at every rate of profit. When the techniques are listed in order of the flow per man employed of a homogeneous net output, it can be seen that a higher output is not necessarily associated with 'more capital,' that a technique that is eligible at a higher rate of profit may require a larger value of capital at the corresponding prices, and that the same technique may be eligible at widely different rates of profit. This killed off the doctrine of 'marginal

---

[37] *Exercises in Economic Analysis*, London, Macmillan, 1960, pp. vii–x.

[38] J. E. Meade, *A Neo-Classical Theory of Economic Growth*, Second edition, London, Allen and Unwin, 1967.

productivity of capital' associated with the production function (though it has refused to get buried),[39] but it does not, by itself, provide the basis for an alternative analysis of accumulation. If techniques are invented, one after the other in historical time, there is no reason to expect them to be mutually non-superior. A new technique is normally adopted because, at existing prices and wage rates, it promises a higher return than the one in use, per unit of financial investment. It does not have to wait for a change in prices to make it eligible. But it will not remain exceptionally profitable for long. Copiers wipe out the initial competitive advantage of new commodities and rising real wage rates, of higher productivity. Meanwhile, new, more eligible techniques are being introduced. At each moment, the prospect of higher profits is inducing change, while, over a run of years, the *ex post* average realized rate of profit may be constant or falling.

To sort out the analysis of this turbulent scene involves the whole of economics and, as Hicks says, we must approach it bit by bit.

The first use to which the golden-age method was put was to examine the relation between accumulation and the rate of profit. Take Kalecki's assumptions that wages are currently consumed as they are received; gross investment is financed out of profits, which are also partly distributed to rentiers. On a steady growth path, g, the rate of growth per annum is equal to I/K, the ratio of net investment to the value of the stock of capital at the ruling rate of profit, and the rate of profit is equal to g/s_p where $(1 - s_p)$ is the proportion of profits consumed by rentiers' households. Thus, if two economies are alike in all respects except for the share of saving from profits, with equal growth rates and the same level of money wages, then prices are higher in the economy where rentiers are less thrifty.

This kind of argument is not confined to strictly steady growth. When each firm finances its own investment out of its own cash flow, and plans to invest its own retained profits, there is no problem of effective demand; the financial system, as Hyman Minsky[40] puts it, is robust, and investment has great inertia. When firms can raise outside finance direct from rentiers or through the banks, the system is liable to instability. The rate of investment is not tethered by a particular ratio to the value of the stock of capital. Any rise in investment above the former ratio increases the current

[39] See Martin Bronfenbrenner, 'Ten Issues in Distribution Theory', in *Modern Economic Thought*, edited by Sidney Weintraub, Philadelphia, 1977, p. 419.

[40] *John Maynard Keynes*, London, Macmillan, 1976; New York, Columbia University Press, 1975.

flow of profits and encourages further investment and a rise in the proportion of borrowing to own finance. Soon schemes of investment are being planned that will be viable only if the overall rate of investment continues to rise. A fragile debt structure has been built up. When the acceleration in the rate of investment tapers off, some businesses find current receipts less than current obligations, and a financial collapse occurs. During the boom, equity holders have been experiencing capital gains and increasing the ratio of expenditure to income; when the boom breaks, thriftiness increases. Thus long-run average growth may occur in cycles.

There is no guarantee, because growth has been maintained on the average for a run of years, that it will continue. At any stage in the process of accumulation, a sufficiently drastic financial collapse may throw the investors into a state of self-fulfilling pessimism, which postpones recovery indefinitely.

The monetary characteristcs of a growing economy would generate instability even if the 'real forces' developed smoothly, but (even apart from wars and political upheavals) technology has never developed smoothly. As Joseph Schumpeter observed, great fundamental discoveries and inventions occur at random intervals and each is followed by a boom, or a series of booms, as investment is made in innovations embodying new techniques. When the appropriate changes have been made in the stock of industrial capital, investment tails off and recession supervenes.

Another problem also can be analysed by means of the golden-age method. We can distinguish the technical character of an innovation in terms of the cost of investment necessary to install the appropriate means of production. When the equipment involved in employing a man with the latest best-practice technique has required the same investment (at unchanged real-wage rates) as that which it replaced, the innovation has been neutral. When it has required a greater investment, the innovation has been capital-using, and when less, capital saving.

The 'stylized facts' – a run of years with a constant rate of profit, constant share of wages in proceeds, and a constant ratio of the value of capital to the flow of net output – are possible only if technical progress is neutral, though neutrality by itself does not guarantee a constant rate of profit.

To allow a constant rate of profit when a series of neutral innovations are being made, the real-wage rate must rise at the same rate as average net output per man employed. Then, if a steady rate of accumulation is being maintained, the value of the stock of capital is rising at the same rate as the flow of net output and the capital to output ratio is constant.

A round of capital-using innovations, with a constant rate of profit, requires real wages to rise in a smaller proportion than net output (to allow for the rise in the capial to labour ratio). Conversely with capital-saving innovations.

On an orthodox production function, there are no articulated techniques. 'Capital' is a kind of mush and, for some unexplained reason, a higher ratio of 'capital' to labour is eligible only at a lower rate of profit.

With neutral technical progress, it is possible to maintain both a constant rate of profit and a constant capital to output ratio. Neutrality is a necessary, not sufficient, condition. Steady growth requires not only that innovations are neutral, but also that the rate of accumulation is constant and that real wages rise at the appropriate rate. These are the characteristics of a golden age.

When real wages fail to rise in step with output, demand fails to expand as fast as supply (unless investment is expanding sufficiently to make up the difference). Underconsumption discourages investment, and the economy falls out of the golden-age into stagnation.

The analysis is quite complicated even on this high plane of abstraction, and this plane is very far removed from the turbulence of actual history. Here is a field where mathematical expertise combined with real-life observation has plenty of work to do. Meanwhile we may hazard some general remarks.

First consider the formation of prices. Innovating firms have to set prices *ex ante*. They may be supposed to aim at a price that will cover average total cost (including the interest bill) at some standard level of utilization of plant, plus an allowance for selling costs, plus an allowance for net profit. As well as the choice of technique, the choice of the standard of utilization, of selling costs, and of the ratio of net profit to price depend upon the policy of the individual firm. There is too great an element of luck in the game for an outside observer to tell which policies are proving the most successful in any particular circumstances.

The design of new commodities is a very important element in innovation. Here the large firms with an ample flow of finance have a great advantage. They can employ research staffs and try out a large number of innovations in the expectation that one will take off and become a winner.

Old commodities are constantly being dolled up with changes of design in the attempt to maintain demand.

The evolution of the general level of prices depends very much upon the strength of the labour movement. With constant prices and money-wage rates, a firm that has made an innovation which raises the value of output per man by more than the cost of investment per man is enjoying a higher rate of profit for the time being. Trade unions feel that it is a right and a duty to get a share of this profit for their members. They demand higher money-wage rates and the prosperous firms may concede this without a fight and without a fully-offsetting rise in selling prices. They may actually welcome a rise in real-wage rates because it helps them in competition with smaller and more backward firms, which cannot survive a rise in costs.

In a closed economy (without foreign trade), a general rise in average wage rates proportional to the average increase in productivity would keep the overall price level constant, but this cannot occur. Wages rise fastest in the most profitable industries. Less profitable industries have to raise the wages that they pay in response, and the firms in those industries have to raise their selling prices in order to survive. Thus, a general rise in real wages is accompanied by a change in the pattern of prices. As the cost of labour in terms of commodities rises, some lines of employment (say, domestic help) are squeezed out. Others (say, collecting garbage) have to be mechanized to maintain a necessary service, for in many cases machines have become cheaper than men. Here we find a grain of truth in the orthodox conception of substitution between capital and labour.

When accumulation has been going on vigorously while the population has ceased to grow, a condition arises of scarcity of labour in the sense that the flow of investable finance from retained profits has risen relative to the number of employable workers. This enhances the bargaining power of labour. (Marx failed to emphasize that growth of population is inimical to the interests of the proletariat.) It also stimulates inventions of all kinds. Even capital-using innovations save labour in the sense of raising output per man of the work force as a whole.

When there is a strong capital-using bias in technical progress, it requires a higher flow of gross investment to maintain a constant long-run level of employment. If sufficient gross investment is not forthcoming, a reserve army of long-period unemployment is created again.

Even when they are not capital-using, innovations may require a greatly increased minimum size of investment. This enhances the competitive advantage of large against small businesses.

A major side effect of technical change is on the nature of work. It is characteristic of modern industry to require highly trained personnel, while it has no use for the labour power of a great mass of unskilled workers.

Thus (as Ricardo admitted) technical development, which from the point of view of capitalism is progressive, may reduce the share of wages in the proceeds of industry and generate long-period unemployment. For a long time, this was hushed up in orthodox doctrine, but now it is becoming too painfully obvious to be ignored.

6

INTERNATIONAL TRADE

The most powerful and all-pervasive doctrine in pre-Keynesian orthodoxy was the case in favour of free trade. This was not invented by the neoclassicists, but derived via Marshall from David Ricardo.

Ricardo intended his model to exist in historical time; he claimed that *removing* protection would *increase* wealth, but in two important respects his argument runs in terms of timeless equilibrium. In the famous story which begins with England and Portugal both producing both cloth and wine,[41] resources can be moved instantaneously, when trade begins, from one industry to another in each country. Labour-value prices rule in each country. This means that there is a uniform rate of profit and a uniform capital to labour ratio in each. Output per man of each commodity determines their relative prices within each country. When it becomes profitable to expand one industry, resources are moved out of the other without trouble or loss and without changing the capital to labour ratio in the country concerned. (It is curious that wine, as well as cloth, is produced in conditions of 'constant returns'.)

Here is the first case of analysis couched in terms of a movement through time, which is really a comparison of equilibrium positions.

The second case is even more striking. Ricardo did not allow overseas investment (which he disapproved of) into his model. The value of the flow of imports and exports had to be equal for each country. He relied upon gold flows and the quantity theory of money to establish equilibrium in the price levels of trading countries.

It is not legitimate to complain of Ricardo, who was hacking a pioneering path through unknown problems, but it is certainly permissible to reproach his successors for keeping the so-called theory of international trade on this narrow track ever since.

[41] *Works and Correspondence*, edited by Piero Sraffa, Cambridge University Press, 1951. Volume 1, *On the principles of political economy and taxation*, Chapter VII.

To broaden the discussion, the first question that we must ask is: What is a nation? In the equilibrium theory, from Marshall to Paul Samuelson,[42] and till today, a country is treated as a compact bundle of 'factors of production', at first in isolation, which remains physically unchanged as trade takes place. Samuelson prudently named his two factors 'land' and 'labour', but many of his followers postulate that each country is endowed with a particular 'quantity of capital'; though profit rates may differ, no financial flows take place.

Among modern industrial countries there is a great interpenetration of production of specialized components of traded commodities; rentiers in each country own placements in others; banking systems are interlocked; great corporations (sometimes operating under 'flags of convenience') install facilities in many countries and employ labour and technostructure personnel of many nationalities. They have become independent entities, each larger and more powerful than many nations, not burdened with patriotism for anything except their own command of capital. The native-born workers of a country regard themselves as a nation, but great capitalist businesses feel it their duty to 'maximize profits' by seeking cheap labour wherever they can find it.

There is one respect, however, in which a modern nation is a distinct economic entity: it has a current account of foreign payments and receipts and an exchange rate, which are of concern to its government and monetary authorities.

For monetary equilibrium, it is not necessary for the current account to be balanced. It is necessary that a surplus of foreign receipts is matched by equal net foreign lending or a deficit matched by borrowing. A surplus is correctly described as a *favourable* balance. It means that citizens of the home country are acquiring foreign assets and so improving its balance for the future. A deficit covered by borrowing may be welcomed if it is due to a high rate of investment at home, which is developing resources that will yield a surplus of exports in the future to repay the debt. But a deficit that is due merely to competitive weakness is highly unfavourable; moreover the interest on the loans necessary to meet it imposes a growing burden on the balance of payments, which makes it progressively more unfavourable.

---

[42] See Alfred Marshall, *Pure Theory of Foreign Trade*, originally published in 1879, republished 1930 in Scarce Tracts in Economic Political Science, No. 1, London; Paul Samuelson, 'International Trade and the Equalisation of Factor Prices', *Economic Journal*, Vol. 58, June 1948, pp. 163–84.

Ricardo, to make his case as dramatic as possible, gave Portugal a competitive advantage over England in the initial position. The output (say, per week) of Portuguese workers both of cloth and of wine was higher than that of English workers. If money wage rates (in terms of gold) had been more or less the same when trade began, England would have been unable to export anything and would have had a drain of gold equal to the total value of her imports. Substituting a Keynes–Kalecki theory of prices for the quantity theory of money, we may say that equilibrium could not have been reached until relative money-wage rates were higher in Portugal in the same ratio as average productivity.

There is a certain tendency for wage differentials to adjust to trade balances. Where output per man is higher in one country than in others, if wages are *not* sufficiently higher there is a competitive advantage in trade leading to high exports and so to high employment and a high rate of profit. Both influences tend to cause money-wage rates to rise. Unemployment and low profits may not actually push down wage rates, but prevent them from rising, so there is tendency towards balance. But the mechanism of differential wage rates is weak and sluggish in its operations.

It was found in the 1930s that British and German costs were roughly equal, while productivity in comparable lines was double in the United States, and wage rates 50 per cent higher.[43] Then the high real-wage country was the cheap labour country.

In recent times, with both money-wage rates and productivity rising everywhere, there has been some tendency for a faster rise of wage rates to accompany a faster relative increase in productivity,[44] but this has been much too weak to maintain equilibrium. It has been supplemented by large deliberate appreciations and depreciations of exchange rates, but these have proved to be less efficacious than economists once expected. Unbalance between the major industrial countries still continues to cause great strain in the international financial system.[45] (The problems of trade with so-called developing nations and with the OPEC countries are not discussed here. Nor is the trade of the socialist world. There are more than

[43] László Rostás, *Comparative Productivity in British and American Industry*, Cambridge, 1948.

[44] Richard Kahn, quoted in Joan Robinson, 'Reflections on the Theory of International Trade', *Collected Economic Papers*, Vol. V, p. 141.

[45] Martin Fetherston et al., *Economic Policy Review*, Dept. of Applied Economics, Cambridge, March 1977, Chapter 6.

enough questions to raise in one article about the problems of the advanced industrialized capitalist nations.)

The authorities of each nation desire to see a surplus on its current account balance of payments, though not all can succeed.

A surplus of exports is advantageous, first of all, in connection with the short-period problem of effective demand. A surplus of value of exports over value of imports represents 'foreign investment'. An increase in it has an employment and multiplier effect. Any increase in activity at home is liable to increase imports so that a boost to income and employment from an increase in the flow of home investment is partly offset by a reduction in foreign investment. A boost due to increasing exports or production of home substitutes for imports (when there is sufficient slack in the economy) does not reduce home investment, but creates conditions favourable to raising it. Thus, an export surplus is a more powerful stimulus to income than home investment.

In the beggar-my-neighbour scramble for trade during the great slump, every country was desperately trying to export its own unemployment. Every country had to join in, for any one that attempted to maintain employment without protecting its balance of trade (through tariffs, subsidies, depreciation, etc.) would have been beggared by the others.

From a long-run point of view, export-led growth is the basis of success. A country that has a competitive advantage in industrial production can maintain a high level of home investment, without fear of being checked by a balance-of-payments crisis. Capital accumulation and technical improvements then progressively enhance its competitive advantage. Employment is high and real-wage rates rising so that 'labour trouble' is kept at bay. Its financial position is strong. If it prefers an extra rise of home consumption to acquiring foreign assets, it can allow its exchange rate to appreciate and turn the terms of trade in its own favour. In all these respects, a country in a weak competitive position suffers the corresponding disadvantages.

When Ricardo set out the case against protection, he was supporting British economic interests. Free trade ruined Portuguese industry.[46] Free trade for *others* is in the interests of the strongest competitor in world markets, and a sufficiently strong competitor has no need for protection at home. Free trade doctrine, in practice, is a more subtle form of Mercantilism. When Britain was the workshop of the world, universal

---

[46] See Sandro Sideri, *Trade and Power: Informal colonialism in Anglo-Portuguese relations*, Rotterdam University Press, 1970.

free trade suited her interests. When (with the aid of protection) rival industries developed in Germany and the United States, she was still able to preserve free trade for her own exports in the Empire.[47] The historical tradition of attachment to free trade doctrine is so strong in England that even now, in her weakness, the idea of protectionism is considered shocking.

After 1945, the United States was far and away the strongest competitor and used her great influence to arrange free trade agreements. GATT, IMF, etc., but she has no objection to protection for her own industries when they are strongly pressed by Japan.

What Now?

The present situation raises new questions. The long boom of twenty-five years after 1945, interrupted only by shallow and local recessions, blew up into a violent inflation in 1973 and collapsed into a world-wide slump. The economists had sunk into complacency and now do not know what to say. Relatively high employment and continuous growth in the indicators of production and accumulation had been taken to show that an age of permanent prosperity had set in. It was natural scientists, not economists, who first pointed out that exponential growth in perpetuity is an impossibility for any physical entity. On the plane of doctrine, Keynes had been smothered in the neo-classical synthesis, and a new 'dynamic' version of Say's Law had come into operation.

Now that the Juggernaut car has come more or less to a halt, we must take stock of the problems that its passage leaves behind.

The consumption of resources, including air to breathe, has evidently impoverished the world; the long struggle over relative shares has implanted a chronic tendency to inflation in the industrial countries, which no resort to monetary stringency can master. The uneven development of trading nations has set insupportable strains on the international financial system. Growth of wealth has not after all removed poverty at home, and 'aid' has not reduced it abroad. Now unemployment exacerbates social problems and embitters politics.

In this situation, the cry is to get growth started again. The European countries in a weak competitive position plead with West Germany to

[47] Eric J. Hobsbawm, *Industry and Empire: An economic history of Britain since* 1750, London, Weidenfeld and Nicolson, 1968.

spend money on something or other to improve the market for the rest so that they can permit employment to increase. Any up turn in the indicators in the United States is greeted as a sign that we shall once more be pulled up out of the slough.

Here we come upon the greatest of all economic questions, but one that in fact is never asked: what is growth for? Under the shadow of the arms race and its diffusion into the Third World, perhaps no merely economic questions are really of great importance; but even if it is a secondary question, we ought to consider it.

The obvious answer is that there is apparently no way to reduce unemployment except by increasing industrial investment. There is no question of choosing between alternative uses for given resources. Past development has dug deep grooves by physical investment, creation of financial property, and specialization of the labour force; existing resources cannot be redeployed; our only hope is to pour more resources down the old grooves.

The problem of the use of resources, and the institutional setting that controls it, cannot be confined within the bounds of theoretical economic analysis, but the economic aspect of the matter ought to be discussed. What is the object of production in a modern industrial nation, and if we could have more of it (through technical change and capital accumulation), what should we use it for?

For the classical economists, such a question did not arise. The wealth of a nation was its investable surplus; real wages were part of the cost of production, like fodder for cattle, and luxury consumption was deprecated; the neoclassicists conceived the object of production to be provision for consumption. But consumption by whom, of what?

The question was supposed to be settled by appeal to the individual's freedom of choice, but there are three very large objections to such a solution.

The first arises from inequality of the distribution of purchasing power between individuals. The nature of accumulation under private enterprise necessarily generates inequality and is therefore condemned to meeting the trivial wants of a few before the urgent needs of the many.

Do we want renewed growth in order to maintain and enhance disparities in consumption? Have we not become disillusioned with the doctrine that 'disease, squalor and ignorance' will soon be cleared away by the 'trickle down' from ever-growing conspicuous consumption?

Secondly, many kinds of consumption that are chosen by some individuals generate disutility for others. The leading case is the spread of private motor cars — the higher the level of consumption, the more uncomfortable life becomes; this fact is painfully obvious, but orthodox doctrine has not been able to accommodate it.

Thirdly, to keep the show going, it is necessary continually to introduce new commodities and create new wants. In a competitive society, a growth of consumption does not guarantee a growth of satisfaction.

Here is the problem. The task of deciding how resources should be allocated is not fulfilled by the market but by the great corporations who are in charge of the finance for development.

These questions involve the whole political and social system of the capitalist world; they cannot be decided by economic theory, but it would be decent, at least, if the economists admitted that they do not have an answer to them.

THE AGE OF GROWTH

THE slump from which we are told the United States economy is now recovering has been an extremely important event. It was the first serious recession since World War II. It brought to an end the epoch in which continuous steady growth in the industrial economies was generally taken for granted. Certainly, there were quite sharp setbacks, particularly in 1958 and 1966, but the very fact that they were overcome maintained confidence that a real recession was a thing of the past.

It was believed that this was a new era in which government policy could be relied upon to control the levers of economic activity. The spokesmen for capitalism were saying, in effect: we have to admit that the unemployment that prevailed in the interwar years was a serious defect in the free-market system. Now we are going to give you capitalism with full employment, so what have you got to complain of?

Indeed, capitalism without a serious slump for 25 years was something new in history. In Western Europe and in Japan, statistical GNP per capita had been growing for a long run of years at never less than per 4 per cent per annum. In North America growth was only at 2·5 per cent, but starting from a higher base, the great mass of consumption grew prodigiously, though poverty, which is largely relative, was not much reduced.

High consumption struck a blow in the cold war. When tourists from the affluent countries began to pass through the ex-iron curtain, they naturally came from the affluent classes; the slum dwellers stayed at home. The display of the tourists' possessions was quite a shock in the socialist world, creating envy and discontent.

Experience of *almost* continuous prosperity built up a belief in perpetual growth as a normal state of affairs.

The Gildersleeve Lecture delivered at Barnard College, New York, 2 March 1976. Reprinted in *Collected Economic Papers*, Vol. V, 1979.

It is for this reason that the slump from which we are now assumed to be recovering was a unique event. It has been a very great shock, all the more because recession was accompanied by rising prices, so that all the old rules fail to hold — inflation no longer makes profits buoyant and rising unemployment no longer keeps inflation in check.

BASTARD KEYNESIANISM

The doctrines of the new era have been attributed to Keynes, but the dominant economic theory of the time, in North America and spreading from there over the world, was what I have called the bastard Keynesian doctrine. I do not use this term just as abuse. It has a definite meaning. The old orthodoxy, against which the Keynesian revolution was raised, was based on Say's law — there cannot be a deficiency of demand. Spending creates demand for consumption goods, while saving creates demand for investment goods such as machinery and stocks. Keynes pointed out the obvious fact that investment is governed by the decisions of business corporations and public institutions, not by the desire of the community to save.

An increase in household saving means a reduction in consumption; it does not increase investment but reduces employment.

According to the bastard Keynesian doctrine, it is possible to calculate the rate of saving that households collectively desire to achieve, and then governments, by fiscal and monetary policy, can organize the investment of this amount of saving. Thus Say's law is artificially restored, and under its shelter all the old doctrines creep back again, even the doctrine that any given stock of capital will provide employment for any amount of labour at the appropriate equilibrium real-wage rate. Then unemployment occurs only because wages are being held above the equilibrium level.

Keynes, and Kalecki, who found out the same theory independently, were diagnosing an inherent defect in the laisser faire system but the bastard Keynesians turned the argument back into being a defence of laisser faire, provided that just one blemish was going to be removed.

The complacency of the age of growth covered what, in the legal phrase, can be called *inherent vice* in the free-marked system. The present situation was quite unexpected. Economists lost track of their formulae and the politicians got their slogans mixed up.

First consider inflation. A major point in the theory of Keynes and Kalecki is that the general level of prices in an industrial economy depends mainly upon the level of money-wage rates. The Keynesian revolution began by refuting the then orthodox theory that cutting wages is the best way to increase employment. Keynes argued that a general cut in wages would reduce the price level more or less proportionally, so raise the burden of debt, discourage investment, and increase unemployment. Kalecki added that if prices do not fall, it is still worse, for then real wages are reduced and unemployment is increased directly by the fall in purchases of consumption goods.

Such arguments obviously cut both ways. If falling money wages reduce prices, rising money wages must increase them.

Keynes expected that a long run of high employment and high profits would lead to continuously rising prices though he did not suggest what to do about it. Any rise of prices leads to a demand for a compensating rise in wages and every rise in wages leads to rising prices again.

Professor Weintraub and his disciples drew this moral from Keynes' theory, but the bastard Keynesians somehow managed to sweep it under the carpet.

It is sometimes said that the trouble arises from monopoly. But according to the textbook theory competitive prices are governed by marginal costs. A rise in wage rates raises marginal costs for a whole group of competitors and prices go up proportionately.

But of course perfect competition never did exist except in the textbooks, and a growth of huge monopolistic corporations is a necessary consequence of competitive growth in a long run of prosperity.

THE CLASS WAR AND INFLATION

The trouble does not lie in monopoly but in the class war – workers must struggle to keep their share in the product of industry and corporations must struggle to prevent them from increasing it.

There is not only a class war between employers and workers as a whole. There is an internal struggle of each group to maintain its relative position. Looking back now, after experience of inflation at 20 per cent per annum, anything less than 5 per cent seems moderate and acceptable. But even 3 and 4 per cent, year after year, was a great nuisance.

Expectations of 3 per cent were quite enough to set going speculative booms in property of every kind, causing huge arbitrary redistributions of wealth and falsification of values. There was a joke after a sudden dip in the art market. One dealer was saying to another: Do you think we could get them to buy paintings because they *like* them?

The long run of what now seems mild inflation gave rise to the cynical doctrine that the private enterprise economy *needs* unemployment to preserve the value of money. The spokesmen of capitalism were saying: Sorry, chaps, we made a mistake. We are not offering full employment, but the natural level of unemployment.

Of course, they suggested that a *little* unemployment would be enough to keep prices stable, but now we know that even a lot will not do so.

Inflation at 3 or 4 per cent was quite enough to set going the struggle for relative shares and to break through the solid belief that a dollar is a dollar. Resistances and conventions were progressively undermined so that any chance shock would set the vicious spiral spinning in earnest.

The shock came from the other part of the price system. The price level in the market economy is in two parts – the cost-plus system in the industrial sector and the supply and demand system in the markets for primary commodities. A sharp rise in activity in the industrial sector raises the prices of raw materials, puts up the cost of manufactures relative to money-wage rates and so sets up a demand to raise wages in turn.

Even before OPEC threw a spanner in the works, a sharp rise in material prices had occurred. This was the spark that fell upon the inflationary tinder that had been accumulating over the years. It was bound to happen sooner or later. For my part, I was surprised that the era of mild inflation (which survived the Korean war boom) could last for so long, not that it finally gave way.

Now that this element of inherent vice in the free-market system has broken out in a virulent form, it is not easy to see any way to return to the era of continuous growth with an 'acceptable' level of inflation.

THE POLITICAL TRADE CYCLE

The next point to observe is that so-called Keynesian policy was not really applied in such a way as to maintain stability. It turned out to be very much like the political trade cycle predicted by Kalecki. A continuous high level of employment is not acceptable to the leaders of industry. It is true that it is accompanied by high profits, but it weakens their position in the class war. As Kalecki remarked, ' "discipline in the factories" and "political stability" are more appreciated by business leaders than profits,' though, of course they require profits as well.

Near-full employment can be established by means of a government deficit, but if it goes on too long the captains of industry fear that the workers will get out of hand and want to 'teach them a lesson'. Rentier interests grow tired of a boom that generates inflation, and, as Kalecki presciently observed, more than one economist will be found to say that the situation is manifestly unsound. Then government outlay is cut, dear money imposed, and unemployment emerges again. But after a year or two it is time for the next election. No government wants to go into an election with too much unemployment. The tap is turned on again and employment and profits revive.

A particular feature of the political trade cycle as it is played out in the United States is that when a political boom is required, it is arms expenditures that expand; when a political recession is required, it is social services that are cut.

One of the contributing factors to the outbreak of inflation in 1973 is that both Mr. Heath in Great Britain and Mr. Nixon in the USA were playing up for a political boom in 1972 with exceptional vigour.

Another Keynesian diagnosis of instability has been developed by Professor Minsky. He maintains that a capitalist economy in general, and in the USA in particular, is inherently incapable of steady growth. When investment is increasing from year to year, the flow of profit is increasing and providing finance to maintain the growth of investment. Then good prospects of profit lead corporations to increase their investment plans beyond their capacity for self-finance, and raise their leverage. The more cautious hold back at first, but when they see that the daring ones are successful they are led to follow suit. Now the ratio of payments required to service debt is continually rising relative to the flow of actual cash receipts. Sooner or later some industrial businesses have to curtail their investment or financial businesses to sell out assets. With the indebtedness that has grown up, the system is vulnerable, and any check to expansion sets the dominoes of credit falling; the search for liquidity spreads from one business to another and a real slump grows out of the financial crisis.

The Minsky thesis and the Kalecki thesis are not mutually exclusive. Rather, the expansion and collapse of credit act as an amplifier of the political cycle, bringing an undesigned, exaggerated reaction to a political stop and preventing a political go from sustaining itself.

Minsky also has a more long-run diagnosis of recent history: when the war ended, both the industrial and the financial systems had a fat hump of liquidity, which was gradually eaten up in successive crises and is now pretty well exhausted. Moreover, the very fact that the authorities would never allow a financial crisis to go too far meant that a residue of debt was left each time so that a robust state of liquidity was never restored.

Nowadays, it seems that even the political trade cycle has come to an end, and the governments of all the capitalist nations are stuck in immobility, dithering between the fear of inflation and the fear of unemployment.

WHERE DO WE GO FROM HERE?

An American economist might very well reproach me: You call me a bastard, but what would *you* do? I could only answer with the quip about the motorist who asked the way to Oklahoma. The man by the roadside answered: If I wanted to go to Oklahoma I should never start here.

The problem has developed far beyond the point where it makes sense to discuss any simple remedies. Keynes himself did not propose *simple* remedies. It was the bastard Keynesians who concocted bromides from his acid treatment of orthodox nonsense. Now the old guard, who stood out against him in the thirties, are saying Keynes has failed. We must return to strict laisser faire and sound finance. If you are uncomfortable in the frying pan you can jump into the fire.

In the famous last chapter of the *General Theory*, Keynes describes his political philosophy as 'moderately conservative'. This was offered as a paradox. All his life he had been treated by the establishment as an *enfant terrible*, so that to present himself as a conservative was partly ironical. Moreover, the preceding chapters of the book were a powerful polemic against received ideas. It was because Keynes was shocked by the force of his own indictment of capitalism that he wrote the last chapter in a mollifying tone.

On inflation, he agreed with my deduction from the *General Theory* that rising prices would prove to be the great unsolved problem of full-employment policy. When money-wage rates do not rise as fast as productivity, the market economy falls into stagnation through sluggish demand, but when the bargaining power of organized labour is sufficient to keep wages rising enough, it will generally raise them too much to maintain stable prices. Keynes regarded this as a political problem which, when he died, still lay in the future.

Kalecki took a more radical view:

'Full employment capitalism' will have, of course, to develop new social and political institutions which will reflect the increased power of the working class. If capitalism can adjust itself to full employment a fundamental reform will have been incorporated in it. If not, it will show itself an outmoded system which must be scrapped.

It is precisely because changes in social and political institutions did not occur that the age of growth has been so uneasy and is now in danger of bringing itself to an end.

In Great Britain, the trade unions were in a strong position while employment was high but they did not want to ask for the kinds of changes that Kalecki recommended. They only asked for freedom in wage bargaining. However, inflation rising to a rate of 25 per cent per annum has been a great shock and the trade unionists found that they were alienating all the rest of the population, including their own wives. Now they are willing to discuss the possibility of restraining wages and asking for other concessions in return.

But there are great difficulties in the way of a thoroughgoing incomes policy. We are told that if the higher salaries are cut the 'best brains' in the country will be drained to the United States. I wish you joy of them.

In Western Europe, particularly in France, there are interesting experiments that have been going on. But in the USA an important new development during the age of growth is not at all favourable to labour's side in the class war. Here, business has always been able to play divide and rule with the work force at home – setting 'WASPs' against blacks and immigrants. Now that game is being played overseas as well. The diligent, dextrous workers of East Asia can be got at a cut price to make components for the sophisticated products of modern industry.

UNEVEN GROWTH

Another serious element of inherent vice in the age of growth was the unevenness of development of various capitalist nations. Differences in competitive power, whatever their origin, set up a spiral of divergence. A country such as West Germany, with growing exports, can maintain a high rate of investment and therefore of growing productivity which enhances its competitive power, and causes real wages to rise so that workers are less demanding; in the miserable United Kingdom, an increase in employment causes an increase in the deficit in the balance of payments so that every *go* has to be brought to an end with a *stop*. Thus strong competitors grow stronger so that the weak grow weaker.

Because of its mere size, the United States' overseas trade plays a small part in national income, but not a small part in the world market. It can move from deficit to surplus without much disturbance at home but with a great deal of disturbance to the other trading nations.

These disequilibria have set great strains on the international monetary system. According to the old rules of the gold-standard game, a deficit country could borrow to develop a source of exports that would service its debt; a lender could support a net outflow of capital no greater than its surplus on income account. Now, the UK has to go on borrowing because to cut imports would be an injury to foreign exporters. The USA was able to take advantage of the dollar being the world currency to run an ever greater outflow on capital account with an ever growing deficit on income account, until President Nixon suddenly tried to reverse the position by decree. A contributory cause to the great inflation was that the devaluation of the dollar in 1971 sent funds in search of liquidity to speculation in commodities and helped to drive up their prices.

Now it seems that gold after all is going to come back into the game, but lumps of metal will not establish rules of play that can bring modern chaos in the international money market into working order.

I said that the great rise in material prices was already under way before the 'oil crisis'. Certainly the sudden rise in the price of a commodity in inelastic demand helped to precipitate the recession. In the United States, the rise in consumers' expenditure on petrol, reflected in the large profits of the oil companies in 1973, was drawing purchasing power away from other goods and services. But I do not support the view that the change in the balance of monopoly power in the world market is a serious menace to the capitalist system. Modern capitalism suffers chronically from deficiency of demand. It can easily stand a depreciation in terms of trade. Expenditure of the oil money is useful to capitalist industry, especially the arms industry, and is one of the elements in the present recovery from the slump.

There used to be an old Soviet joke which today has rather a sour taste:

Q: What is the greatest problem facing the President of the United States?
A: Is it possible to have capitalism in one country?

I believe the oil sheiks are a great help to the United States in spreading capitalism hand over fist.

INVESTMENT AND SOCIAL CONTROL

The oldest element of inherent vice in the private enterprise system is still the most important, that is, the anarchy of unplanned growth. Keynes' last chapter was not so conservative after all, for he thought that it would be necessary to have a comprehensive social control of investment to overcome the short-period instability of capitalism. Its absence is even more serious in the long run. The textbooks teach us that in the free market economy demand 'allocates scarce means between alternative uses'. How are investible resources allocated?

Here, unfortunately, Keynes made an ill-considered remark, quite contrary to his main argument. He suggested that, provided governments make sure that there is enough investment to maintain full employment, 'the classical theory comes into its own again, from this point on'. Provided only that there is enough production, 'there is no objection to be raised against the classical analysis' of the determination of what in particular is to be produced and how the factors of production are allocated between different uses.

Here is the bastard Keynesian theory in its purest form.

But what does it mean? What theory has ever been advanced of how private self-interest directs *new* investment into the lines that best provide for the needs and desires of society as a whole?

It is true that there is nowadays a great deal of public support for certain lines of research and development. But whose needs is it designed to meet? Big money leads to an alliance of big science and big industry, which results in technological megalomania rather than a careful study of human needs. I will not be so unpatriotic as to refer to Concorde, or so ungracious as to remark that putting a man on the moon did nothing to make the earth more habitable. But I must add my voice to the protest that the great concentration upon atomic energy, not only here but in the Third World, is largely due to the snobbery of being 'advanced', which attracts the scientists away from the search for safer, less costly, and so less glamorous ways of economizing and generating power.

In the sectors which are left to private enterprise, the great corporations, pursuing hoped-for profits, choose what lines to develop, and how the population is to be employed. A community grows up around the site where some corporation has found it convenient to install a plant, and is devastated when the corporation finds it convenient to shut the plant down.

As for the sovereignty of choice of the consumers, it rules only so long as they all choose the same thing. When a supermarket has killed off the neighbourhood shops, an individual housewife who regrets them cannot *reveal* her *preference* for buying from them any more.

The leading case of the dominance of production over consumers' tastes is, of course, the motor car. By taking away demand from public transport, raising its costs, and finally making it unable to exist, the motor-car industry increases its own market, until everyone who is not destitute is obliged to run a car, and those who are destitute have to stay at home.

Then television creates a whole new style of social life, and electronics, it seems, is creating a new style of politics.

Is all this what the free individual consumer chooses, or what he has been trapped into thinking that he needs?

The bastard Keynesian theory never even pretended to discuss the use of resources. It fell back upon the old defence of laisser-faire: what is profitable is right. The most remarkable application of this doctrine is now to the problem of pollution. The argument is that antipollution rules are hampering investment and reducing profits. Pollution should be allowed a little longer, so as to help recovery from the slump. Amenities and health have to be sacrificed to profits, because if we hinder the freedom of the corporations to employ the resources of the nation as they choose, they will not be able to employ them at all.

The workers in each industry line up with their employers. They do not *want* their children to be poisoned, but they are more anxious about losing their jobs.

Similarly with the problem of exhaustible resources. The great corporations must be allowed to go on chewing up the planet, else they will not be able to make profits and provide employment.

Now we are stuck with it. We must keep the show going. Private enterprise is wonderfully flexible in jumping from one profitable market to another, but it is very rigid in resistance to social control. Now that the authorities want employment to revive, they can only push industry further down the grooves that it has worn for itself. There is no point in thinking of what we really want, such as abolishing poverty and restoring peace. All we can ask for is what they choose to give us. We must keep the show going or else they won't give us anything at all.

3

STAGFLATION

THE most striking difference between the Great Depression of the 1930s and whatever you want call it in the 1970s is that *then* growing unemployment was accompanied by falling prices, while *now* we suffer from the unprecedented combination of misfortunes called stagflation.

The great slump was accompanied, indeed partly caused, by the sharp fall in the prices of raw materials, including foodstuffs. This killed off purchasing power from one sector of the world economy and so destroyed demand for another. As industry contracted, real demand for primary products was reduced and prices fell all the more. In one sense, this was a mitigation – if you are going to have massive unemployment it is better to have it with cheap food than with dear food.

Looking back, we can see now that straightforward Keynesian remedies – cheap money and public works – would have been effective in the 1930s. Indeed they were. If the democracies had been converted before Hitler proved Keynes right, we might have been saved from a terrible experience.

Now, though the mechanism of the system is understood much better, the remedies are not so simple. The extended period of rapid growth, in socialist as well as capitalist industry, had led to the limits of capacity in many lines. So long as demand from industry for materials is slack, prices are depressed (except when, as with oil, monopoly power keeps them up), but as soon as industry returns to its former rate of growth, it runs into bottlenecks and prices shoot up again. In the 1930s there was poverty in the midst of plenty in an obvious sense – families going hungry while food rotted on the farms. Now there is a more complicated contradiction – present investment to widen the bottlenecks to permit future growth would drive demand into the bottlenecks before they could be widened and so cause scarcities.

The David Kinley Lecture, University of Illinois at Urbana, published in *Challenge*, November/December 1979 and in *The Quarterly Review of Economics and Business*, Autumn 1979.

In the 1930s, deliberate remedies for unemployment would have been feasible, but the authorities refused to understand them. In England, Say's Law and the Treasury view, in spite of all Keynes could say, held sway right up to the outbreak of war, while in the United States the New Deal was a weak mixture of helpful and harmful measures. Now the policies that could reduce unemployment are much better understood but their application is inhibited by the fear of inflation.

These general reflections are obvious enough. Nevertheless, if we try to understand the relation of inflation to employment, we must look more closely into the mechanisms of a modern economy.

1

What do we mean by inflation? It used to be said that inflation is a rise of prices that is the fault of money as opposed to the fault of goods. This puts the theory into the definition so that we are stuck in it. More broadly, inflation usually means a continuing rise of the general price level. But the general level of prices is an abstraction. Different prices behave differently and goods and services being sold alter their character as time goes by. To describe movements of the price level, some conventions have to be adopted and the movement can be described only *ex post*.

To see how inflation occurs we have first to inquire how prices are formed.

The formation of the prices of goods and services by supply and demand is the central topic of so-called microeconomics, which occupies a major part in elementary teaching and proliferates into levels that are by no means elementary. Yet micro-economics has been cut off from any connection with the world that we are living in by eliminating the passage of time and postulating perfect competition. It is shut up in the box of 'general equilibrium', which insulates it from connecting with actual problems. There was a brief vogue for imperfect and monopolistic competition, but this soon faded out and, in my opinion, it was not really much of an improvement. The proposition that prices are determined by costs of production would entail that prices normally fall in a boom when unit costs are reduced by high utilization of capacity and rise in a slump as utilization falls. The theory that they are determined by the quantity of money has never been explained.

I wrote in 1942, 'It seems that economic science has not yet solved its first problem. What determines the price of a commodity?' I think that this is still largely true, but meanwhile we have made some advance in formulating hypotheses that are worth pursuing.

Economic theory operates at three levels. First, it propounds doctrines, such as that the free play of market forces tends to establish an optimum position of equilibrium. Second, it uses the method of thought experiments, in which arbitrarily defined concepts are manipulated to exhibit the logical relations between them. This is necessary in the process of formulating the problems to be discussed, but it is all too apt to develop into the idle amusement of setting up insoluble puzzles and then disputing about how they might be solved. The one most fashionable at the moment is how a market would operate if every trader had correct foresight of what the others were going to do. The third level in economic analysis, the only one that is serious, is to choose hypotheses about the behaviour of an economy that have sufficient *a priori* plausibility to be worth confronting with evidence, and then to search for evidence to see whether they hold water.

To find plausible hypotheses about prices, we must first distinguish various types of markets. Primary commodities — animal, vegetable, and mineral products — are mainly dealt with by merchants acting as intermediaries, buying in order to sell. Here, in the main, supply and demand rule. Their interaction by no means tends to establish equilibrium; rather, it sets up continual oscillations as current experience influences expectations of what will happen next. But, nowadays, even here, it is rare for the 'free play of market forces' to be entirely free: support prices to defend the interests of one sector of the community against another are common and so are political manipulations. Was it just an accident of supply and demand that when Allende was President of Chile her receipts from the export of copper fell sharply? (See *Challenge* Sep./Oct. 1980, p. 61).

In manufactures, the sphere of operation of dealers has been shrinking ever since the great slump of the 1930s and large-scale industry and large-scale retailing have developed the organization of sales and of purchases for themselves so that the sphere of operation of independent merchants has been much reduced.

The manufacturers set their prices for themselves. Here the old theory used to be that prices were determined by marginal costs, but this was more in the nature of a doctrine than a hypothesis.

The received view now is that businesses distinguish costs that vary directly with the flow of output, then calculate the average overhead cost (including an allowance for depreciation) at a standard rate of operation of plant, and, finally, add a margin for net profit more or less according to their judgment of what the traffic will bear. Thus the full cost principle and the degree-of-monopoly principle are combined. This, of course, is a loose generalization to cover a varied scene; a great deal more natural history study is required of how the animals in the competitive jungle actually behave. So far, however, it seems to be standing up to statistical investigation fairly well.

According to this view, supply and demand, with given productive capacity, have very little influence on prices. Once margins have been fixed, they do not vary much with the flow of sales. When output exceeds the standard, superprofits flow in at the previously determined price. If demand is running at a level that carries a plant up to capacity, delivery dates are lengthened rather than prices being raised. When utilization falls below the standard, as Adam Smith remarked, it is considered very bad form to start cutting prices, and sometimes they are even raised 'in order to cover costs.'

Indeed, variable costs contain quite a large element of quasi-fixed expenses, so that marginal costs fall rather than rise as output expands, but the whole level of prime cost is raised when there is a new agreement setting higher money-wage rates than before, or when there are higher costs for materials and energy.

The essence of this hypothesis is that *prices of manufacturers are quite insensitive to swings of demand, but react quickly to changes in costs.*

2

Now turn to the other side of the story. What determines the level of employment?

The questions opened up by Keynes and Kalecki have been smothered in mainstream teaching of macroeconomics by being stuffed back into concepts of equilibrium, much like what happened to price theory in the microeconomic sphere. With the present uneasy situation in the world economy, however, complacency is giving way to doubts and fears that get these crucial questions a hearing once more.

Keynes wrote in the preface to *The General Theory*: 'The ideas which are here expressed so laboriously are extremely simple and should be obvious.' Certainly, it should be obvious that a free market economy does *not* have a strong tendency to establish equilibrium with full employment of its available labour force.

Keynes' alternative hypotheses are stated clearly in short-period terms. Here and now, there is a certain specific amount of productive capacity — factories, machinery, rolling stock embodying particular techniques — brought into existence by past history; certain natural resources and means of consumption — housing, theatres, stocks of goods in the shops; a certain available labour force with particular training and skills; a certain distribution of financial resources, and a state of expectations in the minds of businessmen that has caused them to make certain plans for investments to enlarge capacity. Then there is a certain flow of expenditure that determines which goods will be produced and what incomes will be earned.

In a modern industrial economy, there is almost no production for self-consumption except housework within the home, and even that is growing less and less. Everyone's income, therefore, depends on other people's expenditure. If there were no expenditure this month except out of last month's income, the system would quickly run down. Not all income is spent. Some is used to pay off debts and some is saved to add to private wealth or financial reserves of businesses. Thus, even to maintain, still more to expand, the flow of income there must be some booster to expenditure over and above expenditure out of the income being currently received.

The main boosters, of course, are budget deficits of governments and various authorities, that is, expenditure in excess of tax receipts and rents; the excess of business investment over and above what is financed out of current cash flow, and consumer's expenditure covered by borrowing — say, for housebuilding — or by drawing upon balances saved in the past.

There is another element in the relation of expenditure to income that we shall have to discuss in a moment, namely, the national balance of payments. A booster to income comes from receipts from overseas — foreign earnings — a damper comes from foreign payments — for imports or financial obligations. When the internal boosters are working, increasing income leads to increasing expenditure and part of this goes abroad. It helps to boost incomes in other countries by increasing *their* export earnings and dampens expansion at home. The most reliable booster, then, is an increase in export earnings, for this will automatically cover the damping effect in increasing imports and still leave some boost for home activity. Unfortunately, however, export-led growth for some countries accompanies import-led stagnation for others.

What about the quantity of money? It is quite true that, properly defined, $MV = PT$ (money times velocity equals price times turnover), but why do they always say that causation runs from M to P, that is, that an increase in the quantity of money raises prices? No one has ever explained a mechanism by which this happens.

When I asked Milton Friedman about this, he replied with a thought experiment drawn from Keynes' theory. When there is an increase in the quantity of money *relative to requirements*, the rate of interest is reduced. If other things remain the same (as of course they never do), investment by business and households readjusts their stocks appropriately. But he unfortunately overlooked the fact that this is a once-over change, not a permanent rise in expenditure.

The other way round, there is a simple causal mechanism running from T to M. When employment and output are expanding, businesses finance the growth of working capital by bank loans. Even if the basis of credit is tightly controlled by the Federal Reserve, banks can always make advances to good clients by selling off securities that are less profitable to them. But in any case the basis of credit cannot be so tightly controlled as all that; liquidity normally increases with the need for it.

Now, if our hypothesis is correct, when the boosters are working output can expand so that in many lines it passes standard utilization rates and there is an increase in profits at constant prices. T and M keep more or less in step, while V and P can stay as they were.

Stating the argument in very short-period terms exaggerates instability; when the operation of any of the boosters raises expenditure, therefore employment, therefore income, therefore the flow of profits, then expectations of profit are raised, the supply of internal finance for businesses is increased and borrowing made easier – therefore plans for investment are expanded and the booster boosts itself. When the boosters act rapidly, the system may run into bottlenecks and the upswing be brought to a halt. But an upswing may take some years to play itself out. Meanwhile investment has been going on and if projects have been well chosen, embodying improved techniques, capacity has been growing and productivity increasing. The upswing *may* be able to keep itself going for quite a time, though of course there is no guarantee that it will.

3

Then where does inflation come into the story? Here we must turn to another element in Keynes' *General Theory*, which was even more subversive of received doctrines than his revocation of Say's Law. This was the discovery that there is no meaning whatever to be attached to an equilibrium set of prices in money terms. At any moment, in a free market economy, the level of prices is an historical accident brought about by events in the recent and remote past. It has not much inertia to prevent it changing in response to events taking place today.

This was so shocking that economists for the most part failed to take it in. (Hicks has confessed that he saw the point only recently.)

Keynes was confronted in the early 1930s with the then prevalent doctrine that cutting wage rates would reduce costs relative to demand and so restore equilibrium. He pointed out that when money-wages are cut, prices fall more or less commensurately, so that costs in real terms are not reduced. All the strife and bitterness and relative injustices of trying to push wages down are incurred in vain; furthermore, if they did succeed, it would actually do harm by increasing the burden of liabilities fixed in terms of money and embarrassing the banking system. A cut in wages in one trading country relative to others may give it a competitive advantage, but if so, a depreciation of the exchange rate is a relatively painless way of getting the same result.

On the other tack, in prosperous times, prices are volatile upwards, for it is always easier to redress any discrepancy by raising some prices than by lowering others. Any chance rise in prices, coming, say, from commodity markets, raises some costs and so is likely to spread. Moreover, it reduces real-wage rates. At the same time, capital accumulation with technical progress is increasing profits and trade unions have a right and a duty to ask for a share.

Keynes foresaw that in a period of continuous high employment, money-wage rates would be likely to rise faster than producitivity. The theory of industrial pricing sketched above is that the ratio of gross margins to variable costs has greater inertia so that prices are raised more or less in proportion to unit variable costs. The rises are not uniform. Strong, technically progressive firms do not put up much resistance to wage demands and even welcome them as a means of embarrassing weaker competitors. The traditional relativity of incomes is upset and losers have to fight to restore their position. Service workers such as garbage collectors have no leverage except to conduct malodorous strikes. After some hesitation, the noble professions such as teachers and physicians have to join the scramble.

I do not think that inflation should be defined simply in terms of a rise in prices as such. When the boosters to effective demand increase employment and real output, if they operate too fast, they are likely to increase demand relative to supply for primary products and push up prices in those sectors. But the lateral movement of effective demand pulling out employment and activity should not be called inflation. Inflation is, so to say, a vertical movement of prices due to increasing rates of pay for the same activity. Of course, rises of agricultural and raw material prices do contribute strongly to inflation, for they enter into variable costs and (with constant proportionate gross margins) raise prices relative to money-wage rates and thus lower real wages — and so give another turn to the screw of irresistible demands for more pay.

Looking at inflation this way round, we see that the relation between the movements of employment and prices are quite different from what used to be supposed. The old idea was that, in a boom, employment and prices went up together. With more money to spend, there is a demand-pull on prices. But demand works laterally to pull out real output, employment, and utilization of capacity: more money to spend and more goods to spend it on.

Will it not inevitably boost itself up till it meets a physical limit and comes to a halt? Not inevitably. The short period is not so short as all that. Keynes' crack that in the long run we are all dead was quite unfair — we are living in the long period every week, from Monday to Friday. Long-period movements are those that take place through capital accumulation and technical change. They are slow relative to swings of effective demand, but in prosperous times they are going on at quite an appreciable pace.

Thus, output per unit of employment is constantly growing so that the vertical movement of inflation is absorbed, to a greater or lesser extent, and prices rise less than pay. This may help to slow down the inflation itself for, with rising real-wage rates all round, consciousness of relativities may be less sharp and money-wage demands less insistent.

While prosperity lasted, we had the unexpected experience of rapid all-round growth with a rate of fall in the purchasing power of money that, looking back, seems mild and tolerable, while nowadays the value of money falls fast and real income rises slowly.

There is a similar contrast between nations. A country whose balance of payments is strong can keep up investment and continue to gain in productivity so that real wages can go on rising and so preserve industrial peace, while a weak country is bedevilled with strikes and unrest.

The age of growth was divided from the age of uncertainty by a period of violent upheavals that might be regarded as an historical accident, but continued inflation even at 3 percent per annum tends to accelerate as more and more bargains are made in the light of expectations of higher prices in the immediate and further future, and this makes the system accident-prone. There was a wage explosion in several countries in 1968 (the 'événements' in France). Nixon's bright idea of freeing the dollar from gold in 1971 drove speculative funds into the commodity markets and pushed up prices and, of course, there was oil in 1973.

The action of the Organization of Petroleum Exporting Countries illustrated an old-fashioned textbook argument that had fallen into oblivion: a rise in the price of a commodity that is in inelastic demand reduces expenditure on everything else. The sharp increase in the receipts of the Arabs and the oil companies could not possibly be spent quickly and took a large bite out of worldwide effective demand. This was certainly a rare kind of accident, but accidents will happen and who knows what is yet in store?

4

Now we come to the crux of the argument. Stagflation: how does it happen and why has it set in?

Inflation is admittedly a great nuisance and unemployment a serious evil, but they do not affect the different strata of the population all in the same way. Inflation is the greater nuisance to the middle classes – rentiers, professionals and business executives, civil servants, and politicians. Unemployment is the greater evil to industrial workers, to blacks, ethnic minorities, and the anxious parents of school leavers.

The articulate part of the public readily accepts the doctrine that inflation is the more serious of the two problems and is willing to support the efforts of the authorities to check inflation by means of policies that reduce employment.

The boosters are put into reverse. Monetary restriction puts up interest rates and curtails investment both by business and by households. Government and municipal outlay is reduced and taxes raised. As the growth of expenditure falls, profits decline and plans for further investment are cut down. Now, as in the 1930s, both businesses and households are forced to economize. Quite apart from human misery, there is a great loss of potential real output and of accumulation for future growth, even while the ominous threat of a general financial collapse hangs over the scene.

Inflation, however, is not eliminated. At any moment, there are recent past rises of costs in the pipeline that have yet to be passed on. Strong trade unions, business executives and organized professions still continue to get themselves raises.

Monetary influences work backwards as we saw them working forwards. There is a strong connection between M and T and a weak and indirect relationship between P and M. Credit restriction can reduce real activity and bring down prices in the supply and demand sector, but the vertical inflationary raising of money incomes is only partially slowed down. Taxation reduces expenditure but excise and sales taxes go straight into prices, while taxes on business profits are treated as costs so that margins are raised in order to cover them.

The remedy of exchange depreciation for a weak balance of trade turns out to be ineffective. It acts slowly to reduce the foreign price of exports; meanwhile the rise in the home price of imports is spreading and pouring oil on the fire of wage demands.

The monetarists, seeing that their old doctrines have grown less convincing, have taken up a new line. This is the concept of a 'natural level of unemployment'. There is some level of unemployment at which the expectation of rising prices can be eliminated and, when that point is reached, money-wage rates will cease to rise and inflation will be brought to an end.

It is found in practice, however, that reducing the supply of goods is not very helpful to getting prices down and that great misery among unorganized workers does not break the power of the strong trade unions to maintain real-wage rates for their own members, so this policy does not work very well. For the newfangled monetarists, however, if prices are still rising, that only shows that the natural level of unemployment has not yet been reached — we need more restrictions, more cuts, and more taxes to get employment down further.

This is a return to the policies of the early 1930s, which Keynes, in his day, described as brutal and sadistic.

Yes, you may say, that is all very well, but what do you want us to do?

That is a political question. What powers do you give me? A national treaty, such as they had in the 1930s in Australia, would make it possible to limit *all* incomes, so that a return towards full employment and growth could be pushed without a vertical inflationary rise of prices and pay.

Ad hoc temporary restraint, only on wages, creates so many anomalies, as we have found in Britain, that it always explodes before its work has been done (we have even tried Professor Weintraub's plan of penalizing firms that agree to pay wages above a norm, but that lasted only a week).

For orderly international trade, the Keynes Plan at Bretton Woods proposed that surplus countries should be penalized so as to encourage them to raise wages and import more, thus relieving the pressure on the deficit countries. But in this nationalistic world, the strong countries do not see why they should put themselves out to help the weak ones.

Finally, if incomes were more equal in the United States, there would be a permanent stable mass of consumption demand and the need for boosters to maintain employment would be much reduced.

Of course, all this is a daydream. The dominant doctrine is still laisser faire. Free markets are a sacred creed. The Chicago school has almost as strong a grip in the United States as in Chile and the International Monetary Fund goes round the world strangling deficit countries one after another.

I do not want to suggest that there are no difficulties except pernicious policies. There are deep-seated differences between the advantages of different countries in industry. The English are lazy and the Americans individualistic, while the Japanese are diligent and disciplined.

The turbulence of accumulation and technical change cannot easily be tamed. Trade cycle models are generally brittle thought experiments, but there is one hypothesis, now out of fashion, that I would like to back. That is Schumpeter's theory of bouts of investment induced by major technical discoveries. While the new methods are being installed, there is brisk investment and general prosperity, but, after a time, an overshoot is bound to occur, so that excess capacity emerges and brings investment down.

I should be prepared to bet that, when the detailed history of the twenty-five years after 1945 comes to be written, it will be seen to have had the character of a boom – for instance in substituting mechanical horse power for four-legged horses all over the world (oxen and camels are still surviving in some places) while there is a formidable overexpansion of the motor car industry.

In several lines there had been an overshoot in the early 1970s. I do not think the oil crisis would have caused such prolonged stagnation if the boom had not been near exhausting itself already.

But that is another story.

THINKING ABOUT THINKING

MY first publication, in 1932, was devoted to the methodology of economics. It was a small pamphlet called *Economics is a Serious Subject*. This was during what Professor Shackle has called the years of high theory[1] when it seemed that 'imperfect competition' was going to revolutionize the analysis of prices and when the discussions that brought Keynes from the *Treatise on Money* to the *General Theory* had already begun.[2]

It seemed, at the time, that economics was emerging from the long sleep of laisser faire doctrines, 'marginal products' and equilibrium under Say's Law and that it was an important subject, dealing with urgent problems. The title of my essay, however, turned on a pun. It opens as follows:

> The student's heart sinks when he is presented with a book on the Scope and Method of his subject. Let me make a start, he begs, and I will find out the scope and method as I go along. And the student is perfectly right. For a serious subject, in the academic sense, is neither more nor less than its own technique.

I never had the pamphlet reprinted because I soon ceased to believe in its main argument – that if the economists could avoid certain bad habits and arrive at a consistent set of assumptions, however abstract, they could approach reality step by step merely by making more complicated models.

I soon realized that to avoid unacceptable methods of argument is a necessary but not a sufficient condition for establishing a genuine discipline. But some of the negative points in the essay still seem to be

[1] G. L. S. Shackle, *The Years of High Theory*, CUP, Cambridge 1967.
[2] See JMK, Vol. XIII.

valid forty years after it was written. One of those points concerns controversy among economists.

> Economic controversies sometimes occur in which one of the contestants is right and the other is wrong. One has made a logical error, and the other has seen it. But this is the rarest kind of controversy. More often, like the two knights in the story, they are fighting about whether a shield is black or white, only to find, after it is all over, that one side was black and the other was white. Now, conducting an economic controversy is a delicate business. It is fatal to be too rude – an interchange of: It's black. No it's not, it's white – never leads to any results. On the other hand it is fatal to be too polite. When you are looking at a black shield, and the other man says it is white, it is of no use to say: Perhaps so, but I think on balance the evidence in favour of its being black is stronger; and then, when he politely replies: But I think it is white, to part from him saying: Of course there is a lot of difference of opinion nowadays, and we each have a right to our own. The proper technique of controversy is to say: That's interesting – what makes you say it is white?
>
> Now when the argument is approached in this spirit the differences, other than logical, boil down to a difference of assumptions. One side of the shield is white, and the other is black, and there is no need to quarrel.
>
> But when the two rival sets of assumptions are examined and compared, the argument can continue in an amicable manner.

Some people consider the style of argument prevalent in Cambridge, England, too rude, but it is aimed at getting points clear. I have suffered far more, especially in the USA, from politeness, being fobbed off with compliments just when I was hoping to clinch an argument.

The children's story of the knights illustrates an important point. When controversies arise through confronting contradictory conclusions, they can easily be resolved by examining the arguments that led to them. Each party should set out clearly the assumptions on which his argument is based; by mutual criticism they can arrive at agreement about what consequences follow from what assumptions and then they can join in an amicable discussion about what evidence must be found to show which set of assumptions (if either) is relevant to the problem in hand.

For this method to be successful, both parties must follow it. An attempt by one party to proceed in this way is frustrated if the other continues to reiterate his conclusions or insists that his own set of assumptions is the only one that can legitimately be made. Unfortunately, the greater part of economic controversies arise from confronting dogmas. The style of argument is that of theology, not of science. This has grown with the growth of a large and flourishing profession, in which jobs depend on supporting opinions acceptable to those in authority.

The concept of a change of paradigm, introduced by T. S. Kuhn,[3] has become very fashionable among economists. The Keynesian revolution had many features in common with the scientific revolutions that Kuhn describes, but the subsequent development of the subject was not at all like that of any natural science when a shift of paradigm has occurred. In economics, new ideas are treated, in theological style, as heresies and as far as possible kept out of the schools by drilling students in the habit of repeating the old dogmas, so as to prevent established orthodoxy from being undermined.

On the plane of practical affairs, the importance of the Keynesian revolution was to break through the inhibitions of laisser faire and make governments accept, in principle at least, responsibility for maintaining a 'high and stable level of employment'.

On the plane of academic theory, the importance of the Keynesian revolution was to show that all the familiar dogmas are set in a world without time and cannot survive the simple observation that decisions, in economic life, are necessarily taken in the light of uncertain expectations about their future consequences.

Orthodox theory reacted to this challenge, in true theological style, by inventing fanciful worlds in which the difference between the past and the future does not arise and devising intricate mathematical theorems about how an economy would operate if everyone in it had correct foresight about how everybody else was going to behave.

Professor Hahn defends this manoeuvre; he maintains that it is an important achievement to have formulated the orthodox theory 'so sharply as to enable such an unambiguous verdict to be reached' as that it has no practical application.[4] But the labour that has gone into that achievement could have been saved by recognizing that, at any moment in real life when a decision is taken, the past is already irrevocable and the future is still to come.

The Economics of Imperfect Competition, on which I was working with

---

[3] See *The Structure of Scientific Revolutions*, University of Chicago Press and Routledge and Kegan Paul, 1968.

[4] 'The Winter of our Discontent', a review of Janos Kornai, *Anti-Equilibrium, Economica*, August 1973, p. 324. Note the misprint in the last complete line of the page.

R. F. Kahn in 1932, was pre-Keynesian and it is based on a fudge – confusing comparisons of possible alternative equilibrium positions with the analysis of a process taking place through time. I postulated that every manufacturing firm is faced by a demand curve for its own product, showing how much could be sold at various prices, and that the firm finds out its position and shape by trial and error. For this to be feasible the demand curve would have to remain rigidly fixed for long enough for the firm to discover it, and the experiments of raising and lowering the price to find out the response of sales would have to have negligible cost and no reaction upon the behaviour of the firm's customers.

Keynes himself fudged his own argument. He defined aggregate supply price as 'the amount of the proceeds which the entrepreneurs expect to receive from the corresponding output' and appended this footnote:

> An entrepreneur, who has to reach a practical decision as to his scale of production, does not, of course, entertain a single undoubting expectation of what the sale-proceeds of a given output will be, but several hypothetical expectations held with varying degrees of probability and definiteness. By his expectation of proceeds I mean, therefore, that expectations of proceeds which, if it were held with certainty, would lead to the same behaviour as does the bundle of vague and more various possibilities which actually makes up his state of expectation when he reaches his decision.[5]

Furthermore he treated long-term expectations in the same way; the 'marginal efficiency of capital' is derived from the profits expected from investment, allowing for risk; the level of investment at any moment is said to be such as to equate the marginal efficiency of capital to the rate of interest (the cost of finance). Interest charges represent an obligation to pay certain definite sums of money. What is said to be equated to the rate of interest is an uncertain expectation of profit. But this statement is vacuous, for it is impossible to separate out the expected rate of profit from the allowances for the degree of uncertainty with which expectations are held. Keynes later denounced the conception that uncertainty in economic affairs can be reduced to calculable risks as one of the 'pretty, polite techniques, made for a well-panelled board room and a nicely regulated market' which 'tries to deal with the present by abstracting from the fact that we know very little about the future.'[6]

[5] *The General Theory*, JMK, Vol. VII, p. 24, note 2.
[6] 'The General Theory of Employment', *Quarterly Journal of Economics*, Feb. 1937, JMK, Vol. XIV, pp. 109–23.

This kind of fudging comes from a sort of instinctive self-defence mechanism. At a time of crisis (in Kuhn's sense) there is nothing solid and reliable in traditional theory – everything has to be thought out afresh. No question can properly be asked before every other question has been answered. In pursuing one line of argument, it is necessary to block off others, by fair means or foul, or else no question can ever be posed. I remember pointing out (when I was going through the proofs) that that footnote in the *General Theory* would not do, but Keynes left it unaltered – he could not afford to remove the block that was temporarily providing some space within which he could develop his system.

This, of course, is not a legitimate excuse for fudging; it is a fact about how original work gets done in our ill-disciplined discipline.

The basic fault in the method that I was pursuing in *Imperfect Competition*, and defending in my pamphlet, was to start the argument from a purely *a priori* set of assumptions – the assumptions that Pigou had distilled from Marshall – and then to introduce a minor improvement in them, instead of making a radical critique of the relationship between the traditional assumptions and the actual economy that they pretended to describe. All the same, the work was not wasted because, over the bridge of Kalecki's 'degree of monopoly' it led on to the modern theory of the determination of profit margins and so was linked up with the theory of employment.

My twin, Professor Chamberlin, spent many years protesting that his 'monopolistic competition' was quite different from my 'Imperfect Competition'.|(It used to be said at Harvard at one time that any student could be sure of getting a good degree by abusing Mrs. Robinson.) This was partly, I think, due to human weakness. We had to share reviews and footnotes that Chamberlin would rather have had to himself. (The fact that I was quite bored with the subject annoyed him all the more.) But there was a deeper reason. I was delighted to find that I had proved (within the accepted assumptions) that it is not true to say that wages equal the marginal productivity of labour, while Chamberlin wanted to maintain that advertisement, salesmanship and monopolistic product differentiation in no way impaired the principle of consumer's sovereignty and the beneficial effect of the free play of market forces.

The one-sided controversy of Chamberlin against Robinson was a bad case of confronting the conclusions of two arguments without examining their assumptions. Where he and I set up the same questions (errors and omissions excepted) we found the same answers and where the questions were different, the answers were too. In some respects Chamberlin's assumptions were more realistic than mine, though he did not want to draw realistic conclusions from them.

Nowadays we have both been swept aside in the revival of neoclassical orthodoxy which cannot admit any realism at all.

Keynes had to break out of the orthodoxy in which he had been brought up because he was considering a real problem – the causes of unemployment in an industrial economy – and he had to examine how the economy really works. Even in the well-disciplined natural sciences, it is recognized that an original idea comes in the first place by a flash of intuition. Keynes certainly was an intuitive thinker. In a serious subject, intuition must play over reality and draw hypotheses from it, to be worked over consciously and critically to see if reality does not reject them. Originality means discovery, not invention. It is not like designing an elegant façade for a new building but like exploring an old ruin and trying to make out what its ground-plan must have been.

Because Keynes was trying to understand how the economy works, he was unwittingly following the line of Ricardo and Marx, who were engaged in the same quest, each trying to understand the operation of capitalism in his own day. Keynes was clearing up a particular element in it (effective demand) that Ricardo had ignored and Marx imperfectly understood. This explains the apparent paradox that the post-Keynesians in Cambridge find an affinity with the classics.

Jevons declared: 'That able but wrong-headed man David Ricardo shunted the car of economic science onto the wrong track'. In fact Jevons himself shunted the train onto a loop line round which it still circulates, but Keynes and Kalecki managed to detach a few coaches and got them back onto the main track.

I had a very literary education and to this day I know only the mathematics that I was able to pick up in the course of trying to formalize economic arguments, but it seemed to me obvious that a quantity that is to be manipulated by the methods of applied mathematics must be specified as a number of some unit, and that the very definition of a unit implies its method of measurement.

I was quite naïve when I wrote my pamphlet. I thought that this fact had only to be mentioned to receive universal recognition.

I observed that, to make economics into a serious subject it was necessary to

continue the labour of removing out of the tool-box of the analysts all tools which appear to involve conceptions that are not capable of measurement. If any reader of this essay practises any other serious subject, I must pause to explain why this is still necessary. Economists are subject to many vices, and one of them has been to talk about 'utility', which is a quantitative conception that there is no known way of measuring. Such a scandal must be frankly admitted. For confession and penitence must precede the recognition of economics as a serious subject.

Not all economic concepts can be reduced to strictly quantitative terms. To treat something that is in principle unmeasurable as though it were a quantity is a confusion of thought pretending to be scientifically precise.

Twenty years later when I made a similar point about the meaning of a 'quantity of capital', I was still naïve. I really thought that if I asked a reasonable question I ought to get a reasonable answer. I was quite surprised at the rage and indignation that my question aroused. 'Everyone except Joan Robinson knows perfectly well what capital means.' It became quite a joke in the profession. I once happened to hear a tape of a meeting at which a speaker was saying 'As Mrs. Robinson is not in the room, I suppose you do not object to my talking about capital.'

I only recently discovered that Thorstein Veblen had made my point, much better than I did, in 1908.

> Much is made of the doctrine that the two facts of 'capital' and 'capital goods' are conceptually distinct, though substantially identical. The two terms cover virtually the same facts as would be covered by the terms 'pecuniary capital' [finance] and 'instrumental equipment'.
>
> . . .
>
> The continuum in which the 'abiding entity' of capital resides is a continuity of ownership, not a physical fact. The continuity, in fact, is of an immaterial nature, a matter of legal rights, of contract, of purchase and sale. Just why this patent state of the case is overlooked, as it somewhat elaborately is, is not easily seen.[7]

In the natural sciences, controversies are settled in a few months, or at a time of crisis, in a year or two, but in the social so-called sciences, absurd misunderstanding can continue for sixty or a hundred years without being cleared up.

[7] 'Professor Clark's Economics', *Quarterly Journal of Economics*, Feb. 1908, reprinted in *The Place of Science in Modern Civilization*, B. W. Huebsch, 1919, pp. 195–7, and see below p. 116.

The cause of this difference, of course, lies in the difference of methods. My saying: 'A serious subject is neither more nor less than its own technique' was a half truth, but it is the important half. In the natural sciences, experiments can be repeated and observations checked so that a false hypothesis is quickly knocked out. I agree with Kuhn's view of science as a particular kind of social activity which is carried on for its own sake, with a particular set of accepted rules. That it enables us to understand an aspect of the universe is, so to speak, an accidental by-product of this activity. Economics is also a social activity but its rules are such that its by-products are much less impressive.

The modern style of so-called mathematical economics came into fashion after the period when my pamphlet was written. Mathematical logic is a powerful tool of thought, but its application in economic theory generally seems to consist merely of putting circular arguments into algebra. Mathematical theory of statistics, also, was developing fast. At first there were high hopes that observations of reality by the method of econometrics would produce truly scientific results.

Since I have confessed that I am no mathematician, my views on this subject might be thought to be those of the fox who had lost his tail, but that reproach could not be made to Norbert Wiener.[8]

> An econometrician will develop an elaborate and ingenious theory of demand and supply, inventories and unemployment, and the like, with a relative or total indifference to the methods by which these elusive quantities are observed or measured. Their quantitative theories are treated with the unquestioning respect with which the physicists of a less sophisticated age treated the concepts of the Newtonian physics. Very few econometricians are aware that if they are to imitate the procedure of modern physics and not its mere appearances, a mathematical economics must begin with a critical account of these quantitative notions and the means adopted for collecting and measuring them.

He continues: 'Difficult as it is to collect good physical data, it is far more difficult to collect long runs of economic or social data so that the whole of the run shall have a uniform significance.' This means that an attempt to test hypotheses by data in the form of time series is posing two questions at once — whether the forces at work were correctly diagnosed for one period and whether they have remained the same over subsequent

---

[8] See *God and Golem, Inc.*, cf. Chapter 1, note 7.

periods. When there are elements in the forces involved such as the militancy of trade unions or the effect of advertising on household expenditure, this difficulty appears to be insuperable.

Keynes' review of Tinbergen[9] pouring cold water on the pretentions of econometrics caused a great deal of offence but it seems to have turned out in the main to have been correct. Ragnar Frisch, himself a great practitioner, has sadly remarked that most of the work done in this field has been playometrics not econometrics.[10] Only for a few narrow and tightly specified questions has the method turned out to be fruitful.

Yet there have been some notable cases where hypotheses drawn from economic analysis have been broadly vindicated. Keynes in 1925 predicted that the return to the gold standard at an overvalued sterling exchange rate would be followed by a period of pressure to reduce wages which would be bitterly resisted. (In 1926 there was a general strike.)

In 1931, he pointed out that falling prices were putting a great strain on the banks. (In March 1933 the banking system in the USA came to a standstill.) In 1936 (following Keynes) I observed that a period of continuous near-full employment would lead to continuous inflation; and (most remarkable of all) Kalecki predicted in 1944 that after the war we should be living under the regime of a political trade cycle (stop-go). These predictions were not at all exact; they were not derived from studying time series, but from a diagnosis of how the contemporary economic system operated. It seems as though what success economics has had depends more upon insight than upon precision and that its affinity must be with history as much as with mathematics.

History can never give a final knockdown answer to any question. Each generation rewrites its own past in accord with its current ideology. Certainly, economics can never escape from ideology. In every human activity or line of inquiry there is always a right and a left, orthodox and radical views, defence of the status quo and demand for change. This is true even of the natural sciences at a time of crisis. As long as I have known economics, it has always been in crisis.

At the present time [1970], it seems that the neo-classical orthodoxy is quite discredited but I do not think that the swing of opinion against it owes so much to the exposure of its logical defects by Gunnar Myrdal, Maurice Dobb and Piero Sraffa as to the revolt of the young generation

[9] JMK, Vol. XIV.
[10] 'Econometrics in the world today' in *Essays in Honour of Sir Roy Harrod*, ed. W. Eltis, Oxford, 1970.

against an unjust society that began with the Civil Rights Campaign in the USA. Myrdal and Dobb have been available for thirty or forty years and no one would have understood Sraffa who was not in revolt already.

Then, the question may be raised: if the choice between one theory and another is always made by their ideological colour, not their logic, why is a reasonable theory any more use than a spurious one? Is there any point, after all, in trying to make economics into a serious subject?

At the present time, there are a great many radicals who seem to feel that any argument is justified by being anti-neoclassical no matter whether or not it is internally coherent or in accord with evidence.

I believe, however, that there is a lot of difference between good analysis and bad, apart from ideological tendencies. Logic is the same for everyone (though I could never get Professor Solow to admit it) and the reading of evidence, though always biassed to some extent, can be more or less fair. I do not think it was a waste of time to try to understand the great slump, post-war growth and the present crisis and, for understanding, an adequate system of analysis is indispensable. It was not a waste of time, either, to try to examine the neo-classicals to find out why their logic is at fault, as well as their opinions.

It is often said that one theory can be driven out only by another; the neoclassicals have a complete theory (though I maintain that it is nothing but a circular argument) and we need a better theory to supplant them. I do not agree. I think any other 'complete theory' would be only another box of tricks. What we need is a different habit of mind — to eschew fudging, to respect facts and to admit ignorance of what we do not know.

Honesty and hard work are required of radicals, while the orthodox can doze over their dogmas. But I do not think that radicals need fear that they will have to sacrifice their convictions in order to make economics a serious subject. My old saying about technique was a half truth. The other half concerns the subject to which technique is to be applied. I believe that the proper subject matter of economics is an examination of the manner of operation of various economic systems, particularly our own, and as long as our economy system continues to survive, a clear-sighted examination of it is more likely to favour radical views than to support the defenders of the status quo.

5

ACCUMULATION AND EXPLOITATION: AN ANALYSIS IN THE TRADITION OF MARX, SRAFFA AND KALECKI

With Amit Bhaduri[*]

PIERO SRAFFA was completely successful in his aim of providing a basis for the critique of neoclassical theory but the model in *Production of Commodities by Means of Commodities* (1960) provides a very narrow basis for constructive analysis.

The model presents a strictly one-technique economy. In the system of equations, each input used up in one period is replaced in kind as production goes on. This entails that the same technique is going to be used in the next period. In itself, this is a merit of the construction, but it needs to be emphasized; Sraffa himself blurs the point by introducing changes into his self-repeating story.[1]

The characterization of a technique has two elements – the engineering specification of the physical input–output equations and the pattern of applications of labour through time. In Sraffa's story, in Part I, the reproduction of the system takes place in a single period; the turnover of each commodity takes the same time. Thus, in the production of each commodity, the stock in existence at a moment of time, in the pipelines of production, is the same multiple of its flow of output. The rate of profit is expressed as a percentage per period. (When fixed capital is introduced in Part II, time patterns are more varied. Here both types are treated together.)

There is no discussion of the realization of surplus as profit. It is merely taken for granted that whatever is produced is disposed of at such prices as to result in a uniform rate of profits in all lines of production.

Finally, the determination of the distribution of net output between

---

[*] Centre for Economic Studies, Jawaharlal Nehru University, New Delhi.
[1] See for example Sraffa, (1960), p. 81.

Cambridge Journal of Economics, Vol. 4, no. 2, June 1980. The original mathematical appendix has been omitted here.

wages and net profit is left completely open (apart from the inexplicable suggestion that the rate of profit on capital might be governed by the rate of interest). In this sense, Sraffa presents a scheme more fruitful than Ricardo's. Since it does not specify the real wage, it presents a challenge to attempt to diagnose what forces do determine the distribution of income between profits and wages.

Ian Steedman, in *Marx after Sraffa* (1977), refutes the various objections that dogmatists have raised against this analysis and shows that, if we are supposed to have full information in physical terms (including the real wage), there is no advantage in introducing *value* as a unit of measurement. But in his own argument, he follows Ricardo in making the real wage a given basket of specified wage goods, which are therefore basics in the system. This entails the determination of distribution from the technical data, leaving no room for class conflict, and it does not touch on the question of realization.[2] Presumably, to complete this story, we must suppose that a capitalist uses part of net profit for consumption and invests the rest, each in his own business. Here we are in a pre-Keynesian setting where savings govern accumulation and there is no discussion of what form investment takes, or how it could result in a feasible rate of growth of the system, unless in a one-commodity economy.

To avoid these objections, we present a Sraffaesque model, or rather a family of models, including distribution according to Marx and realization according to Kalecki.

Our method is to elaborate Sraffa's model, first dealing with one problem at a time and then recombining them. Like his, our models depict a two-class society in a 'pure' capitalist economy, without foreign trade or taxation. For the most part, the argument is conducted in terms of a one-technique system with long-run normal prices – thus it is a set of highly abstract intellectual experiments. It is intended, however, to clear the logical ground for a discussion of real issues involved in the analysis of capitalist accumulation.

[2] Was Marx a neo-Ricardian? Marx argued that labour power is sold as a commodity and that all commodities exchange at their *values*. The *value* of labour power is a real wage sufficient to maintain the customary standard of life. If the *value* of labour power remains constant through time, then distribution is determined by technology as Ricardo believed. But if real-wage rates can rise or fall under the influence of changes in productivity and the balance of power in society, as Marx clearly contemplated that they would, then the *value* of labour power is an unnecessary and misleading concept. Sraffa is certainly not a neo-Ricardian in this sense, but he has never gone into the question of the realization of physical surplus as profits, leaving his logical scheme open-ended with one degree of freedom in the system of equations.

A STATIONARY STATE

Sraffa did not need to ask whether his system was growing or not. Net output may or may not include some physical items to be added to stock, and the workers receive a share in the value of net output, not a supply of specific wage goods. Here our system is a modification of his. We make a physical distinction between means of production, which are basics in Sraffa's sense, each entering directly or indirectly into the output of all commodities, and consumption goods, which are non-basic.

We first consider simple reproduction (a stationary state). This means that there is a constant labour force, working standard hours per day and per year and a stock of means of production which is being kept intact by continual replacements of items as they are used up, while the whole flow of net output is being consumed. The notion of a capitalist economy dwelling contentedly in a self-perpetuating stationary state is evidently artificial. The assumption of stationariness is here introduced provisionally in order to separate out for analysis the time-pattern aspect of the stock of means of production required for a given technique.

The quantity of each item in the stock depends on the amount of it required in the general flow of production and on its turnover period.[3] For a type of machine that, say, takes one year to build and has ten years of life at full efficiency (a one-hoss shay), an annual output of a single machine maintains a stock of 10 machines of ages zero to ten. Each year one falls out of use. The production of one machine per year keeps the stock of balanced age composition in being. Along with each item of long-lived equipment there is a stock of working capital corresponding to the short-period throughput of production with that equipment.

The length of the period of turnover of the self-reproducing state is the least common multiple of the turnover period of all the items. The stock of each item is then represented by the amount of labour time directly and indirectly required to produce it and the time pattern in which the labour was applied. In the stationary state, the whole labour force maintains the whole basic stock (and also produces a flow of non-basics for consumption) but, by the method of sub-systems, the labour embodied in each particular item can be distinguished from the rest.[4]

It is to be observed that stocks of animal and vegetable products can

[3] Cf. *Collected Economic Papers*, Vol. II, p. 201.

[4] This point is drastically simplified in Robinson (1978). The simplification was made in order to meet the Marxian argument on its own terms.

have been built up in this way, but minerals (including coal and oil) are not replaced but taken from the earth's crust and dissipated into the air or crumbled into the ground. In contrast, there are installations, such as hydro-electric stations, which required a large investment in the past and are kept permanently in being by a relatively low rate of expenditure on maintenance thereafter.

When these two types of investments are excluded, the existence of the whole self-reproducing stock can be traced back through logical time in the manner which Sraffa applies to working capital. This is not a process in historical time. It never reaches a moment when the stock was first completed (at the end of a supposed initial gestation period) but continues indefinitely into the past. At any stage in the process, however far back it is taken, there is a stock of means of production already in existence in the correct proportions, because the same technique is assumed to have been in use ever since time began.

The question was raised by Keynes on an early draft of the book as to whether Sraffa's system allows for variable returns to scale (Sraffa, 1960, p. vi). The question seems to be irrelevant to a one-technique model. One total stock of basics is appropriate to one flow of work being performed with one technique. A differently employed labour force would require a correspondingly different stock. If there were differences in returns to scale between the two cases, the items in the two stocks would not be in the same proportions and they would represent two different techniques. Thus, once the existence of stocks in a stationary state is explicitly recognized, the question of changing the scale of output does not arise. As we shall see, the one-technique model can be adapted to deal with steady growth, but growth with changing proportions of inputs requires a historical analysis of the manner in which a new stock is built up to support a changed technique of production.

At the same time, when joint production is excluded, the pattern of prices, with any one technique, is independent of the proportions in which commodities are produced. This was misleadingly called by Samuelson 'non-substitution' (see Pasinetti, 1977) and by Pigou (1932) 'constant supply price' for individual commodities.

THE RATIO OF EXPLOITATION AND RATE OF PROFITS

Sraffa set out to provide the basis for a critique of the economic theory that was prevalent when he began work in the 1920s, before the first rumbles of the Keynesian revolution had been heard. The dominant theory of distribution was that of Alfred Marshall vulgarized by J. B. Clark (1891): What a social class gets is, under natural law, what it contributes to the general output of industry.

Sraffa opposed to this the argument that, with a given flow of production defined in physical terms, the share of real wages in physical net output may, in principle, be anything between unity and zero with the corresponding rates of profit between zero and the physically possible maximum.

Given the physical specification of the model, a particular rate of profit, uniform throughout the economy, entails a particular pattern of prices for all the items in the flow of production (including non-basics) and for the stocks of inputs, and a pattern of the ratios of gross profits to wages in each industry.

Sraffa's argument was largely concerned with the construction of a numeraire in physical terms — the standard commodity. It seems equally satisfactory to use as numeraire the labour time performed by a representative worker, say over a week. We can postulate an arbitrary money-wage rate per man-week, say 10, and specify all the relationships within the system in terms of dollars. We then have a wage bill, say per annum, as a flow of dollars, independent of the rate of profit. Corresponding to any given rate of profit (with its appropriate pattern of prices and gross margins) there is a particular flow of net profits in dollars received by capitalists.

Comparing a higher with a lower rate of profit, the pattern of prices may be widely different but the overall level of prices must be higher and the real-wage rate lower.

It seems appropriate to express the ratio of the flow of net profits to the wage bill as the rate of exploitation. (Marx defined this in terms of labour *values*; here we are translating into a system of prices of production.)

The rate, or better the ratio, of exploitation is not determined by the technical specification of the system. It is an independent element in the situation which may be explained by the fortunes of the class war. This freedom of the distribution parameter enabled Sraffa to break out of the 'iron-law of real wages'. He was himself somewhat reluctant to make such a departure from classical traditions but for us it is this liberation that enables us to integrate the problem of realization into our analysis.

In the formal model there is no causality. The rate of profit entails and is entailed by the ratio of exploitation whatever it may be. But when we want to step down from the model into an interpretation of reality we have to consider which determines which. It is certainly easier to do the sums if we start from a given rate of profits, but Marx's instinct was correct; the causal factor is the *share* of profit from which the uniform *rate* can be derived only as a postulate of the long-run normal configuration of prices.

A Variety of Non-Basics

To concentrate upon the main argument, we have so far said nothing about the physical nature of the output of non-basics. We now introduce into the model the fact that rentiers and workers consume different physical baskets of non-basics – luxuries and wage goods. (There may be some items in common but in different quantities; thus the luxury basket contains less bread than the wage-good basket, and more whisky.) The value of the flow of luxuries in dollars is equal to the flow of rentier income, and the value of wage goods is equal to the wage bill. This requires a somewhat different basic stock of means of production for each ratio of exploitation; the main bulk of the stock is not affected but there must be appropriate productive capacity for the flow of output of the physically different non-basics.

Now we come to a puzzle. The ratio of exploitation is logically prior to the flows of luxuries and wage goods, yet the stocks to produce them must already be in place. The Marxists have long recognized the problem as the 'crisis of proportionality' – to each given real-wage rate must correspond a certain division of productive capacity between the investment sector and the consumption-goods sector. To a *different* real wage rate, entailing a different ratio of exploitation, must correspond a different proportion between sectors, while a sudden *change* in the real wage would throw the proportions in the stock out of line with the flows of production.

The answer is that, when the stocks are in balance with outputs, it must be supposed that the investment in the two stocks was made in the light of correct expectations of the returns to be enjoyed on each.

A uniform rate of profits can be imposed upon a set of prices by an economist describing his model, but in terms of the behaviour of the inhabitants of the system, the equalization of the rate of profits can take place only through investment decisions influenced by expectations of future profitability. Only when expectations have turned out exactly correct is there a perfectly uniform ex-post rate of profits in the system.

It is sometimes objected that expectations introduce an illegitimate subjective element into analysis, but the subjective expectations held in the past are manifest in the objective stocks in existence today. Not to recognize stocks explicitly is then tantamount to ignoring the importance of expectations – correctly or falsely held – as an essential characteristic of time in the analysis.

The same consideration applies to the formation of prices. When a uniform rate of profits rules, gross profit margins (the excess of proceeds over prime costs) for baskets of non-basics are determined. A product which requires a higher capital to output ratio has correspondingly higher gross margins at any given level of the rate of profit. Each type of product in the flow of output requires a certain rate of gross investment to keep its stock intact and a certain allowance of net profit to yield the given rate of profit on the value of its stock of long-lived and short-lived basics, which we may now describe as its capital. 'Capital' is thus seen as a two-edged concept, in the tradition of Marx, involving both the physical aspect of means of production and property rights which give rise to profit as the source of capitalists' income.

Now, in industry, prices have to be set in advance of sales. The level of unit costs, with long-lived equipment, depends on its level of utilization. Gross margins in each line are fixed in such a way as to cover costs and yield a 'subjective-normal' rate of net profit at a standard level of utilization of capacity. The ex-post rate of profits for each will be normal when the standard rate of output is realized. If actual output were higher than standard, profits would be more than normal, and vice versa.

Our earlier puzzle – the proportionality crisis revisited in the form of the question of how stocks can be exactly right to fit with whatever may be the distribution of income – is precisely the outcome of an assumption that expectations in the past have been exactly correct. On the composition of the basket at least of luxuries, there must be some influence of consumers' tastes. But consumers are not choosing between 'n' ready-made commodities, as in so-called general equilibrium. Rather, producers have to guess what they will be able to entice consumers to buy.

These considerations show that it is unreasonable, except in a pure thought experiment, to postulate that an absolutely uniform rate of profits is ever realized, for expectations can never be exactly correct. In the type of model in which the rate of profit is technically determined, it may be postulated to be uniform, but then the conditions for the realization of the physical surplus as profit are left in the air.

CHANGING EXPLOITATION

In a steady state, with confident expectations, the ratio of exploitation is, so to say, built into the stock of basics. A change from one ratio of exploitation to another would require an appropriate adaptation in the stock.

A rise in the exploitation ratio might come about from an increase in monopoly power and weakening of trade union resistance, causing a rise in profit margins and an increase in distribution to rentiers. This generates a rise in expenditure on luxuries, which may run them up to full capacity and raise their profitability all the more. A fall in the consumption of wage goods checks and may even reverse the increase in the flow of profits in that sector.

Suppose that there has been a once and for all change and that new situation lasts, and is expected to last, indefinitely so that there is now a new state of long-term expectations. We can trace a traverse with gross investment below replacement in the wage-good industries and above it in luxury industries until the rate of profit has been equalized between the sectors, at a new higher level, and the composition of the stock of basics has been readjusted accordingly.

A fall in the exploitation ratio might be caused by a growth of trade union strength combined with more intense competition among capitalists that prevents them from passing raised money-wage costs fully into prices. Now the flow of profits has been reduced in both sectors.

Technical conditions do not exclude a traverse to a lower rate of profit, the mirror image of the above, for as Keynes (1936, p. 374) observed, there is no reason why the game should not be played for lower stakes once the players are used to them. But the experience of a fall in net proceeds from one quarter to the next may have given the capitalists a shock. They jib at maintaining the former rate of gross investment. An increase in capacity for wage goods fails to balance a decline in that for luxuries so that the total stock of basics is allowed to shrink, and the full-capacity level of employment is reduced. Thus the neoclassical dictum that high wages reduce employment may turn out to be true for quite un-neoclassical reasons: the capitalists' reaction, in terms of the volume and composition of investment, to a lower ratio of exploitation may lead the course of the traverse to a new stock configuration appropriate to a permanently lower level of output and employment.

Accumulation without Rentier Consumption

We now introduce a model in which there is no consumption out of profits, but net investment is going on. There is a growth rate which is given by the overall ratio of the value of the flow of net investment to the value of the stock. In this case, since we are in a one-technique economy, eployment must be growing in step with the growth rate. The analysis is familiar (see von Neumann, 1945). We need only remark that the growth rate must have been built into the system from the first; a single technique is being reproduced on an ever-widening base. Thus economies of scale are here ruled out.

When the growth rate is given, the corresponding ratio of exploitation is determined, but it is not true that the exploitation ratio, by itself, determines the rate of growth. The ratio determines the potential surplus of the system, but investment decisions by active capitalists are needed to turn the surplus into profit. Professor von Weizsacker (1973) has argued that there can be no exploitation in such a case because the entire profit is needed to finance accumulation.[5] But he failed to observe that realization of surplus as profits is possible only through accumulation, which capitalists arbitrarily decide upon in their own interests, without consulting workers. Thus the workers' share in net output is still governed by the ratio of exploitation, while accumulation (without the aid of capitalists' consumption) turns the potential share of the capitalists, set by the ratio of exploitation, into the corresponding rate of profit by creating enough effective demand to realize it. It is to be observed that we are here comparing different growth rates with a single technology. When actual capitalist economies are compared, it often happens that the one with a higher growth rate uses superior techniques and has a higher rate of innovation so that faster growth is associated with higher rather than lower real wages in a particular phase of development.

The General Model

When we combine growth with rentier consumption, net output consists of net additions to the stock of basics plus the flow of non-basics. The flow of output contains three physical elements, the complex of basics (replacements and additions) and the baskets of luxuries and of wage goods.

The flow of realized net profits is now composed of two elements, net

[5] Cf. p. 74 below.

investment and rentier consumption. This accords with Kalecki's famous epigram: the workers spend what they get and the capitalists get what they spend.[6]

We may suppose that the rate of growth has emerged from the decisions of the active capitalists (entrepreneurs) who manage business and that they also decide upon the amount of profit to be distributed to rentiers, subject to the limitation upon the overall share of profit set by working class resistance.

In the former model, the rentiers simply spent whatever profits they received. If they also have a propensity to save, then: $C = a + (1 - s) D$, where C is the flow of rentier consumption and D distributed profits. The savings of the rentiers are lent to the capitalists to finance investment. Now, if each capitalist financed the whole of his gross investment out of gross profits, he would automatically be financing net investment out of net profit. There could not then be any savings by rentiers. If rentiers fail to spend part of the distributed profits that they receive, profits are realized on a reduced scale and distributions are correspondingly lower. Rentier income then could not rise above the constant, a, in the above equation, which is all consumed.

When investment exceeds retentions, rentiers' income exceeds expenditure for consumption and their savings are exactly what is required to finance the excess of investment over retained profits.

The Anglo-Italian formula, $\pi = g/s_p$ (the rate of profits, on a steady growth path, is equal to the rate of growth divided by saving out of profits) is formally correct when there is no saving except out of profits, but it obscures the mechanism of the financial system by failing to distinguish between saving out of profits in the form of retentions and saving out of rentier income.

The foregoing argument shows that to postulate a given physical real wage in advance would require the rest of the model to be draped around it so that technical conditions, the ratio of exploitation, the realization of the potential surplus and the rate of profits are all consistent with it. Starting from the other end, we find that the level of real wages in a particular economy depends, first of all, on technical conditions and the stocks of means of production in existence, which determine the net output that the system can yield in a self-reproducing state. Secondly, it depends upon the

---

[6] Saving out of earned income may be treated as saving to spend later. Workers may lend and borrow among themselves without providing any finance to the capitalists through the banking system.

share of profits in net output, which is governed by the rate of accumulation and of non-wage consumption, subject to the limit on the ratio of exploitation permitted by social conditions.

On this view, capitalists, in the various sectors of industry, set their selling prices in relation to costs, according to various profit-seeking strategies. The interaction among them establishes the 'degree of monopoly', that is, the overall mark-up on the total wage bill. But until flows of output of commodities are sold at those prices in the market, the mark-up over the wage bill remains only a *potential* surplus. Investment and consumption expenditure by the capitalists determines how much of this potential surplus is realized as actual profits.

This is as far as a one-technique model will take us. A one-technique economy is not to be found in the history of capitalism, for accumulation is always accompanied by innovations and at any moment the stock of means of production in existence is mainly composed of fossils from earlier phases of technical development while current gross investment is installing the latest types of equipment. To set the model in historical time, we must take account of change.

OUT OF THE STRAIT-JACKET

In a steady state all events are predetermined. Anything that happens 'today' is fully determined by the past, including expectations about 'today' that were held in the past. It is precisely those expectations, confidently held, which are now reflected in the various stocks in existence in the appropriate configuration 'today'.

To discuss the effects of change in any element in our story, we must break this link between the past and the future and treat 'today' as a gap between the two in which unpredetermined events may occur. This is necessary to set the analysis in historical, not logical, time.

There is one point on which all schools of thought can agree – that the actual process of capitalist accumulation goes on through historical time. In spite of this, contemporary economic methodology applied to the analysis of the process of accumulation does not usually make a distinction between past and future time. A case in point is the neoclassical 'production function' with its treatment of 'malleable capital' made of putty as a factor of production.

The 'pseudo-production function', which emerged in the course of the still-unsettled controversy over capital theory, purported to exhibit a number of steady states, in logical time, with different technologies. By the very construction, each such steady state had to be independent of the rest. For, as our argument has shown, each had to have its appropriate stock configuration fully determined by its own past. Consequently, there could be no way of moving from one steady state to another without undoing their past histories. And, since history is not malleable, there can be no question of moving from one quantitative stock configuration to another; each configuration entails its own individual history of expectations on which its own particular stock was built up. Thus, the concept of *switching* techniques with *changes* in the rate of profit has been an unfortunate aberration.

PRELUDE TO A CRITIQUE

Students brought up on contemporary textbooks may have some difficulty in seeing the bearing of Sraffa's 'critique of economic theory'. Current neoclassical teaching is rooted in general equilibrium and 'scarce means with alternative uses'. No heavy guns are needed to bring that structure down. As Kornai has shown, it falls apart of its own accord as soon as it is set in historical time (Kornai, 1971: also Robinson, 1979). Sraffa's critique was aimed at a different target — the amorphous moralizing Marshallian theory of 'factors of production' receiving 'rewards' consonant with their respective productivities. This still underlies much neoclassical doctrine, although nowadays it is not openly spelled out.

Sraffa shows that the influence upon distribution in capitalist industry must be divided into two separate elements. On the one side are the technical factors — the productivity of labour and the stock of means of production required to implement it. In reality, this will not be in a pure form as in his model. It will generally be a 'job lot', brought into existence by the evolution of technology and accumulation over the more or less recent past. At any moment, the requirements for depreciation lie partly in the future, so that relation of gross to net output is not exact. However, by and large, potential productivity is governed by technical factors while the current level of utilization depends upon the state of effective demand.

Against this, the share of wages in net output (and therefore the potential rate of profit on capital) depends upon commercial, social and political influences and the fortunes of the class war.

In principle, a given technical situation is compatible with any proportion of relative shares. This rules out the notion of earnings determined by productivity. Now the time gives it proof, for we can see more or less the same technology being used in 'developing' as in 'developed' industry with a small fraction of the real-wage rate.

There is no difficulty in releasing the second set of influences into historical time; indeed, in describing the model it was hard to hold them back. We know something about how the share of wages in the value of net output is affected by monopoly power and the pricing policy of corporations, by particular scarcities, by effective demand, by bargaining power and the social and political climate in which it operates; and about the 'inflation barrier' which drives money wages irresistibly upward when real wages are pushed too low.

The first half of the story – the influence of changes in technology on demand for labour, on accumulation and on effective demand – has been very little discussed. This is a serious defect in our theoretical apparatus, for the evolution of technology is the most important of all aspects of capitalist development. A start on the subject was made in the 1950s (Robinson, 1956), but it was smothered with neoclassical putty, while the anti-neoclassicals were distracting themselves with reswitching. Now it is time to take up the challenge afresh.

BIBLIOGRAPHY

Clark, J. B. 1891. 'Distribution as Determined by the Law of Rent', *Quaterly Journal of Economics*, Vol. 5, April.

Kahn, R. F. and Champernowne, D. G. 1953–4. 'The Value of Invested Capital', *Review of Economic Studies*.

Keynes, J. M. 1936. *The General Theory of Employment, Interest and Money*, London, Macmillan.

Kornai, J. 1971. *Anti-equilibrium: On Economic Systems Theory and the Tasks of Research*, Amsterdam, North-Holland.

Neumann, J. von, 1945, 'A Model of General Equilibrium', *Review of Economic Studies*, Vol. XIII.

Pasinetti, L. L. 1977. 'On "Non-Substitution" in Production Models', *Cambridge Journal of Economics*, December.

Pigou, A. C. 1932. *The Economics of Welfare*, Fourth edition, London, Macmillan, Chapter XI.

Robinson, J. 1956. *The Accumulation of Capital*, London, Macmillan.

Robinson, J. 1960. *Collected Economic Papers*, Vol. II, Oxford, Basil Blackwell.

Robinson, J. 1978. 'The Organic Composition of Capital', *Kyklos*, Vol. 31.

Robinson, J. 1979. 'History versus Equilibrium', in *Collected Economic Papers*, Vol. V, Oxford, Basil Blackwell.

Sraffa, P. 1960. *Production of Commodities by Means of Commodities*, Cambridge, CUP.

Steedman, I. 1977. *Marx after Sraffa*, London, New Left Books.

Weizsacker, C. L. von, 1973. 'Modern Capital Theory and the Concept of Exploitation', *Kyklos*, Vol. 26.

6

KEYNES AND RICARDO

To me, the expression *post-Keynesian* has a definite meaning; it applies to an economic theory or method of analysis which takes account of the difference between the future and the past.

When Keynes replied to his critics in 1937,[1] he examined the nature of the basic difference between his theory and those that he was opposing. He showed that the difference lay in his recognition of the fact that, at any moment of time, the future is unknown. 'It is generally recognized', he wrote 'that the Ricardian analysis was concerned with what we now call long-period equilibrium.'[2] It is characteristic of a position of equilibrium that it is fulfilling expectations (as to prices, flows of output, profits, etc.) which were held in the past and is therefore recreating expectations that will be fulfilled in the future. In reality, this situation is never realized. 'Thus the fact that our knowledge of the future is fluctuating, vague and uncertain, renders wealth a peculiarly unsuitable subject for the methods of the classical economic theory.'[3]

THE SHORT-PERIOD

The notion of *getting into* equilibrium is 'a metaphor based on space to explain a process which takes place in time.'[4] In space, it is possible to go to and fro and correct misdirections, but time goes only one way.

[1] 'General Theory of Employment', JMK, Vol. XIV, pp. 109 et seq.

[2] Op. cit., p. 112.

[3] Ibid.

[4] See Joan Robinson, 'A Lecture Delivered at Oxford by a Cambridge Economist', 1953. Reprinted in *Collected Economic Papers*, Vol. IV, Oxford, Blackwell.

The Moving Finger writes, and, having writ,
Moves on: nor all your Piety nor Wit
Shall lure it back to cancel half a line,
Nor all your Tears wash out a Word of it.

This is why equilibrium cannot be achieved by a process of trial and error.

Whenever equilibrium theory is breached, economists rush like bees whose comb has been broken to patch up the damage. J. R. Hicks was one of the first, with his IS/LM, to try to reduce the *General Theory* to a system of equilibrium. This had a wide success and has distorted teaching for many generations of students. J. R. Hicks used to be fond of quoting a letter from Keynes which, because of its friendly tone, seemed to approve of IS/LM, but it contained a clear objection to a system that leaves out expectations of the future from the inducement to invest.[5]

Forty years later, John Hicks[6] noticed the difference between the future and the past and became dissatisfied with IS/LM but (presumably to save face for his predecessor, J.R.) he argued that Keynes's analysis was only half *in time* and half in equilibrium.[7]

The *General Theory* is set in a strictly 'short-period' situation. A short-period is not a length of time but the position at a moment of time. Fixed capital, stocks, the organization of business, the training of workers and the habits of consumers are all whatever they are. In such a situation, a particular level of effective demand determines a particular level of output and flow of incomes; a change in effective demand at that moment brings about a particular change in output. Thus, in that situation, there is a short-period supply curve or utilization function, expressing the relation of the amount of employment to the level of effective demand.

Keynes inherited from Marshall the notion of rising short-period marginal costs but this is inessential; the modern treatment of the subject would have suited him better. Taking money-wage rates as given:

> Fixed or 'sticky' prices are found in manufacturing and distribution, where products are not homogeneous and labour costs are constant or decreasing up to the limits of capacity. The result . . . is that

[5] JMK, Vol. XIV, p. 70.

[6] For the change of signature, see 'Revival of Political Economy, the Old and the New', *Economic Record*, September 1975.

[7] 'Some Questions of Time in Economics', in *Evolution, Welfare and Time in Economics: Essays in honor of Nicholas Georgescu-Roegen*, edited by Anthony M. Tang et al., Lexington, Mass., Lexington Books, 1976.

productivity in industry increases with short-run increases in output, while prices are sticky.[8]

Rising marginal costs are associated with fixed natural resources.

A state of expectations, controlling a given level of effective demand, is given only momentarily and is always in course of bringing itself to an end. Perhaps it was a misnomer to describe such a position as equilibrium, but without a concept of the character of an existing short-period situation it is not possible to say anything at all. John Hicks, once his eyes had been opened, ought to have been able to see in what sense Keynes used the concept of equilibrium and not made it an excuse to provide an apology for J. R. Hicks's distortions.

RICARDO VIA SRAFFA

Keynes hardly ever peered over the edge of the short period to see the effect of investment in making addition to the stocks of productive equipment. He used to say: The long period is a subject for undergraduates. He dealt only with forward-looking expectations of profits which would never be exactly fulfilled. All the same, he hankered after the concepts of a normal rate of profit and value of capital though he could not get them clear.[9] Here it was Ricardo who could have helped him out.

All the time that the explosions of the Keynesian Revolution were going on overhead, Piero Sraffa was sapping and mining away to prepare a revolution of his own. He first broke surface in 1951 with the *Introduction* to Ricardo's *Principles*.[10] Ricardo was concerned with the distribution of the product of the earth between the classes of the community. Leaving rent aside, this is the question of the relative shares of wages and profits in net national income. The classical theory that had come down to Keynes through Marshall was a travesty of Ricardo. There is a kind of ghost of a long-run normal rate of profit on capital in Marshall's *Principles*, but it is expressed only in terms of departures from it with unexpected changes in demand and it was tied up with the moralizing concepts of 'profit as the reward of enterprise and interest as the reward of waiting'. Marshall did not commit himself to the notion of 'the marginal productivity of capital'

[8] R. Kahn, 'Malinvaud on Keynes', *Cambridge Journal of Economics*, December 1977.

[9] Cf. Murray Milgate, 'Keynes on the "classical" theory of interest', *Cambridge Journal of Economics*, November 1977.

[10] *Works and Correspondence of David Ricardo*, ed. P. Sraffa, Vol. I.

but his doctrine that the 'real costs' of production are the 'efforts' of the workers and the 'sacrifices' of the capitalists lent itself to being vulgarized in that way by J. B. Clark. Keynes knew very well that this would not do, but he had nothing to put in its place. Sraffa replaced it by re-establishing Ricardo's theory that the rate of profit is determined by the technical conditions of production in physical terms and the share of wages in net output.

Ricardo himself got lost when he departed from a one-commodity economy in which all inputs and outputs are quantities of corn. In *Production of Commodities by Means of Commodities*, Sraffa set up a multi-commodity input-output system and showed that, corresponding to any share of wages, there is a particular pattern of normal prices that yields a particular uniform rate of profit on capital valued at those prices.

The book was not published until 1960. Sraffa had shown a draft to Keynes in 1928. Keynes evidently did not make much of it and Sraffa, in turn, never made much of the *General Theory*. It is the task of post-Keynesians to reconcile the two.

Keynes was right in showing that Ricardo was blind to the nature of effective demand but it was not right to throw him into the same box as Pigou in timeless equilibrium. Ricardo was observing a historical process of accumulation going on through time and, like Keynes, he was applying what he believed to be a realistic analysis of the actual situation to problems of policy. His stationary state was not an equilibrium, but an awful warning. If they did not abolish the Corn Laws so as to reduce the real cost of wages, which were fixed in terms of bread, the rate of profit would go on falling as employment in agriculture increased with 'diminishing returns' until, sooner or later, accumulation would be brought to an end.

Ricardo overlooked the possibility of a deficiency of effective demand; he supposed that both workers and landlords would spend all their incomes currently as they were received while capitalists would devote most of their profits to financing additions to stock. Thus he made saving govern investment. This became the orthodox dogma of J. S. Mill and of Marshall (though he had some reservations)[11] and it needed the whole force of the Keynesian revolution to overturn it.

There was another stumbling block to Ricardo's system. He took the real-wage rate to be given in physical terms. Therefore distribution was determined entirely by the technical conditions of production and there

[11] See *Principles*, Eighth edition, p. 711.

was no room for bargaining power, monopoly or the needs of accumulation to influence relative shares.

Marx, at one level of his thinking, postulated a given real wage. He maintained that labour power, like any other commodity, is exchanged for its *value*. The *value* of labour power is a real-wage rate sufficient to maintain the customary standard of life. But as his argument goes on, the *rate of exploitation*, which governs relative shares, may be pushed up or down with the fortunes of the class war.

Sraffa's system was designed precisely to show that technical conditions do *not* determine relative shares, thus knocking out the 'marginal productivity of capital' as the determinant of the rate of profit.

The neo-neoclassics cannot give up marginal productivity because of its deep roots in the moralizing ideology of J. B. Clark. They resort to all kinds of sophistries to defend it, including abolishing the difference between the future and the past by making machines malleable. The post-Keynesians must make use of Sraffa to build up a type of long-period analysis which will prevent neoclassical equilibrium from oozing back into the General Theory.

THE SHARE OF PROFITS

Confining the argument to a 'pure' capitalist economy, without foreign trade or government activity, where can we find a post-Keynesian theory of relative shares? Keynes himself did not say much about it but Kalecki showed that, in a simple two-class society in which workers spend all their wages currently as they are received, the flow of gross profit per annum is equal to the value of gross investment plus capitalists' consumption.

The same flow of profits is compatible with different levels of profit margins, a higher level being consonant with lower real wages, less employment and a lower level of utilization of the plant in existence. Each firm is assumed to reckon its costs on the basis of a standard ratio of utilization of its plant. The short-period level of effective demand is then in balance with the long-period situation when all equipment throughout industry is being utilized at its standard ratio and prices have been set at the level at which the corresponding outputs can be sold. This is not a position of equilibrium, for if effective demand happened to move away, there is nothing to bring it back to the point of balance.

Such a situation could exist only if there had been correct expectations of what the situation would be like while investment was being undertaken to create the equipment now in use. This is the link between the future and the past which is required for long-period analysis.

Long-period balance could be continuously maintained only on a steady growth path where confident expectations about the future can be maintained, continuously fulfilled and so renewed. This is not something that actually happens. It might be called a subject for graduate students. But, as we shall see, it has interesting implications.

The Rate of Profit and Technical Change

When we have accounted for the share of profit in the flow of value of output, in a steady state, we still have not found the rate of profit on capital, for that involves the value of the stock of means of production in existence. Here we come upon the problem of technical change, for accumulation never takes place without innovations.

The Sraffa model represents a strictly one-technique economy. Inputs used up in production are continuously replaced in kind and there is a clear physical distinction between gross and net output. The great controversy that the book aroused unfortunately went chasing after the red herring of 'reswitching'. This arises in the context of a pseudo-production function, comprising alternative techniques. Each technique must have had its appropriate stock of inputs built up by past accumulation. There is no way of switching from one to another unless we could go back into the past and rewrite history, or go into the future with a long course of investment and disinvestment to change one stock into another.

Different stocks, appropriate to different techniques, do not coexist in time and space. Change takes place by inventions and discoveries which cause innovations to be introduced successively through time. Now, the principal requirement for steady growth is that each round of innovations should be neutral to the last. This means that new best-practice techniques require the same 'degree of mechanization' as before. Then, at a constant rate of profit, the capital to output ratio, in wage units, remains constant while the capital to labour ratio rises at the growth rate.

When accumulation and innovations are raising productivity at a steady rate, to maintain balance, the real wage rate must be rising at the same rate. Here is where bargaining power and the class war come into the argument. When real wages fail to rise sufficiently, effective demand fails to absorb the growth of production and the economy sinks into stagnation.

It is also necessary that the supply of money and of finance in general expands in such a way as to keep the rate of interest constant.

Assuming steady growth to be maintained, then at any moment there are a number of vintages of equipment in use, each being operated at standard utilization. The oldest, which is just about to be scrapped, can barely cover its costs at the wage rate ruling at that moment; the latest is yielding the highest quasi-rent. The distance between them, corresponding to the share of gross profits in proceeds, determines the length of service life of a vintage, and so the number of vintages in use. The higher is the share of profit the lower is the real wage rate at any point on the path and therefore the longer the tail of older, less efficient vintages in use.[12] But the share of gross profit is determined by the short-period relationships – gross investment and rentier consumption. Thus technical conditions and the share of profit determine the level of real wages at any moment, the value of the stock of capital, the rate of profit and the prices of all inputs and outputs 'in any numeraire' as Sraffa has shown.

Is this all just a rigmarole? I think not, for it helps to illuminate a problem of urgent importance. When technical progress is neutral, older plant is continually being replaced by new which employs the same amount of labour at normal utilization, producing a higher rate of output. The overall level of employment is then maintained provided that the real-wage rate, the level of consumption and gross investment are all rising at the same rate as output. The rate of profit and the ratio of value of capital to value of output are then both constant, and the capital to labour ratio is rising at the same rate as output per man employed.

What if innovations take on a capital-using bias so that, over a certain range, the capital to labour ratio is rising faster than output?

Marx believed that rising organic composition of capital would cause a fall in the rate of profit, but no one has ever succeeded in making this comprehensible. Ricardo held the opposite opinion, that the introduction of machinery was not against the interests of the capitalists but might be against the interests of the workers. His argument is the more cogent. When the same ratio as before of gross investment to the value of the stock of capital is being maintained when innovations take on a capital-using form, then the new plant that is being created requires less employment at normal utilization than that which is being replaced. It would need a sharp increase in gross investment to prevent this from happening but there is nothing in the situation to cause gross investment to rise.

[12] Cf. Joan Robinson, *Economic Heresies*, Basic Books, 1971, and Macmillan, 1972, pp. 129 et seq.

The condition of increasing long-period unemployment seems to be prevalent at the present time (1978). This cannot be prevented by operating on effective demand; it requires fundamental structural remedies. On top of it a short-period, Keynesian recession has reduced the level of utilization of plant.

Post-Keynesian theory has plenty of problems to work on. We now have a general framework of long- and short-period analysis which will enable us to bring the insights of Marx, Keynes and Kalecki into a coherent form and apply them to the contemporary scene, but there is still a long way to go.

7

TIME IN ECONOMIC THEORY

'TODAY' is at the front edge of time. It moves continuously forward with an ever lengthening past behind it. Any event that occurred at any date in history occurred when that date was 'today'. We attempt to understand its causes, which lay in its own past and to trace its consequences which followed in its own future. The future up to today of any event in the past has already happened. As would-be social scientists – historians and economists – our relations to an event in the past and an event taking place 'today' are radically different. The consequences of past events can, in principle, be known, or at least discussed, while the consequences of a present event can, at best, be predicted with a range of possibilities which may turn out not to have been correctly anticipated. This is a necessary condition of human life. Life as we experience it would not be possible if the future was known for certain.

> There was a young man who said 'Damn!
> Now I perceive that I am
> A creature that moves
> In predestinate grooves
> Not even a bus, but a tram'.

He was wrong. 'Today' is influenced, but not completely bound, by the past. Any action or decision taken today is either the result of blind habit and convention or it is directed towards its future consequences, which cannot yet be fully known.

There is a third kind of time which is met with in economic theory, that is, logical time in a specified model.

1

LOGICAL TIME

In a properly specified stationary state, there is no distinction between any one day and any other. On a properly specified growth path, such as a von Neumann ray, exhibiting a particular pace of expansion of employment and of a specified stock of means of production, there is no movement forward and upward or backward and downward, except the movement of the reader's eye along the curve.

Unfortunately, the great majority of models in the textbooks are not properly specified. Take, for instance, the familiar Marshallian cross of supply and demand curves showing an equilibrium point in the middle. At a price above the equilibrium level, offer exceeds demand, and below, demand exceeds offer.

Now we are told, if price at any moment is not at the equilibrium level, it will tend towards it. This means that historical events are introduced into a timeless picture. As Professor Samuelson kindly explained to me, 'When a mathematician says "y rises as x falls", he is implying nothing about temporal sequences or anything different from "When x is low, y is high".'[1]

To move implies a temporal sequence. To fill in the story of a movement towards equilibrium, a complicated dynamic process must be specified and to specify a process that will actually reach equilibrium is by no means a simple matter.[2]

The other favourite diagram in elementary neoclassical textbooks is an isoquant showing a given output produced by different combinations of 'capital' and labour. The question, raised by Thorstein Veblen in 1908 and by myself in 1953, as to whether a 'quantity of capital' is a number of dollars or a stock of productive equipment, has not yet been answered, but even if we allow them to specify it as a number of tons of putty, they are not out of the wood. Two points on the isoquant represent two different techniques of production, one with a higher ratio of putty to men employed than the other. A movement from one to the other would involve augmenting the stock of putty or dismissing some workers. Before we can go on with the story, we want to know which.

[1] See below, p. 138.
[2] See A. Medio, 'A Mathematical Note on Equilibrium in Value and Distribution', *Economic Notes*, Siena, Vol. 7, 23, 1978.

Marshall was aware of the difficulty.[3] He drew a long-period supply curve going forward through time, with economies of scale and learning by doing. At any date that had once been reached, he conceived that there was a curve running backwards showing lower costs than on the forward curve because economies that have once been achieved would not be lost if demand were to shrink so that output had to be reduced. But this device raises more problems than it solves.

A pseudo-production function (though I confess I was the first to draw one) is not a legitimate construction. It exhibits different techniques, each with the appropriate stocks of equipment already in being. This was a protest against a production function with putty capital but it did not go far enough. It led on to a protest against confusing comparisons of imagined equilibrium positions with movements through historical time.

Sraffa's model escapes these difficulties if we interpret it in terms of comparisons of possible self-reproducing states. There are two completely separate sets of comparisons. One is of different technological systems, which is hinted at in Part III of *Production of Commodities . . .* The other is of different distributions between wages and profits of the net output in a single system. There is a great deal to be learned from this model, particularly in a negative direction. It is a *Prelude to a Critique of Economic Theory*. The theory which cannot survive the critique is the notion that the rate of profits in a capitalist economy is determined by the relations between 'factors of production' expressed in the concept of the 'marginal productivity of capital'. But as the basis for analysis in a positive direction there is a difficulty about the specification of Sraffa's model in terms of logical time. The difficulty arises already in the first part of the argument before joint products and fixed capital are introduced; in the present context we need not go beyond it.

The technical conditions of the model are described in a 'system' of input-output equations in physical terms. There is the same turnover period for each element in the system. The labour force, working with inputs, replaces them with a surplus which is divided between wages and net profits at the end of the period. This entails that at the beginning of the period there were stocks of the required inputs in existence in the correct proportions.

Sraffa conducts the analysis in terms of *changing* the share of wages in net output but this cannot be taken literally for a given share puts the model on to a predestinate tramline. The argument must be conducted in terms

---

[3] *Principles*, Appendix H.

of *comparing* different shares with the same technical system. To any given share, there corresponds a particular rate of profits, uniform throughout the system, a pattern of prices of inputs and outputs, and a pattern of ratios of gross profits to the wage bill (profit margins) in the various industries.

Many high-theorists are fastidious about mentioning money but I do not see any objection to introducing an arbitrary money-wage bill per period, and reckoning prices and profit margins in money terms.

Now, the difficulty is that there is no relation between distribution and the physical composition of net output. The wage is a share of net output, whatever it may be made of. If growth is going on, part of net output consists of investment goods which workers' households cannot consume. We can evade this problem by putting the model into a stationary state so that all net output is consumed – throwing the wage, as Sraffa says, into the limbo of non-basics. Then net output may be conceived to be made up of homogeneous baskets of consumable goods, but still it is unnatural to postulate that rentiers take their share in the same proportion of various items that go to workers' households.

This problem arises because there is no causality in Sraffa's system. The capitalists do not decide what labour to employ, what prices to set and what investment plans to draw up. All they can do is meekly to fulfil the equations that the observing economist has written down. The only limitation on what the equations may be is that the workers' share of consumable goods is enough to support life.

But if we are to introduce decisions into the model, we must introduce time. Decisions are taken in the light of beliefs about their future consequences. To make the model coherent, we must endow the capitalists with correct foresight as to what composition of output and what pattern of prices will maximize their profits. Then the division of net output as between wage goods and luxury items is made to fit the distribution of income between workers and rentiers. Each rate of profits, with a given basic technology, must be conceived to have an appropriate composition of the flow of net output.

In a short-period model, there is not correct foresight. There are individual expectations which need not be consistent with each other and which may turn out later to have been mistaken. Productive capacity – the stocks of inputs and training of the labour force – has been brought into existence by past events; it is whatever it is. Capitalists, taken one with another, are offering employment at certain wage rates in order to produce a particular flow of output and households are deciding upon a particular flow of purchases. The consequent interaction of individual decisions is seen in the total composition and prices of the total flow of output and its distribution between wages and gross profits. This brings about the realization of surplus value, in Marxian language, or the equalization of savings with investment, in Keynesian language.

In working out the relationship between the share of wages in net output, and the corresponding uniform rate of profits on capital, Sraffa's model cannot evade the distinction between the future and the past.

2

HISTORICAL TIME

We certainly would not expect, in studying past history, to find a date at which a uniform rate of profit was ruling in the capitalist world, or in any one country comprised by it. The construction of a long-run model does not lead up to any plausible hypotheses about reality. It is useful for eliminating contradictions and pointing towards causal relations that will have to be taken into account in interpreting history. Nor should we expect to find a period in which technology can be represented in a single system of equations or in an orderly series of vintages. The analysis for comparing technologies has unfortunately run up the blind alley of the pseudo-production function, which has held up the development of long-period theory for the last twenty years. To construct models that cannot be applied is merely an idle amusement. It is only by interpreting history, including the present in history, that economics can aspire to be a serious subject.

A notable practitioner of the discipline, E. H. Carr, has maintained that the study of history is of the same nature as the study of physical science:

> All thinking requires acceptance of certain pre-suppositions based on observation which make scientific thinking possible, but are subject to revision in the light of that thinking. These hypotheses may well be valid in some contexts or for some purposes, though they turn out to be invalid in others. The test in all cases is the empirical one whether they are in fact effective in promoting fresh insights and adding to our knowledge. The methods of Rutherford were recently described by one of his most distinguished pupils and fellow-workers:
>
> > 'He had a driving urge to know how nuclear phenomena worked in the sense in which one could speak of knowing what went on in the kitchen. I do not believe that he searched for an

explanation in the classical manner of a theory using certain basic laws; as long as he knew what was happening he was content.'*

This description equally fits the historian, who has abandoned the search for basic laws, and is content to enquire how things work.[4]

* Sir Charles Ellis, *Trinity Review*, Cambridge, Lent Term, 1960.

The study of history and of natural phenomena are social activities. There is no point in trying to justify them. Like climbing Everest, the motive for studying society is because it is there. Knowledge of physics has produced enormous practical consequences for good and ill. Knowledge of history, as it filters down to the man in the street, produces political consequences. But if any study is conducted with a view to its consequences, it is liable to become corrupted. A serious subject must be studied, with an open mind, for its own sake.

Here the study of society and of the physical universe are, in principle, alike but the difference of degree is enormous. The inclination to bend the evidence in favour of a pre-conceived result is much more prevalent when human beings are studying human society than when they are studying the external world, and the discipline of the subject to prevent it is much weaker.

Professor Ziman describes procedures in the physical sciences:

In order that science may continually break through the invisible barriers of its own paradigmatic categories, each scientist is encouraged to be an imaginative source of interpretation, both of his contributions and of the work of other scientists.

On the other hand, nothing may be published as scientific information without careful, critical scrutiny by editors, referees and reviewers. The highest standards of instrumental accuracy and logical necessity are imposed on all scientific communications. Experiments are conscientiously repeated and theoretical calculations tested by alternative procedures. Every scientific paper, ostensibly building on the preceding work that it cites, carries an implied or open criticism of much of that work, which it seeks to validate or disconfirm and supersede. Review articles, colloquia and research monographs delineate controversial issues, and delicately point out the deficiencies of many reputable research contributions.

Experienced scientists know, indeed, that real progress in research is slow and painful, and that many experimental observations and

[4] E. H. Carr, *What is History?*, London, Macmillan, 1961, pp. 5394.

plausible arguments will not stand up for long under expert questioning. If science is to evolve, it must continually purge itself of mis-
conceptions, follies and practical errors: there must be preserved a
central store of absolutely reliable knowledge, from which to draw in
evaluating novel ideas and on which, very slowly and carefully, to
build. In order that science may retain its reliability and credibility,
each scientist is expected to exercise critical vigilance over his own
work and the claims of his contemporaries.

This truly remarkable and civilized behaviour amongst scientists
we take for granted: these are the standards against which occasional
pathologies are judged. And if those who rule society — aristocrats or
democrats, capitalists or socialists, conservatives or radicals — want
scientific knowledge on which they can rely, they must not allow the
inner tension of science to slacken, break, or overbalance. According
to the narrow logic of bureaucratic planning, it is a wasteful,
irrational system that ought to be made efficient and economical. But
by encouraging innovation, yet conserving past achievement, by
calling the gambling competitive spirit from each of us, yet making us
also the guardians of truth and the judges of quality, it is remarkably
successful as the source of many wonders.[5]

These standards do not prevail in the social sciences and it seems vain to
expect that they ever could. In the absence of a decisive and agreed
method for reading the evidence from history, the choice between rival
hypotheses is influenced by psychological and political factors not
susceptible to pure reason. Thus hypotheses are turned into doctrines.

Marx set out to discover 'laws of motion' of the capitalist system as it
had emerged in the Western world and he made bold predictions about
what for him was the future. Now a good stretch of that future is our past.
Here we have an opportunity to apply scientific method to the study of
our own society, checking his hypotheses with actual results. In the
writing of history, this has borne good fruit but in economics it has been
wasted, for the most part, in a theological style of verbal disputes.

The short-period theory in Marx — the process of the realization of
surplus — as it has been developed by Kalecki — has laid the foundation for
an analysis of employment, distribution and effective demand and of the
consequences (though not of the causes) of changing technological
knowledge.

[5] John Ziman, *Reliable Knowledge*, CUP, 1978, p. 132.

Nowadays, hypotheses based on this line of thought are swamped in orthodox teaching by the doctrines of monetarism. At the present time (1979) a policy based upon those doctrines is actually being carried out in the UK. This will provide a rare chance to show which of two rival hypotheses is going to prove to be the least correct.

3

WHEN IS THE LONG RUN?

In expounding economic theory, the statement is often made that such and such will happen 'in the long run'. For Marshall, the long run is a period of *future* time after some event has occurred. An unforeseen rise in the demand for fish, at a certain date, causes its price to rise. High profits attract investment into the business and the subsequent higher flow of output will bring the price down. Marshall implies that the price will come back to more or less where it was before, but predictions of this kind are usually guarded by the phrase 'other things equal'. The Marshallian method of exposition is to attempt to trace the effects over the future of a particular event happening 'today' by the one-at-a-time method, that is to say by assuming that we know what would have happened over that particular period of future time if this event had not occurred. This could be specified in a model where all elements are under the control of the observing economist: Marshall makes the step from a model to reality by an act of faith. He knows that other things in fact will not be equal – history marches on – but he supposes that it is possible to trace the effects of a single specified event *as though* it was the only change that occurred at a particular date.

The weak point in the argument is that he cannot specify *what* would have occurred in the absence of this event. He has a concept of the level of the normal rate of profit, but he has no theory whatever of what causes it to be at any particular level or of a mechanism that causes it to be maintained at a constant level 'in the long run'.

This arises from the basic fudge in Marshall's theory of the long-term rate of interest (which means the rate of profit) as the 'reward of waiting'.

Ricardo postulated a mechanism which keeps real wages from remaining, over a stretch of some years of historical time, much above or below the level necessary to support the customary standard of life of the workers. Marshall removed this mechanism from his system and put nothing in its place.

The search for a theory of the normal rate of profit is proverbially like looking in a dark room for a black cat that probably is not there. If we had complete information about a period of past history we could see what were the flows of gross profits in various industries, what allowances were made for depreciation and so what were the flows of net profits and we could see what changes were made over the period in stocks of productive capacity and the ownership of financial wealth. To account for what happened, we should have to enquire what conventions and expectations were guiding conduct at dates in the period when decisions were taken by firms and households. Thus we could choose between the hypotheses that theorists have put forward and see which were the least unplausible.

Then we should have a long-run theory based on past experience and we could use it to predict what will be the future provided that no relevant change takes place in the conditions prevailing in the past.

Unfortunately, when our predictions turn out to have been incorrect, we should have the fresh task of finding out whether there has been a relevant change or whether our theory was not correct in the first place.

4

WORK IN PROGRESS

Economics can never be a serious subject on the plane of physics but we can make it a great deal less frivolous than it is at present.

We must throw out concepts and theorems that are logically self-contradictory, such as the general equilibrium of supply and demand, the long-run production function, the marginal productivity of capital and the equilibrium size of firms.

In the space thus cleared, we can assemble the hypotheses about the world we are living in which seem to be surviving best. In commodity markets, prices fluctuate under the influence of changes in the relations of supply to demand, without ever tending towards stability. In corporate industry, prices are set by the producer in relation to costs, but since costs include depreciation, *net* proceeds can be known only after the event. These prices are not much affected by the volume of demand but are sensitive to changes in money costs and in taxation.

The most reliable part of our apparatus is the analysis of effective demand initiated by Keynes and Kalecki. Swings of activity must be seen, not as starting up from cold, but as overlaying slow long-run changes in productive capacity produced by accumulation, technical change (including changes in methods of operation of the labour force) and alterations in the composition of output. The interaction between the long-run and the short-run consequences of technical innovations is a complicated subject which requires more study.

The evolution of business activity and trade-union policy should be approached in the spirit of natural-history observation of the behaviour of classes and groups.

The analysis of international trade should be preceded by an inquiry into the meaning of a 'nation' in the relevant respects – a question which nowadays is not so simple as used to be supposed.

All this, and much more, indicates work to be done, provided that we give up the search for grand general laws and are content to try to enquire how things happen.

8

THE DISINTEGRATION OF ECONOMICS

PROFESSIONAL economics grew and flourished on an unprecedented scale, especially in North America, after the end of World War II. At the same time, the Western industrial nations were enjoying a period of continuous growth and high employment, interrupted only by brief and shallow recessions and accompanied by only a mild rate of inflation in the price level. The central teaching of orthodox economic theory was the natural tendency to 'equilibrium' in the free market system, and this did not appear to be in obvious contradiction to the facts of experience.

Since 1974, the occurrence of a serious world-wide recession accompanied by increased inflation has left the economists gaping. Othodoxy has nothing to offer and all kinds of fanciful notions are floating around.

HOLLOW ORTHODOXY

However, it is not only the slump which has exposed the bankruptcy of academic economic teaching. The structure of thought which it expounds was long ago proved to be hollow. It consisted of a set of propositions which bore hardly any relation to the structure and evolution of the economy that they were supposed to depict. The reason for this intellectual aberration seems to have been that the very notion of an economic system, as a particular historical phenomenon, developing through time, was associated with the doctrines of Marx. The aim of teaching was to build up a screen to prevent students from glancing in that direction. This was reinforced during the McCarthy period by the fear of being suspected of dangerous thoughts. Thus the academics were anxious

---

A lecture, first published in *Collected Economic Papers*, Vol. V, 1979.

to present the economy in a pleasing light and did not care to examine it to see what it was actually like.

As a matter of fact, a very robust defence of capitalism can be derived from Marx's analysis. Exploitation, that is the payment as wages of less than the value of the net proceeds of industry, is necessary for the emergence of profits. Profits provide both the motive and the means for the accumulation of capital and the competitive struggle amongst capitalists to accumulate leads to technical innovation which 'ripens the productive power of social labour as though in a hot-house'.

The academics (except for Joseph Schumpeter) did not follow up this line. They pretend that the Marxian 'labour theory of value' means that workers have the right to the whole product industry — the view of the Utopian socialists whom Marx despised — and protest that capital also produces value and has a right to its share.

Before the great slump of the 1930s, Alfred Marshall was the dominant influence on economics in the English-speaking world. He was a subtle thinker who allowed for exceptions to every rule that he propounded but the effect of his doctrines as they were generally interpreted was to support laisser faire — government intervention in economic life, however well-intentioned, will do more harm than good; belief in a natural tendency to equilibrium in the free-market economy at a level of real wages consonant with full employment of the available labour force; the beneficial effects of free trade; the defence of the gold standard and of sound finance. Many arguments drawn from this complex of ideas are being trotted out again now, as they were in the 1930s; for instance, the view that there cannot be any 'involuntary' unemployment, because any individual could always get a job by offering to work at less than the going wage rate, or that government borrowing draws upon a given fund of savings (or is it of finance?) and so 'crowds out' private-sector investment. However, during the great debate that was broken off by the war in 1939, the arguments of Keynes were gradually prevailing over orthodoxy, and by the end of the war Keynes had become orthodox in his turn.

In the course of his endeavour to understand the causes of unemployment, Keynes had reintroduced the concept of capitalism as a particular economic system, evolving through history. He saw it as containing an essential flaw — its inherent instability and chronic failure to make full use of its potential resources — but he thought that his theory showed how this could be patched up and in any case, as an economic system, it 'was the best in sight'.

This was not good enough for the new orthodoxy burgeoning in the United States. The subject was split into two parts; Keynes was safely corralled in the section called 'macro economics' while the main stream of teaching returned to celebrating the establishment of equilibrium in a free market.

This section of theory was described as 'micro economics', that is, the study of prices of particular commodities and the behaviour of individual sellers and buyers; however, it is obviously impossible to discuss the behaviour of individuals in a vacuum without saying anything about the legal, political and economic setting in which they are to operate. The setting in which the equilibrium of supply and demand in analysed has no resemblance to modern capitalism. It is suited, rather, to the discussion of a rural fair where independent peasants and artisans meet to exchange products that are surplus to their own requirements.

A great point is made of the freedom of the consumer to choose what commodities to consume, according to his individual 'tastes', but obviously the main influence upon the pattern of demand for commodities is the distribution of purchasing power between families. Nothing is said about this except that each individual has an 'endowment' of some 'factor of production', such as the ability to work, or property in land or (though this is scarcely consistent with the rest of the story) property in various types of industrial equipment.

In the old Marshallian theory there had been a discussion of 'welfare' and it was admitted that a given flow of production of commodities would provide more 'satisfaction' to a given human population the more equally it was distributed amongst the consumers concerned. Marshall himself favoured a more equal distribution of national income provided it could be brought about without any revolutionary upheaval. This whole question, however, was eliminated from the analysis of the equilibrium model, first by passing very lightly over the question of the relative amounts of 'endowments' possessed by different individuals while concentrating on the determination of the relative price per unit of the various 'factors'; secondly, by concentrating upon the choices made by a single consumer under a 'budget constraint', that is, with a certain amount of purchasing power to spend. When it has been shown that his 'tastes' and the prices of the commodities determine what he buys, the suggestion is slipped in that the choices of consumers in the aggregate determine what is to be produced. In acclaiming the 'sovereignty of the consumer', the problem of distribution of consuming power amongst the population somehow gets lost to view.

The great claim of equilibrium theory was that it showed how scarce means are allocated between alternative uses in accordance with consumers' tastes. The existence of scarce means (materials, energy, cultivable land) has recently come very much to the fore in public discussion, while consumers' tastes run to large cars, overheated rooms, and an excessive consumption of meat. The central doctrine of orthodox economics is the defence of the freedom of anyone who has money to spend, to spend it as he likes.

SMOTHERING KEYNES

In the other department, so-called macro economics, the discussion is all about instability and how slumps could be prevented by applying Keynes' conceptions of demand management. This complete break, like a geological fault, between the two departments of economic theory, makes it impossible for students to form a coherent view of what it is all about. If there is a natural tendency in the free market system to equilibrium with full employment, why do we need Keynes; and if Keynes was right, that the capitalist system is inherently unstable, why do we have to spend so much time working out the mathematics of an equilibrium system? Such doubts, however, were smothered by reducing 'Keynesian' theory to a kind of equilibrium in its turn and swallowing it up in the 'neo-neoclassical synthesis'.

Keynes himself, when he had worked out the argument of the *General Theory*, was startled by the indictment of the free-enterprise system that it seemed to represent and he wrote the last chapter in a very mollifying style which made it possible for orthodoxy to accept it and to pass very lightly over the awkward questions that earlier chapters had raised.

The synthesis was very soothing. A natural tendency to steady growth took the place of equilibrium. The subject split up into a number of compartments – business economics, labour economics, urban economics, and so forth which provided many fields of work for academics to burrow into without questioning the central structure of theory. The elaboration of mathematical theorems (though devoid of empirical content) kept many brilliant practitioners happily occupied. When some dissidents tried to attack the basis of orthodox doctrines from a Marxist point of view, they were absorbed into the profession; now 'radical economics' is one of the standard compartments of the subject along with the rest.

Under this cover a great deal of work has been done and a mass of information collected, much of which is of great interest, but it has been confused and distorted by the need to stuff it into the restricting frame of equilibrium analysis.

A case in point is the so-called theory of the firm. Marshall was a great moralizer. His aim was to justify the ways of Mammon to man. The labourer is worthy of his hire, and the capitalist is worthy of his return. The interest received by a rentier is the 'reward of waiting' that is, of keeping his wealth intact. For an entrepreneur it is the reward of 'business ability in command of capital'.

Marshall knew that the main source of finance for the growth of a business is reinvestment of its own profits, but he refused to accept the corollary that any business which gets a good start will go on growing indefinitely. He maintained that there is an upper limit to the size of firms so that every market will normally be served by a sufficient number of sellers to ensure competitive pricing.

His theory is one of the fossils of nineteenth century doctrine that has been carried down till today in mainstream teaching. The mutation in capitalism which has come about with the establishment of the great, and still growing, multinational corporations is largely ignored. Kenneth Galbraith has examined the characteristics of the *New Industrial State*, but as he writes in a bright, readable style, his views need not be taken seriously. Many realistic studies of actual business performance have been made but they are excluded from the mainstream textbooks which still depict competitive industries composed of a large number of firms each unable to grow beyond the equilibrium size.

ANOTHER VERSION

There was a serious weakness in the neo-neoclassical synthesis to which most of the profession seems to have been oblivious. The theory of market equilibrium, with given 'endowments' and given 'tastes' for a specified list of commodities is essentially static. It can accommodate accumulation and change only by making the assumption that buyers and sellers have 'correct foresight' of the future course of prices. A world of correct foresight is not the world in which human beings live. From this point, the argument takes off into an elaboration of mathematical structures which have no point of contact with empirical reality. But if steady growth had been substituted in the synthesis for static equilibrium, it was obviously necessary to discuss accumulation. This required an account of the nature of capital and of the generation of profits.

There had been another version of the central theory derived from Marshall, often mixed up in the textbooks with market equilibrium. In this, the 'factors of production' are not individual endowments but the total amounts available to the economy as a whole, of land, labour and capital. When all are fully employed, each receives a 'reward', rent, wages and interest, according to its contribution to the product of industry. This doctrine was propounded in the USA by Professor J. B. Clark, at the beginning of the present century. Thorstein Veblen immediately pointed out that the 'capital' which receives interest is rentier wealth that can be lent to business or to government, while the 'capital' that contributes to the product of industry is the technology embodied in equipment and stocks that permits labour to produce output. But no one from the orthodox camp deigned to answer him. Veblen (the most original economist born and bred in the USA) was a maverick whose views could be laughed off.

When the question was raised in Cambridge (England) twenty years ago, the orthodox answer was: let us pretend that 'capital' consists of a physical substance that is just like finance so that the problem does not arise. It is homogeneous, divisible, and measurable, and can be embodied in any variety of equipment, instantaneously, without cost and without change in the initial quantity. The distinction which Keynes had drawn between interest — the price of loans, and profit — the return on invest- ment — was muddled up again and the rate of interest was taken to measure the productivity of this imaginary substance.

Orthodoxy seemed to be quite content with this concoction, until the publication by Piero Sraffa of a book with the eccentric title: *Production of Commodities by Means of Commodities*, roused a sharp controversy. Cam- bridge (Massachusetts) challenged Cambridge (England) and failed to win the point. Professor Samuelson very candidly admitted that his system did not hold water. This knocked the bottom out of the logical structure of orthodox theory, but mainstream teaching goes on just the same.

THE PRESENT AS HISTORY

Piero Sraffa's formal analysis re-established (though in a somewhat cryptic manner) the classical doctrine that the rate of profit on capital depends upon the technical structure of production and the share of wages in net output. The classical economists, such as Adam Smith and Ricardo, had naturally thought in terms of accumulation as a historical process. (The equilibrists are fond of claiming Adam Smith as the founder of their school, but he certainly did not intend to set up a static model of an exchange economy.)

Keynes abused Ricardo for neglecting the problem of effective demand, and he had no time for Marx, but he himself instinctively thought in the classical manner of the institutions of capitalism evolving through time. His own analysis was confined, for the most part, to strictly short-period problems but it fits into a classical, historical approach. (Modern attempts to force Keynes into the equilibrium mould are causing a great deal of unnecessary confusion.) By acknowledging that life is lived in time and that today is an ever moving break between the irrevocable past and the unknown future, he had shattered the basic conception of equilibrium, though he sometimes felt a nostalgic reluctance to give it up.

When we view our problems in historical terms, it is obvious that the twenty-five years of continuous growth after the end of the Second World War was a special epoch (indeed, every decade in the history of capitalism is a special epoch). It was characterized by the rise to dominance of the United States over the free-enterprise world economy, with the cold and hot wars that that entailed. Keynesian doctrines had very little to do with its success, except, first, that the monetary authorities had learned how to prevent a recession in industry from developing into a severe credit crisis, and second, that deficit finance had been made respectable; this was an important contribution to the development of the military–industrial complex, to which President Eisenhower vainly attempted to alert public opinion in America.

The high rate of consumption of natural materials entailed by the growth of industrial production gradually caused demand to overtake supply so that the terms of trade were turned against manufactures. The uneven development of the free-enterprise nations set intolerable strains on the world financial system, and the attempt by Nixon to devalue the dollar in 1971 was a further shock. Trying to counter an incipient recession due to rising costs by cheap money led to a wild inflation in 1973. Then OPEC threw a spanner into the works and the long boom finally collapsed.

Now there is a revulsion against Keynes, and the popular view seems to be that it was really all his fault.

INFLATION

The characteristic of the present slump which makes it markedly different from the slump that Keynes was trying to diagnose in the 1930s, is that it is accompanied everywhere by a greater or less degree of inflation, that is, by world-wide rising price levels. During the long run of high employ-ment, as Keynes predicted, there was a tendency for money-wage rates to rise faster than the general productivity of industry, and so for prices to rise to cover rising costs. This experience led to the concept of a 'pay-off' between unemployment and inflation. Some rather slap-dash historical research produced a statistical 'law' showing an inverse relation between the level of unemployment and the rate of rise of the price level. The concept of a pay-off is typical of the way economists argue from statistics without thinking about human beings. Clearly, the cost of unemployment falls mainly upon workers, while the inconvenience of inflation is felt mainly by the middle class. The economists do not hesitate to tot them up and set one against the other. When the 'law' broke down in the late 1960s, with inflation and unemployment rising together, the economists proclaimed that the terms of the pay-off had shifted, and it was necessary to have more unemployment to keep inflation in check. This is how the matter rests at present (1980).

During the long boom, while 'Keynesian' policies seemed to be working satisfactorily, a dispute developed between two schools of thought as to whether monetary policy, operating through the banking system, was to be preferred to fiscal policy operating through central and local budgets. The prevalence of inflation has given a great boost to the monetarists, who flourish particularly in Chicago, for traditionally infla-tion was always regarded as a 'monetary' problem. The strong point in their case is that a rise in the value of transactions, due to increased activity at rising prices, generally cannot take place without an increase in the stock of money. The weak point is that for the authorities to prevent the quantity of money from increasing requires a severe credit squeeze, which acts directly upon industry, causing bankruptcies and reducing employ-ment, and only indirectly, if at all, on the level of prices.

The monetarist argument supports the idea of a 'pay-off'. If a high level of unemployment can be maintained for long enough (some say two years, some say five) the rate of inflation will gradually fall until stability is established (does this include the price of oil?). Meanwhile, the stock of industrial equipment would be degenerating for lack of investment and the labour force would be degenerating as juveniles fail to get jobs. But that does not matter. Inflation, to the monetarists, is the worst of all evils and there is no remedy for it but keeping production low.

Business opinion seems rather to favour fiscal policy and hopes for an injection of profits into industry through enlarged expenditure on arma-ments. In a wider context, it might be argued that this remedy is worse than the disease.

Permanent Unemployment

The immediate problem of unemployment is serious enough, but the long-period problem lying behind it is still more menacing. Industrial technology is continually developing and continually reducing the requirement for manual labour. From one point of view, of course, it is a benefit to humanity to reduce the burden of heavy toil, but for the individual, the purpose of work is to earn money and it is no benefit to him to reduce the burden of toil if it reduces the possibility of earning a living at the same time.

It is true that modern technology is very destructive of amenities, including fresh air, but the individual would prefer to earn money in the smog rather than not earn it at all.

No less an authority than Arthur Burns (in *Challenge*, January/February 1976) has pointed out that American industry, at its most flourishing, offers employment to a limited number of highly skilled workers. (He might have added that, when the great corporations do require unskilled labour, they often prefer to get it in South Korea and Taiwan, where wages are lower and trade unions not allowed.) Even if growth could be started up again at the old rate, there is no possibility of reaching full employment in the long-period sense, that the economy provides everyone with the opportunity to support himself without resorting to crime.

The most pertinent question to ask is:

What characteristic of the private enterprise system is it that condemns the wealthiest nation the world has ever seen to keeping an appreciable proportion of its population in perpetual ignorance and misery?

The professional economists keep up a smoke-screen of 'theorems' and 'laws' and 'pay-offs' that prevents questions such as that from being asked. This situation is, I think, inevitable. In every country, educational institutions in general, and universities in particular, are supported directly or indirectly by the established authorities and whether in Chicago or in Moscow, their first duty is to save their pupils from contact with dangerous thoughts.

9

SURVEY: 1950s

REFLECTIONS AND REMINISCENCES

DURING the decade of the fifties, in Cambridge, the Keynesian revolution was being consolidated and expanded. Already before the war, Kalecki, Kaldor, Harrod and Keynes himself had made important criticisms and advances on the original formulation. The General Theory of Employment was a growing and variegated body of thought, richer and wider than the book of that name. A new phase began when Harrod's *Towards a Dynamic Economics*, in 1947, threw out a challenge to develop a Keynesian analysis of accumulation in the long run.

POST-KEYNESIAN ANALYSIS

In 1952, I published a 'Generalisation of the General Theory'.[1] The main programme during this period was to go beyond Keynes and develop a long-run analysis 'which has freed itself from the need to assume conditions of static equilibrium'.

The following is taken from the Introduction to the volume in which it appeared:

[1] Reprinted in *The Generalisation of the General Theory and Other Essays*, London, Macmillan, 1979. It originally appeared in *Econometrica* in April 1951. When Ragnar Frisch was President of the Econometric Society, he invited me to be a Vice-President. I said that it was no good for my name to appear on the cover of the journal when I could not understand anything inside it. He replied that he had a campaign to get more prose into *Econometrica*, and asked me to let them have an article. When I submitted 'The Rate of Interest', it was rejected by the editors. Then I sent it to Frisch, who insisted on them taking it. (He paid me the very valuable compliment of saying that I had Ricardo's instinct for making realistic simplifications.) But I do not think that his campaign went any further.

An amended version of the Introduction to *Collected Economic Papers*, Vol. II, Second edition, 1975.

The theme of these essays is the analysis of a dynamic economic system. The characteristic of a dynamic analysis, in the sense intended here, is that it cannot explain how an economy behaves in given conditions, without reference to past history, while static analysis purports to describe a position of equilibrium which the system will reach (or would reach if the given conditions remained unchanged for long enough) no matter where it started from.

We have all been studying dynamic economics all our lives, for no one, can refrain from reflecting, from time to time, on actual economic events, and actual events are always dynamic. Only in the sealed vacuum of the classrooms where equilibrium theory is taught can static problems be discussed, and even there the outside air is always leaking in. Most of the results of the following analysis are therefore obvious and familiar. It seems, however, worthwhile to try to connect the familiar problems with the classroom analysis, for so long as the analysis is static and the problems dynamic the two are for ever at cross-purposes.

Analysis dealing with actual events encounters the difficulty that the answers to economic problems are only political questions. With politics, enters ideological prejudice. As Gunnar Myrdal has pointed out, the very choice of questions to discuss is an expression of ideology; yet I believe that economic analysis, though it cannot help containing an element of propaganda, yet can be scientific as well.

I have always aimed to make my own prejudices sufficiently obvious to allow a reader, while studying the argument, to discount them as he thinks fit, though, of course, this generally leads a reader of opposite prejudices to reject the argument in advance.

Besides its dynamic approach, the hallmark of post-Keynesian theory is that it takes account of the variety of economic systems and aims to show how the same principles work out differently in different social settings. In 1957 a group of visiting economists were kindly entertained at the Academy of Sciences in Moscow. When it was my turn to put a question, I asked how the labour theory of value applies in agriculture. Khrushchev's reforms had recently raised prices for the products of the collective farms. I picked up a lump of sugar, and asked: 'Has the labour value of this increased?' At first, the answer was evasive: 'A lump of sugar is not an agricultural commodity. It is highly processed'. 'Very well. Take the labour value of raw sugar on the farm'. 'That is a very difficult question'.

I was asked to write a piece on this problem for *Voprosi Ekonomiki*, but when I sent in my 'Philosophy of Prices'[2] it was not accepted for publication.

A study of the differences between the various systems existing in the world today, and of the interactions between them, involves a great deal more than economic theory, but at the same time economic analysis is an indispensable element in it. The young radicals today indignantly reject a doctrine which interprets all problems in terms of Robinson Crusoe allocating scarce means between alternative ends; I was trying to show that there is a kind of analysis which could be useful to them.

In the western world, the decade of the 1950s was a time of prosperity, when high employment, rising consumption and a continuously expanding economy were being taken for granted.

A revival was going on, particularly in USA, of pre-Keynesian theory – the defence of laisser faire – while, in practice, more or less Keynesian methods of control were being followed to preserve near-stability. As with the operation of the gold standard, the equilibrium theory was not immediately laughed out of court because the results that it predicted were being established by quite other means.

Neo-Classical Capital

A defect in my 'Generalisation of the General Theory' was the lack of an adequate conception of the rate of profit and of its relation to the choice of technique.[3] In this context I raised the question of the meaning of a quantity of capital as a fund of finance or as a stock of equipment.

'The Production Function and the Theory of Capital' (1953)[4] was met, not only with incomprehension, but with riducule and indignation. I can understand this now better than I did at the time. In Cambridge, the meaning of the capital to labour ratio in a long-period sense was a well-known unsettled question that Dennis Robertson has left in an admittedly unsatisfactory state. Elsewhere, as I since found, there was a convention of agreeing to believe that it was no problem. My article (written in a somewhat light-hearted style) was innocently remarking that the Emperor had no clothes.

Later controversies (still puttering on after 20 years) make it possible to

---

[2] Included in *Collected Economic Papers*, Vol. II.
[3] Remedied (I hope) in the Introduction to the reprint.
[4] *Review of Economic Studies*, and *Collected Economic Papers*, Vol. II.

understand what the conventional belief was. It consisted of three elements.

The first derived from the Walrasian theory of general equilibrium of exchange. The economy has an endowment of various items of productive equipment which appear to be man-made machines but play the role, in the argument, of scarce natural resources, like Marshall's meteoric stones.[5] The second conception, which Professor Samuelson[6] attributes to J. B. Clark, is of a one-commodity world in which investment takes the form of withdrawing part of the flow of output and adding it to the pre-existing stock. In its capacity as a stock of means of production, the commodity takes on the character of 'putty[7] capital'; it is continuously squeezed up or spread out, as it accrues, so as always to preserve equilibrium. The third conception is that of Irving Fisher, for whom saving is merely a means of transferring consumption from an earlier to a later period, without making a permanent addition to stock.

Of these conceptions, putty capital has been the most fully developed. In this story, there is no room for a short-period supply curve or utilization function, depicting output varying as less or more labour is employed with an unchanged stock of fixed equipment. There is no role for expectations, because equilibrium is instantly restored after any change. There is no distinction between gross and net investment; an alteration of technique (that is, a change in the putty to labour ratio) does not require replacement of old equipment by new, for additional putty is just added on to the existing stock and squeezed up with it. Say's Law is restored and household saving governs industrial investment. Full employment of the available labour force is always provided. The distinction between capital as finance and capital as a stock of physical inputs disappears; in the one-commodity world, a unit of the commodity is the same thing as a unit of purchasing power. Above all, there is no room for any distinction between what is profitable for business and what is beneficial to society, since there is only one commodity to produce and one appropriate technique to install. Thus every objective of Keynesian and post-Keynesian analysis is ruled out of court.

This conception of capital, mixed with some elements drawn from the

[5] See *Principles*, Eighth edition, p. 415.

[6] See 'Parable and Realism in Capital Theory', *Review of Economic Studies*, Vol. XXXIX, June 1962, p. 194.

[7] Professor Samuelson calls it jelly, which has a different meaning in England. The best would be to call the flow of consumption ghi and the stock, butter.

other two (Walras and Fisher) was straddling like the impenetrable Boyg across the path to reasoned argument.

ACCUMULATION AND TECHNICAL CHANGE

The pre-Keynesian conception of substitution between capital and labour is generally treated in terms of a process of accumulation raising the ratio of capital to labour, 'in a given state of technical knowledge'. This is a conception from which I have had a 'long struggle to escape'.

In the article on the production function, I had set out what came to be called a pseudo-production function, purporting to list the techniques specified in a supposed 'book of blueprints' representing the state of technical knowledge. Here, I came across the phenomenon of 'reswitching', later so notorious, but I did not make much of it. At this stage, it seemed sufficiently startling to find that, of two techniques, the one that is more mechanized, in the sense of yielding a *higher* output per man employed may well have the *lower* value of capital at the rate of profit at which it is eligible.

I emphasized that this construction can be used only for comparisons of equilibrium positions, but I failed to ask: if each point represents an economy, an 'island', with its own past and expectations of its own rate of profit and level of real wages remaining constant in the future, what is the point of supposing that they all have access to the same book of blueprints? If each has its own real-wage rate and its own stock of inputs, it would be more natural to suppose that it also has its own state of technical knowledge. The pseudo-production function played an important part in the debate over the meaning and measurement of capital, but it was a completely artificial construction with no correspondence to anything in real life.

Yet I was always hankering after the story of accumulation without new inventions, which used to be told in terms of deepening the structure of capital, lengthening the average period of production, or increasing the roundaboutness of inputs of labour. I later called this the 'Wicksell process'. Wicksell made far and away the most useful contributions to capital theory of any neoclassic, but he was liable to confuse a difference in the rate of interest appropriate to different time-patterns of production with a process of pushing the rate of interest down by pulling the time-pattern out. It is not true that at any moment there is

a range of possible techniques, co-existing in time in the form of
blueprints, amongst which choices are made by firms or investment
planners when new productive capacity is being set up.

Investment does not involve merely picking the profit-maximizing spot
on a well-mapped technological frontier. It involves searching for an
appropriate technique, which will be blueprinted only after it has been
chosen, and the very process of search is a process of technical change. The
growth of output itself creates opportunities for specialization and
'increasing returns' in Allyn Young's sense[8] and new inventions and
discoveries are continually being adapted to industrial processes. There is
no such thing as accumulation without change.

Nothing could be more absurd than the picture of investment pushing
down the rate of profit because of 'diminishing returns' from 'capital
applied to labour'. When we can measure physical capital by some rough
indication, such as horse-power per man employed, we certainly do not
expect to find the lowest rate of profit (in moderately prosperous times)
where this indication is highest. Equally, in a situation where profits are
falling, we do not expect to see the rate of accumulation being
maintained.

A rise in the rate of investment along a given utilization function
temporarily raises the share of profits in national income and may depress
real wages somewhat by raising prices relatively to money-wage rates, but
when a high rate of accumulation, over the long run, is increasing
productive capacity relatively to the growth of the labour force, there is a
strong inducement to improve productivity by installing techniques that
raise output per head.

If real wages remained constant, profit would rise faster than the value
of capital. Thus it is possible for trade unions to secure for their members a
share of the increase in productivity that leaves the rate of profit more or
less constant. This, indeed, helps to maintain accumulation, by expanding
effective demand for output so that growing productive capacity can be
utilized.

When productivity is being raised more or less evenly throughout
industry (neutral technical progress) there is not much change in the
overall ratio of the value of capital to the value of the flow of output.
There is also an element of 'substitution of capital for labour' in the
process of accumulation. Rising real wages and low unemployment cause

[8] Cf. N. Kaldor, 'The Irrelevance of Equilibrium Economics', *Economic Journal*, December 1972.

many lines of production and services to be mechanized by adaptation of methods already known. This can sometimes be seen with the naked eye. Dustmen are provided with special carts when it is necessary to economize on manpower; golfers pull their own bags of clubs along on wheels when caddies ask too much.

Small businesses, for which the wage bill is the main cost, must mechanize to increase output per head if they are to survive. Here, not the rate of profit, but the rate of interest, comes into the story, for access to finance on easy terms is necessary for them to do so.

Where large corporations have installed the same central equipment in a number of countries, for ancillary processes such as wrapping and transporting the product, workers in a low-wage country have to use their hands and feet; in a high-wage country they are assisted by mechanical power.

(Nowadays, there is substitution of labour for capital when a factory is set up in the Third World, paying the lowest possible wages, to make components which are brought back to be incorporated in highly sophisticated products.)

Mechanization undertaken in response to high wages leads to the discovery of superior techniques that would have been profitable, if they had been thought of, when wages were lower. Rising productivity makes rising real wages possible, and rising wages promote rising productivity. When accumulation is sluggish, the labour force growing rapidly and trade unions weak, real wages fail to rise and productivity fails to increase.

The spectrum of ready-blueprinted techniques was a misleading formulation; the process of accumulation itself brings techniques into being as they are required.

Mechanization of formerly labour-intensive production tends to increase the capital to labour ratio, but in the general process of accumulation this may be offset or reversed by capital-saving innovations in lines where advanced technology is in use. In the early stages of industrialization, when the foundation is being laid for heavy industry and transport, there is likely to be a capital-using bias in accumulation; this is roughly what Marx called rising organic composition of capital – the labour embodied in equipment grows relatively to current employment. Then, if the overall rate of profit remains constant, the value of capital per man employed, in the economy as a whole, rises by more than the value of output per man. This might look something like 'diminishing returns', but it does not entail that the rate of profit on capital must fall; it merely limits the rise in wages that is compatible with a constant rate of profit.

10

SURVEY: 1960s

THERE is something baffling about our endless dispute with the neo-neoclassicals. I try to play their game in order to find out to what assumptions their conclusions might correspond. Professor Meade conscientiously spells out the meaning of his malleable machines.[1] This seems to me the height of absurdity, but he is quite satisfied with it. Professor Hahn makes what seems to be a blistering attack on his colleagues:

> It cannot be denied that there is something scandalous in the spectacle of so many people refining the analysis of economic states which they give no reason to suppose will ever, or have ever, come about. . . . It is an unsatisfactory and slightly dishonest state of affairs.[2]

Yet he continues to teach and write in the same mode himself. My critical pieces are understood only by those who agree with me and do not need to read them. Evidently, we are in the presence of a clash of paradigms.

In *The Structure of Scientific Revolutions*[3] the examples are drawn from physics, chemistry and biology. So far as the content of the subject is concerned, it is inappropriate to compare economics with these sciences. We cannot command the methods that have led to their success − precise observation of exact recurrences or controlled experiment − and we have no body of agreed and reliable results such as theirs to offer to the world. But as an academic profession, a group of workers in a particular field, we have much in common with the scientific community which Kuhn describes. When I read his account of a 'crisis' in the development of a scientific discipline, I recognized exactly what I had lived through in the

[1] J. E. Meade, *A Neoclassical Theory of Economic Growth*, London, Allen and Unwin, 1961.

[2] *Econometrica*, Vol. 38, January 1970, p. 1–2.

[3] T. S. Kuhn, *The Structure of Scientific Revolutions*, Routledge and Kegan Paul and Chicago University Press, 1957, Second edition, 1962.

An amended version of the Introduction to *Collected Economic Papers*, Vol. III, Second Edition, 1975.

Keynesian revolution. Now it seems we have to live through it all over again.

To understand how this situation has arisen, we must go back to the beginning.

CAPITAL

Adam Smith struck out a number of separate lines of thought only loosely related to each other. One was the notion that labour is the source of production.

> In the original state of things which precedes both the appropriation of land and the accumulation of stock, the whole produce of labour belongs to the labourer. He has neither landlord nor master to share with him.

Landlords who 'love to reap where they never sowed' and employers who organize factories, muscle in and take part of the produce as rent and profit. Ricardo made this conception more coherent. Workers who have no access to land depend upon earning wages in order to live. A capitalist can get command of labour by advancing wages. He undertakes to pay rent, provides the requisite means of production, and manages the business. The rate of profit on capital depends on the value of output per man on marginal, no-rent land, the wage per man and the value of the wage fund and other stock advanced. Ricardo got bogged down in the problem of how to find a common measure for these three quantities. His theory did not become perfectly clear until Sraffa rescued him. But Marx was able to take it up and expand it into a great historical vision of capitalism as a system of exploitation, which would destroy itself through its own success.

Another seminal idea of Adam Smith was the mutual benefits of free exchange between buyer and seller:

> It is not from the benevolence of the butcher, the brewer, or the baker, that we expect our dinner, but from their regard to their own interests. We address ourselves, not to their humanity but to their self-love, and never talk to them of our own necessities but of their advantages.

From this the neoclassicals who came into fashion after 1870 developed the full-blown defence of laisser faire. They concentrated mainly upon questions of exchange and of the allocation of scarce means between alternative uses; they also claimed that the market mechanism, left to itself, guarantees equilibrium with full employment.

They looked at capital almost entirely from the point of view of a rentier, as a fund of wealth which yields interest. (Marshall, however, combined this with some elements of the classical tradition. The conception of the stock of capital as all the equipment and other inputs available at a moment of time was the launching pad from which Keynes' *General Theory* took off.) Irving Fisher treated the investment of savings merely as a way of transferring consumption from an earlier to a later date. Interest was regarded as something that arose out of saving, without considering that it is only because production is profitable that a business is willing to promise interest in the future for a present supply of finance.

It was necessary, however, to offer some kind of account of the role of capital in production. This was supplied by the notion of the superior productivity of roundabout processes. It is obvious to the naked eye that men equipped with machines produce more than men with only simple tools. It seemed to follow that, if part of a given labour force was set to building machines, it would produce more, in time, than if all were employed in the final stage of the process from the start. The question of time was important. More roundabout methods take longer to yield an output and in some cases, such as Wicksell's stand of timber, merely allowing time to pass yields a product.

This was all summed up in a production function, in a given state of technical knowledge, showing how more 'capital' per man gives more output, subject to the condition of diminishing returns (this condition was borrowed from its setting in Ricardo's theory of rent). An 'invention' was conceived to bring into being a whole new range of technical knowledge which would be shown in a new production function.

The defence of laisser faire, with its guarantee of full employment, came to a violent crash in the great slump. From this emerged Keynes' General Theory, and the experience of wartime planning established it as a new orthodoxy. But the theoretical model that it offered had a very narrow coverage. Long-period analysis, concerning capital and accumulation, was almost completely lacking. In this sphere the neo-neoclassicals inherited only the undigested elements of the pre-Keynesian theory and they started putting it into algebra before asking what it meant.

The most obvious difficulty in the pre-Keynesian theory was that it ran in terms of quantities of capital without offering any unit in which it could be reckoned. (Wicksell set out to find one and, being more candid than most of his contemporaries, admitted that he had failed.)

Nearly the whole argument for the last twenty years has circled around this question of measurement. But it is a superficial problem. The real dispute is not about the *measurement* of capital but about the *meaning* of capital.

The neoclassical concept was designed to present capital as a 'factor of production', on a par with land and labour, and interest (rather than profits) as its just reward. J. B. Clark made this perfectly clear, and even Marshall, in a footnote, describes the factors of production as land, labour and waiting – to wait being to own a stock of wealth without dissipating it in consumption.

To present interest as the reward of a factor of production, two steps are necessary. First, productivity is treated as inhering in 'capital goods'. Wicksell's notion of the productivity of the passage of time has something in it of the classical conception of capital as an advance – an outpayment made before receipts come in. But that is a relationship between employers and employed, not something that could be seen as technically embodied in capital goods. The idea of the productivity of 'a machine' was easier to grasp. The essential idea was that the productivity of a machine was something inherent in itself which could be added to the productivity of labour. Then, applying the notion of substitution developed in the theory of exchange, the rewards of the factors emerge from their marginal productivities, determined by the quantity of each in relation to the other.

The second step is to transfer the marginal productivity and the reward from the machines to their owners – the rentiers who have financed the business of production. There is no doubt that it is the interest paid to rentiers which is the reward of the productivity of machines. There was a separate heading for entrepreneurial profit, to be added to interest, as the reward of enterprise or of 'the co-ordinating function'.

A rentier, as Irving Fisher remarked, is interested in spreading consumption through time; he may be nibbling at his stock of wealth or saving to augment it, according to his tastes and his family situation. He is concerned, also, about placing his money to the best advantage on the Stock Exchange. The only link with the 'productivity of a machine' is that a business is willing and able to pay interest on a loan out of the profits that it earns on the finance invested in productive capacity. But this link is left out of the neoclassical story.

Furthermore, the very concept of productivity inherent in a machine is quite wrong-headed. Thorstein Veblen observed, against J. B. Clark, that the difference between one method of production and another does not inhere in physical inputs, but in the technology which dictates how work is to be done and what kind of instruments it requires.

The productive power of the primitive hunter does not reside in his bow and arrows:

> . . . The loss of these objects − tangible assets − would entail a transient inconvenience. But the accumulated, habitual knowledge of the ways and means involved in the production and use of these appliances is the outcome of long experience and experimentation, and given this body of commonplace technological information the acquisition and employment of the suitable apparatus is easily arranged.[4]

It is still true, with all the development there has been in the application of science to industry, that technology is a possession of society as a whole, not of individual capitalists:

> The commonplace knowledge of ways and means, the accumulated experience of mankind, is still transmitted in and by the body of the community at large; but, for practical purposes, the advanced 'state of the industrial arts' has enabled the owners of goods to corner the wisdom of the ancients and the accumulated experience of the race.[5]

The possibility of buying up and cornering research, and the economies of large scale (which for that very reason are much exaggerated), foster the appropriation of technological knowledge by great corporations that can provide finance for large units of equipment, but it is the knowledge, not the equipment that accounts for the level of productivity achieved.

This is well illustrated by the quick recovery of an industrial country after the destruction of its physical capital in war. The economic miracle of North Korea is the most striking case (especially as the knowledge had to be acquired as it was being applied), but there have been examples also in the capitalist world.

The neoclassical paradigm was built on a fallacy.

After solving the puzzle of valuation, Sraffa was able to confront the doctrine of the productivity of capital with a restatement of the classical theory of profits. His model is exceedingly lean and dry, containing only the bare minimum of elements necessary to deploy the argument.[6] He starts from a precisely specified technology − a system of equations of

---

[4] 'Professor Clark's Economics', reprinted in *A Critique of Economic Theory*, Penguin Modern Economics Readings, p. 174.

[5] Ibid.

[6] See Introduction, p. xii, above.

production – showing the net output that a team of workers can produce while continuously maintaining the stock of inputs required for continued production. He then shows that, corresponding to each share of wages in net output – from unity to zero – there is a determinate value of the rate of profit, uniform throughout the system, on the value of inputs, a determinate pattern of prices for inputs and outputs, and a determinate real wage in terms of any basket of goods. As for what determines the share of wages, in any actual case, we must look for it where it is to be found, in the structure of society at large.

The lineage of Sraffa's conceptions is the more ancient, but after the long reign of the neoclassics they appear startlingly fresh. Just now the neo-neoclassicals are showing all the symptoms, described by Kuhn, of a group whose paradigm is disintegrating in face of a new challenge.

THE RATE OF RETURN

The rate of return is the increment of production due to an increment added by investment to the stock of inputs, expressed as a ratio to the cost of the investment involved. This ratio could be discovered only in a strictly one-commodity world. But the broad idea of the benefit to society as a whole of investment increasing the stock of means of production (industrial equipment) and of means of consumption (such as housing) is certainly a valuable – indeed, an indispensable – concept for the analysis of growth. And so is the concept of accumulation as a burden on society in the sense that a higher rate of investment (given near-full employment) entails a lower ratio of consumption to work being done.

If 'capital' is productive and the rate of profit measures the productivity of an increment of capital at the margin, then the rate of return is identical with the rate of profit.[7] It follows that profit-maximizing firms in a regime of perfect competition can be relied upon to dispose of society's investible resources to the best advantage for society,[8] while the

---

[7] An increment of product at the margin must not be confused with marginal productivity in the sense to which Euler's theorem can be applied. Marginal productivity in that sense can be defined in a one-commodity world with continuously differentiable factor ratios. It is concerned with substitutability within a given stock of inputs and has no application to a process of accumulation.

[8] There is unfortunately an echo of this concept in the last chapter of Keynes' General Theory, where it is quite out of place.

abstinence from consumption which provides the funds to invest is duly
rewarded.

The proposition that the rate of profit on capital measures the rate of
return for society as a whole on private wealth is the very heart of
neoclassical doctrine, on which the defence of laisser faire depends. (After
various attempts to demonstrate this proposition for an industrial
economy, Professor Solow has finally retreated into a one-commodity
world, where he can contemplate it at his leisure.[9])

One aspect of this complex of ideas has been discredited by the post-
Keynesian theory of distribution. In a short-period situation a higher ratio
of investment to income is associated with a higher share of profits and
more, not less, rentier consumption. In long-period growth, the system
generates a rate of profit sufficient to provide finance for the accumulation
that is going on. When rentiers do not choose to perform abstinence, the
rate of profit is so much the higher and abstinence imposed on the workers
so much the greater.

This, however, is a realtively minor objection to the concept of a 'rate
of return'. The major objection is that the great corporations dispose of
society's investible resources in forms which best suit their own ends.
They decide what techniques are to be installed, how the labour force is to
be manipulated, what incremental bill of goods is to be produced and
how consumers' tastes can be moulded to make them saleable.

(These fairly obvious considerations often drive the neo-neoclassicals to
set up models of a fully socialist economy, where the notion of investment
planned in the interest of society as a whole might have a run for its
money.)

A striking example of the tenacity of an inappropriate ideology in face
of new problems is the neo-neoclassical treatment of the notorious dangers
of pollution. The prevalence of pollution is admitted, but it must not be
allowed to affect the general presumption in favour of laisser faire. It is a
tiresome exception to the general rule, due to 'externalities' that should be
'internalized' (that is, brought into the system of competitive prices) by
instituting a suitable fee for the emission of each kind of poison. Then the
free play of market forces will reduce pollution to the optimum level

> at which the social costs of reducing pollution by a further unit just
> equal the social benefits of doing so, and where a further reduction in
> pollution would then cost more than the further benefits to be
> obtained from doing so.[10]

[9] *Growth Theory, An Exposition*, 1971.
[10] See W. Beckerman, 'In Defence of Economic Growth', Jonathan Cape, 1974, p. 141.

This would make it possible to return to the old slogans: What is profitable is right. Leave it to the businessmen. Businessmen know best.

The victory of Keynes' theory over the orthodoxy of sound finance was not due to his superior logic but to the pressure of great events in the world. Perhaps we shall finally owe the defeat of neoclassical complacency to public indignation at the devastating accidents which highly profitable technology is always bringing about.

THE PSEUDO-PRODUCTION FUNCTION

The construction of a pseudo-production function is an exercise in taking a question from one paradigm and answering it in terms of another; that is, examining the concept of a well-behaved production function by means of Sraffa's system. It was a pure intellectual experiment without any pretensions at all to real science. We knew what game we were playing, but the neo-neoclassicals were thrown into a distressing state of confusion by it.

The construction consists of taking a number of separate techniques or Sraffa systems. There is a blueprint for each, specifying the physical inputs that it requires, the time pattern of its processes and the amount of net output that a given labour force can produce while continually replacing the inputs as they are used up. For simplicity, workers are all alike and the composition of net output is the same for all techniques, consisting of a uniform basket of commodities. The techniques are listed in descending order of net output per unit of labour.

There is no kind of movement between economies using different techniques. Each is an 'island' with its own past and its own confidently expected future. But to simulate the appearance of a production function representing a 'given state of technical knowledge' the list of blueprints is chosen so that no technique is inferior to any other. The technique appropriate to each 'island' depends on its level of real wages, just as the level of real wages at a point on a production function depends on the 'capital' to labour ratio at that point.

Nothing can change in this scene; there are no events, but we can perform the intellectual experiment of running the share of wages in net output from unity to zero through the whole book of blueprints and observing which is the profit-maximizing technique at each level of wages. When the share of wages is unity, the rate of profit is zero and the technique with the highest net output per man is eligible. As the share of wages falls, the rate of profit rises, faster or slower according to the time patterns of the techniques.

For each technique, at a level of wages at which it is eligible, there is a set of prices for all its ingredients and therefore a value for its stock of inputs, in terms of any numeraire. The most convenient numeraire is a unit of net output.

At zero wages, the rate of profit is at its maximum, and that technique is eligible which gives the highest ratio of net output to the value of the stock of inputs.

All this is quite alien to the neoclassical view, in which the value and the physical specification of inputs are merged together as a 'quantity of capital'.

Between each pair of techniques there is a switch-point, at which the ratio of the values of the two stocks of inputs is equal to the ratio of their net profits. Here, both are eligible at the same rate of profit. The cost of the stock of inputs required by any one technique (equal, where it is eligible, to its value) is composed of the wage bill for the labour time directly and indirectly required to produce it and an interest bill equal to profit at the ruling rate on the value of the inputs at the prices corresponding to that rate of profit.

The value of a given physical stock of inputs rises or falls with a rise in the rate of profit, according to the character of the time pattern of the technique. Since the time patterns of the various techniques may have all sorts of forms, there may be all sorts of twists and turns in the value of capital as we run through the book of blueprints with rising rates of profit. The most striking case is a backward switch-point, at which a small reduction in the wage rate makes the *less* labour-intensive technique eligible.

The existence of a backward switch may be associated with re-switching; that is, the existence of widely separated rates of profit at which the same technique is eligible. There was a great deal of fuss about this point. Some attempts were made to prove that it cannot exist. Professor Samuelson drew up a special case of a pseudo-production function on which re-switching does not occur,[11] and Piero Garegnani replied by drawing one on which every technique is eligible at two discrete rates of profit.[12]

[11] 'Parable and Realism in Capital Theory: The Surrogate Production Function', *Review of Economic Studies*, June 1962.

[12] 'Heterogeneous Capital and the Production Function', *Review of Economic Studies*, July 1970. (Publication of this article was delayed. The main idea was conceived as a comment on Professor Samuelson's article of 1962.)

After boggling for a time, Professor Samuelson accepted the phenomenon of re-switching and took it over into his paradigm, which led to a most ludicrous result. He applied to the pseudo-production function the neoclassical concept of a process of accumulation in which 'society moves from high interest rates to low by sacrificing current consumption goods in return for more consumption later' and supposed that, when it comes to a backward switch-point, society is 'splashed with net consumption rather than having to sacrifice consumption'.[13] (The 'movement' here, by the way, is from a higher to a lower level of net output per man employed.) I took up this point with Professor Samuelson eight years later and he assured me that he was quite satisfied that this argument is correct.[14]

We do not have the method of the laboratory sciences for settling a dispute by a crucial experiment. Mere logic will never prise a writer off his paradigm until he is ready to drop it himself. In a similar impasse with Professor Hayek, Keynes quoted Ibsen:

> The wild duck has dived down to the bottom — as deep as she can get — and bitten fast hold of the weed and tangle and all the rubbish that is down there, and it would need an extraordinarily clever dog to dive after and fish her up again.

Let us leave it at that.

MARX AND KEYNES

Keynes himself never studied Marxian economics (he was quite happy to believe the rumour that it is all nonsense) and Marxian ideology was alien to him. He identified himself as a member of the 'educated bourgeoisie' and had some patriotism for his class. In so far as he had any sympathy with socialist ideals, it was purely intellectual, not from the heart.

Nevertheless, the main lines of the General Theory are identical with the analysis that Michal Kalecki erected on the basis of Marx's schema of expanded reproduction. This is a notable case of the independence of logic from political prejudice.[15]

The function of the theory of effective demand, in a Marxian setting, is to provide an account of the realization of surplus value, which Marx left

---

[13] 'A Summing Up', *Quarterly Journal of Economics*, November 1966.
[14] See below, p. 137.
[15] Cf. below, p. 159.

rather vague.[16] The theory of prices in Kalecki's version of the General Theory is more up-to-date than Keynes'. The monetary aspect is much more fully developed by Keynes, but there is a weak point in his treatment of it. He identifies the Stock Exchange value of the shares of a company with the value of its real productive assets. Thus, in some passages, he makes a fall in the level of interest rates stimulate investment by raising the value of equipment relatively to its cost of production, instead of merely by making finance cheaper relatively to expected profits.

Connected with this is an ambiguity in the definition of the 'marginal efficiency of capital'. Sometimes it means the expected rate of profit on investment, a complex and partly subjective concept; at other times, it means the profit that actually is going to accrue on an increment of the stock of means of production. Moreover, in the last chapter of the *General Theory*, he fails to distinguish between profit to a capitalist investor and benefit to society. Thus an element of neoclassical complacency appears in his conclusions, though not in the main line of his analysis.

Kalecki's version of the General Theory, rather than Keynes', has been incorporated in the post-Keynesian tradition. The function of Sraffa's prelude to a critique is mainly negative – to knock out the marginal productivity theory and clear a space where a Marxian analysis of modern problems can grow up. There is plenty of work still to do.

---

[16] Maurice Dobb seems to suggest that exploitation could somehow exist independently of realization, and accuses the post-Keynesians of regarding realization as independent of exploitation, but, obviously, neither can exist without the other. See *Theories of Value and Distribution since Adam Smith*, CUP, 1973 (in general, a most admirable book), p. 270.

11

DEBATE: 1970s

THE publication of Sraffa's *Production of Commodities by Means of Commodities* (1960) brought an access of strength to the anti-neoclassical polemic, but at the same time it led to a secondary controversy on that side of the question.

The argument was conducted in terms of a modified form of Sraffa's diagram. The y axis represents a flow of net output of commodities per man employed in physical terms, the x axis represents the rate of profit on capital, uniform throughout the economy. The stock of means of production required to operate the technique in use is off stage. Its structure is reflected in the shape of its wage-profit curve. For instance, when, at all rates of profit, the capital to labour ratio is higher in investment industries than in consumption-good industries, the share of wages in net output falls as the rate of profit rises at an accelerating rate. (See, for example, the β curve in Figure I.)

The first round in the renewed debate, after I had visited MIT,[1] was an article by Professor Paul Samuelson in 1962[2] in which he drew what afterwards became known as a pseudo-production function in which the wage-profit curve for each technique is a straight line.

Pierangelo Garegnani[3] objected that this is illegitimate as he maintained that it is equivalent to reducing the economy depicted to a one-commodity world.

After this, there was an informal exchange of papers among the anti-neoclassical group. I objected that a straight-line wage-profit curve merely represents a case of 'labour-*value* prices' — the capital-labour ratio is uniform throughout industry and does not vary with the rate of profit. I

---

[1] See 'Reminiscences', *Contributions to Modern Economics*, 1978, p. xviii.

[2] 'Parable and Realism in Capital Theory,' *Review of Economic Studies*, Vol. XXIX, June 1962.

[3] See 'Survey: 1960s' above, note 12.

maintained that the error lay, not in the shape of the curves but in the notion of switching from one to another with changes in the rate of profit.

I understand the Sraffa model to depict a process of production going on with a single technique represented by the 'system' of equations. The definition of net output requires that all basic inputs are being replaced as they are used up. This implies that the same technique is going to continue to be used over the next period.

Formally, we could bring fixed plant into the model by taking the least common multiple of the turnover period of every ingredient in the process and treat this as the turnover period for the technique in use. This would not be a useful procedure for analysis of reality because in reality a single technique is not in use over a long stretch of historical time. But we might adopt this concept for the intellectual experiment of constructing a pseudo-production function. I regard a pseudo-production function as representing a series of Sraffa systems each with its own inputs being reproduced, that is, with its own future and its own past.

My objection to Samuelson is that he combined this concept with the notion of accumulation 'moving from higher to lower interest rates' along a pseudo production function. This was particularly absurd when he accepted reswitching.[4] When the economy moves over the lower switch point it is 'splashed with net consumption' without extra saving (although net output per man with the Beta technique is lower than with Alpha). But it was not much less absurd when he used his own version of the pseudo production function with labour-*value* prices for each technique. How is it possible to move from one technique to another?

The ingredients for one Sraffa system could be changed into those for another only by a long process of investment and scrapping taking place out of steady state conditions.

Moreover, in real life, different techniques do not co-exist in time in a ready-made book of blueprints; they are evolved as accumulation goes on. In general, it is unacceptable methodology to draw a plane diagram, showing relations between variables, and then to introduce movements about on the page. A movement must take place in time, which can be represented by a third dimension at right angles to the page.

Garegnani failed to see that I was making a purely logical, methodological point and wrote a long, elaborate reply in which he accused me of giving aid and comfort to the neoclassicals.[5]

---

[4] 'A Summing Up', *Quarterly Journal of Economics*, November 1968.
[5] See *Valore e Domanoa Effettiva*, Einaudi, 1979, Appendix B.

Figure I

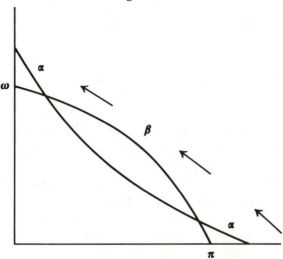

Figure II

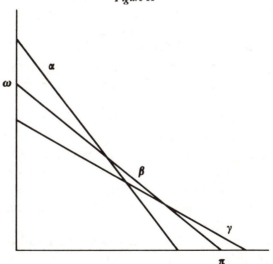

FURTHER THOUGHTS, AUGUST 1978

We are united in rejecting neoclassical ideology in all its manifestations and in attempting to restore and adapt to modern problems the classical theory disinterred by Piero Sraffa. As is natural at the frontiers of a new movement, there are some disagreements amongst us. From the foregoing, it seems that there are two issues that need to be discussed: the meaning and status of a pseudo-production function and the use of the concept of long-period equilibrium in historical analysis.

1

I was the first to produce a pseudo-production function, in 1953[6] inspired by Sraffa's *Introduction* to Ricardo's *Principles*. My attempt was clumsy and defective. I smartened it up later under the influence of Garegnani and Spaventa.

It consists of an imaginary list of techniques or Sraffa 'systems' each one in a self-reproducing steady state, all growing at the same rate, which may be zero. They differ in respect to the rate of output per man and in respect to the physical composition of the inputs that they require and they may differ also in the time-pattern of production.

It is convenient to assume that the labour force is identical for all. It is necessary to assume the specification of a unit of a homogeneous non-basic final output. (Otherwise it would be impossible to compare the productivity of techniques.) The diagram is drawn in the space of net output per man employed and the rate of profit.

The techniques are mutually non-superior in the sense that none has both a higher output per man than the rest and a lower cost of capital at all rates of profit.

Running an eye down the curve from higher to lower output, we observe an inverse relation between wages (the share of labour in net output) and the rate of profit but not necessarily any other regularities. There may be concave or convex stretches, small or large gaps between switch points, reversals of capital values, backward switch points, and reswitches. Garegnani, Pasinetti and others have produced many beautiful and ingenious examples.

When I first put a pseudo-production afloat, I called it a 'book of blueprints' and I drew the ex-ante production function facing a firm or a planning authority choosing between alternative available techniques as though it had somewhat the same form as a pseudo-production function. This was a serious error. The pseudo-production function does not exist in historical time; there are no events and no choices. Moreover, there is no technological change. In real life a *change* in technology will often bring

[6] In *The Accumulation of Capital*, Macmillan, 1956.

into being *superior* techniques which are preferred to existing ones at the same real wage rate and would be preferred at any real wage rate. That an alteration in technique necessarily has to wait for a change in 'factor prices' is one of the neoclassical errors that we are trying to smoke out.

Garegnani regards Samuelson's version of the pseudo-production function with straight lines (as in Figure II) as illegitimate. As an answer to Sraffa, it was a mere evasion but, at this time of day, I think it is rather useful; it enables us to see very clearly where the neoclassical fallacies lie.

For Samuelson, a higher output per man is associated with a higher value of capital per man so that his structure *looks* like a neoclassical production function on which the higher output between one point and the next is attributed to the productivity of the extra 'capital'. As Veblen pointed out long ago,[7] productivity is a function of the technology in use not of the instruments needed to apply it. Technical knowledge is the possession of society as a whole but because of the great cost of modern installations, capitalist businesses can 'corner the wisdom of the ancients' and extracts profits from it.

Secondly, Samuelson's idea that 'society' saves in order to enjoy higher output in the future, and that accumulation begins where productivity is lowest and profits highest, gradually creeping up the curve with a falling rate of profit, is utterly absurd from every point of view.

Thirdly, Samuelson, who takes a patronising attitude to me because I do not know mathematics, has committed a methodological howler. He draws a curve in a plane diagram showing the relationship between two variables and then moves about on it.

Perhaps Garegnani gets so annoyed with me because he has a bad conscience about doing the same thing himself.

2

'Natural prices', 'centres of gravitation' and the rate of profit in 'long-run equilibrium' are all perfectly straightforward concepts on the classical assumption that the real wage is given as a specific quantity of specified commodities. I have not been able to get Garegnani to say what he means by them in a Sraffaesque context where the real wage is a share of net output.

In Sraffa's one-technique 'system', net output is a precise, physical

[7] Cf. p. 124 below.

concept. In historical reality, since inputs used up are usually replaced with something different and the utilization of plant varies over its working life, depreciation has to be reckoned in imprecise, financial terms, so that the demarcation of net from gross output is partly a matter of accounting conventions. The share of wages evolves historically under the influence of broad social and political forces, bargaining power, monopoly, product differentiation, the pace of technical change, and the present and recent past states of effective demand.

When is the long-run position with prices corresponding to a uniform rate of profit? Is it in the future or the past? Or only in a journal article?

I certainly agree that, in any actual situation, there *is* a share of wages (though it is not unambiguously measurable) and there *is* a stock of means of production (though it is a job lot of past vintages). I concede that we might imagine that we could detect the ghost of a long-run rate of profit that would correspond to the momentary actual situation if it were permanent (though it is necessarily in the course of changing). Perhaps the succession of values of this ghost could be traced through historical time, to see whether it has had a falling tendency. But there are so many indeterminacies in such a calculation that probably anyone who attempted it would only get an answer corresponding to his preconceptions, whatever they might be.

Meanwhile, it is the *expectation* of profits, at any moment, that is the operative force. Garegnani distrusts expectations as introducing an illegitimate element into long-run theory, but surely an economic decision must be taken with a view to its future consequences, which cannot be fore-known exactly; this applies with particular force to decisions about accumulation. Uncertainty is a matter of degree but the fact that production has to precede utilisation is a logical necessity. The very description of equilibrium implies that correct decisions were made in the past.

Garegnani uses the long period as an element of his criticism of 'intertemporal equilibrium'. For my part, I have never been able to make that theory stand up long enough to knock it down. What role does Garegnani's long period play in the kind of analysis which aims to help us to understand the world that we are living in?

STILL FURTHER THOUGHTS, APRIL 1979

I feel frustrated by our round of papers because no-one answers me either yes or no. Here I am going back to the beginning. The argument started with my attacking what I believe to be a fundamental, indeed fatal, flaw in neo-neoclassical methodology. This was brushed aside by Garegnani who attacked instead on another point (straight-line wage-profit profiles) which I consider to be perfectly legitimate *within the neo-neoclassical frame*.

After several vain attempts to ring through, I shall in future leave Samuelson to rot in peace, but I am worried about the infection spreading among our friends.

I will take a trivial example first.

Revealed Preference. Samuelson pretends that he can find out the pattern of demand for commodities by pure observation — revealed preference. Suppose that Paul, Joan and Hendrik Houthakker[8] are observing the behaviour of a housewife, Mrs Snooks. On Friday the 1st of the month she fills her shopping basket with a particular selection of goods. On the 8th, prices and her allowance are unchanged but she buys a different selection of goods. Paul observes. Hendrik deduces from the *postulates* of his system of indifference curves that her tastes have changed. Joan, who has not promised to abandon common sense, suggests the *hypothesis* that, since many packets of goods contain more than a week's consumption, the stocks in Mrs Snook's larder have changed over the week and part of her purchases on the 8th are to readjust them. Also, the family likes varied meals. The very fact that she bought baked beans on the 1st is a reason for not buying them on the 8th. There is no particular reason to suppose that tastes have changed. I might even ask her about this. If she says I am right, of course it does not prove my hypotheses correct, but it encourages me not to give them up.

On the 15th, there have been a number of changes in particular prices. Mrs Snooks has been lucky, her routine purchases now cost less and she spends the balance of her allowance on a treat — say a chocolate cake. Samuelson observes. Hendrik is happy. There has been an income effect. He is no longer obliged to *postulate* a change in tastes as the rules of his game are satisfied without it. To form an opinion as to whether tastes really are unchanged, Joan would have to form some new hypotheses and examine them, but she is not much interested. She is, however, happy to see that Mrs Snooks spends her whole allowance every week so as not to precipitate a recession. But what can Samuelson say? He has observed three different preferences revealed on three different days. So what?

[8] See 'Revealed Preference and the Utility Function', *Economica*, Vol. XVII, No. 66, May 1950.

The Pseudo Production Function. Taking over a concept from which I have had a long struggle to escape, Samuelson shows what Solow called a pseudo-production function, a list of techniques each with appropriate stocks of means of production. At first he drew it in such a way that the value of capital for each technique was independent of the rate of profit (this is what Garegnani objected to) so that there could be no reswitching but nowadays he is reswitching all the time; he just loves it.

The rules are that the techniques comprised by the schedule are mutually non-superior so that each is eligible at at least one rate of profit and all have the same growth rate, which may be zero. (In equilibrium, the terms rate of interest and rate of profit are interchangeable.) I do not want to go into the question of how the rate of profit is supposed to be changed by a process of accumulation. I merely point out that the pseudo-production function, as a thought experiment, permits *comparisons* of the equilibrium positions in which it is postulated that the physical composition of the stock of means of production, the rate of output, the share of wages in net output, the rate of profit and the value of capital are already in gear with each other, but not *changes* in the rate of profit to which everything else is adjusted instantaneously.

Obviously, the stocks of inputs for different techniques could not coincide both in time and in space. In a pure thought experiment, it may be useful to imagine different techniques in use on different 'islands'. But how does it happen that they are all mutually non-superior? If the techniques are separated in time, it would be natural to suppose that some of those introduced later are superior to earlier ones because research and development has been going on meanwhile. The whole argument seems to have arisen out of a hangover from the neoclassical conception of 'factor ratios' (eligible at different 'factor prices') within 'a given state of technical knowledge'. (The invention of a superior technique of this view creates a new 'state of technical knowledge'.)

The Keynesian revolution destroyed the basis of this concept of long-period equilibrium and put nothing in its place. Keynes was interested in investment as an influence on current effective demand and paid almost no attention to its consequences in changing the amount and character of future productive capacity. Thus the debris of the old theory has been lying about all this time and we are only now beginning to clear it up.

12

RETROSPECT: 1980

WHEN the dust has settled, we can look back and trace the origin of these misunderstandings.

Sraffa offers long-period analysis in the sense that the stock of means of production for a particular technique is supposed to be always used at its designed capacity. He presents us, first, with a model with a simplified technological specification for producing a particular flow of output in physical terms. The stock of inputs required is already in existence and is being kept intact by replacements of outputs used up in the course of production. The question to be discussed is the pattern of prices that will yield a uniform *rate* of profits corresponding to each possible level of the *share* of profits in the value of net output.

Here we come to a difficulty. The whole of the flow of consumable goods going to workers is being consumed by them and part also may be consumed by capitalists. If the two classes consume physically different commodities – wage goods and luxuries – the composition of output must be supposed to fit with the distribution of income. In such a case, the flow of net output could not be unambiguously specified in physical terms. Following Sraffa's policy of drastic simplification, we dispose of this difficulty by assuming that consumption per head differs between the two classes only in quantity, being composed of 'baskets' of consumption goods of given physical composition.

In the next section, the technical specifications of the model are varied. There are different turnover periods for different ingredients in the stock of inputs; land is distinguished from equipment that has to be kept intact by gross investment; different pieces of equipment have different lengths of service life, and so forth. There is a distinction (which takes up much of Sraffa's argument) between basic commodities which enter directly or indirectly into all outputs, and the non basics which do not. Now three sets of questions are being discussed – differences in technical knowledge, that is, different physical specifications of possible input–output systems;

for each system, different shares of wages and profits in net output and different growth rates of the whole complex representing a given system. In any one technological system where there are joint products (wheat and straw) there must be alternative physical methods of production requiring inputs in different proportions so that existing stock can be used to produce outputs in the appropriate mixture.[1] There must be a correct correspondence between the composition of the stock of inputs, in a particular system, and its growth rate so as to make the flow of saving by capitalists equal to the flow of net investment.

The upshot of these comparisons is that, in a given system or state of technical knowledge, a higher net output per acre of the available land requires a higher input of labour either, say, in ploughing or in maintaining the stock of ploughs, but a higher net output per man of given physical composition does not necessarily require a greater 'quantity of capital' per man employed. The specific inputs required for a given physical flow of net output cannot be expressed as a physical quantity. It can be expressed as a quantity of value, in any unit, when the prices in terms of that unit are known but relative prices depend upon the rate of profit on capital, which in turn depends on the share of profit in the value of net output. Thus we can speak of 'diminishing returns' from labour applied to land in the traditional way, but not of the marginal productivity of 'capital' cooperating with labour. This is the prelude to a critique of economic theory which Sraffa offers.

All this is a purely logical structure – an elaborate thought experiment. There is no causation and no change. At each moment, in any one system, the stock of inputs required for its technology and its growth rate has already come into existence, which implies that in the past, when stocks were being replaced, there must have been correct foresight of what 'today' would be like, so that the profit-maximizing variety of technology has been installed – in short the distinction between the future and the past, as viewed from 'today', has been abolished.

There is no room here for short-period 'Keynesian' movements in the level of utilization of stocks of inputs or employment of labour. The language of change may be used, for it is difficult to describe a map without using the language of moving about on it, but essentially the argument is conducted strictly in terms of comparisons of logically possible positions.

In the last chapter of the book, a new element is introduced into the

[1] See P. Sraffa, *The Production of Commodities by Means of Commodities*, 1960, p. 43.

argument. Alternative methods of production are known for some of the elements in the flow of output. The methods of production are in use which minimize the overall flow of costs at the ruling rate of profit.

There may be switch-points at particular levels of the rate of profits at which two different methods of production of a particular output have the same cost. There is still no discussion of what *causes* the rate of profit to be at one level rather than another, but the *consequence* of a difference in the rate of profit may be to cause one technique to be preferred to another for a particular part of the flow of production. We are no longer discussing merely differences in the pattern of prices corresponding to differences in the share of profits with the same (highly complex) specification of the physical system. We are now discussing differences in the physical system itself induced by differences in the rate of profits.

This produces a profound change into the method of exposition. Instead of describing the structure of the stock of inputs for a technique that has already come into existence, we are now discussing which technique is the more profitable 'for a producer who builds a new plant' (p. 81).

I was myself caught in this trap for some time and elaborated the analysis of the 'pseudo production function' until I realised that two physically different systems could not coexist both in space and time. If two systems exist on 'islands' with no contact, how do they come to be producing net output of the same physical composition? And if they exist at different dates the later one may be superior to the earlier because of inventions and discoveries made in the interval.

It is of no use to try to get out of this contradiction by assuming 'correct foresight' for it is one of the most obvious conditions of human life that, at each moment of time, the future is not known for certain. Here we must abandon Sraffa and descend from purely logical comparisons into historical time.

Switch points, at which two different physical systems operate at the same costs, must be thrown out along with the 'marginal productivity of capital' as an illegitimate concept.

When this has been done, we can set up the simplest possible model for production in long-period conditions in an isolated country consisting of an area of cultivable land, with forests and deposits of iron ore. Workers raise wheat and produce iron ploughs. The stock of inputs (iron, seed, ploughs and a wage fund of wheat) is being kept intact, while a flow of wheat is being produced and consumed. The growth of the economy is at a steady rate that may be zero. The stocks of inputs – seed, iron, ploughs, food etc. – required for the growth rate is in existence today in the appropriate proportions. These are the technical specifications of the model. The control of production may be appropriate to any social and political system — socialist, cooperative or capitalist. Where the land and stocks are owned by a class of capitalists they are paying a certain wage bill per annum in terms of dollars. The dollar price of wheat then determines the real wage rate per man year of employment and the share of gross and net profits in proceeds. The ratio of net profit in dollars to the wage bill is the ratio of exploitation. The prices of wheat, iron and ploughs are such as to make the rate of profit on the dollar value of capital uniform and constant through time. The rate of exploitation (with the corresponding level of the rate of profits) may be anything between zero (which permits only enough gross profit to keep stocks intact) and the maximum which permits the labour force just to exist and reproduce itself.

The complete separation of the technical data of the system from the political and social data is preserved. There are no events in this history and no changes except for, possibly, a steady and unchanging rate of growth. The model does not illustrate the history of a possible economy for history takes place in historical time, when every day the past has already happened and the future is still to come. It represents a pure intellectual experiment showing the boundaries within which events may occur within one state of technical knowledge. It is a mistake in methodology to compare two technical systems (in each of which the ratio of exploitation may be at any level between zero and that which yields subsistence wages) and then to switch from one to the other. A switch is an event in historical time which has to be accounted for by introducing historical causation into the story.

This is where Sraffa leaves us and hands us over to Keynes.

13

MISUNDERSTANDINGS IN THE THEORY OF PRODUCTION

ANY contribution to economic theory that is not merely repeating slogans must pass through a stage of what Janos Kornai (in *Anti-equilibrium*, 1971) calls intellectual experiment. Concepts are defined and logical relations between them worked out under the shelter of 'other things equal' and 'other things remaining the same'. When inconsistencies have been eliminated and implausible assumptions discarded, the next stage is to propose the most promising looking hypotheses to be confronted with evidence from reality.

Unfortunately, the textbooks are littered with broken-down thought experiments. Kornai himself shows that the entire structure of general equilibrium is in that state. Piero Sraffa's critique has done irreparable damage to the 'marginal productivity of capital'.

Sraffa cannot go on from intellectual experiment to the second stage: the *Production of Commodities by Means of Commodities* (1960) is set up in terms of long-period relationships in the sense that inputs are correctly adjusted to outputs and a stock of means of production is being operated by a given labour force at its designed level of utilization. A long-period model cannot be directly confronted with evidence because any actual situation is affected by short-period influences, such as the state of effective demand and the distribution of money income, which occupy the forefront of the picture.

(Looking back now, I see that in the tumultuous years when Keynes' *General Theory* was being written, Piero never really quite knew what it was that we were going on about.)

1

For me, the Sraffa revolution dates from 1951, the *Introduction* to Ricardo's *Principles* (Sraffa, ed., 1951), not from 1960. The thought experiment is simple and robust — the corn model. I set about to dismantle the neoclassical production function by introducing what I called a book of blueprints showing the concrete stock of means of production required for each level of output with a given labour force. From this developed what Professor Solow called a pseudo-production function. (Bob! I thank thee for that word.) I do not think I ever mis-used it as Professor Samuelson does nowadays,[1] but it certainly took me a long time to understand its meaning and its limitations.

A pseudo-production function represents a list of mutually non-superior techniques with a flow of homogeneous final output and given employment of labour, each in a self-reproducing state with its appropriate stock of means of production. Each technique is eligible at at least one rate of profits (with the corresponding share of wages in the value of net output). Between each pair is a switch point at which both yield the same rate of profits.

In the 'Unimportance of Reswitching',[2] I emphasized the fact that this construction permits only of comparisons of imaginary equilibrium positions already in existence, not a process of accumulation going on through time. Samuelson's 'Reply' is instructive.[3] (I checked with him recently; he stands by it today.)

First, in respect to accumulation, it seems that he is still a completely unreconstructed pre-Keynesian neoclassic. He expects to find the rate of interest (which is what he calls what Sraffa calls the rate of profits) lowered by successful saving-investment abstaining from consumption. But let that pass.

SUBSTANTIVE VINDICATION?

Where then does the possibility of misinterpretation arise? It arises from the ambiguity of English speech and grammar. Thus, in my first paragraph, I speak of 'switching back at a low interest rate. . .' and of '. . .as the interest rate falls in consequence of abstention from present consumption. . .' Suppose that here, and in a score of other innocent passages, I had rewritten these as '. . .a switch back had *permanently* occurred at a *permanent* low interest rate to the techniques *permanently*

---

[1] Samuelson was piqued at my saying, 'The professors at MIT took over my book of blueprints'. He says that he used my nickname, as a compliment, for a very well-known concept. But if it was all well-known, how account for the famous error that he had to admit in 1966?

[2] *Quarterly Journal of Economics*, February 1975 and *Collected Economic Papers*, Vol. V.

[3] 'Steady-State and Transient Relations', ibid.

viable at a *permanent* high interest rate *subsequent* to successful saving-investment abstaining in the past from then-current consumption [as envisaged by the neoclassical writers being quoted]'. If I had done this, even a hostile critic could not have managed to fall into a misunderstanding; and a critic of neoclassical views, sensitized to past propensities of some writers to err on related matters, would have had no reason to quarrel with my revised text.

So, to narrow down misunderstanding, I authorize any reader to make such purely verbal alterations at a score of places. This done, how much of my substantive argument evaporates, or is vitiated, or needs amendment and elucidation? None that I can see. No diagram needs redrawing. No substantive contention need be withdrawn or qualified.[4]

Evidently, we are in an era when a slow secular fall in the rate of profits is going on. Each time it passes a switch point (whether towards a technique which requires a higher or a lower value of capital than the last) there must be a certain period of investment and disinvestment installing the stock required for the latest technique and clearing away the debris of the former one. We are not told anything about what goes on in these interludes, which seem to pass as though in a dream.

The whole process may take centuries but all the while there is no technical progress or learning by doing. The specifications of all the techniques were available in the original book of blueprints.

In the reply to Harcourt[5] also there are strange episodes. In a case of double switching, the rate of interest may drop from more than 100 percent to below 50 percent 'without any physical movement at all'. Would not a violent change in the ratio of profits to wages require readjustment in the flows of output?

After a backward switch, a transition is made to a technique with lower net output, but since the value of capital is going to be less than before, there is at the same time a transient period of 'negative abstinence' or excess consumption.

Professor Samuelson raises the question whether such transitions could be made *efficiently* in market or planned economies in the real world.

The reply to Harcourt ends with a declaration of faith by Samuelson in himself:

[4] Ibid., pp. 43–4.
[5] Ibid., footnote 7.

I am not aware that my own part in this discussion contains *invalid* 'habits of thought so ingrained as for him [me] to be unconscious of their presence', but I shall be happy to recant if such logical errors can be found.

Then, patronizingly, to me:

I do not think that the real stumbling block has been the failure of a literary writer to understand that when a mathematician says, '*y* rises as *x* falls', he is implying nothing about temporal sequences or anything different from 'when *x* is low, *y* is high'.[6]

My dear sir! That is *my* point. I really cannot allow you to get away with that.

In 1974, I finally took the pseudo-production function to pieces again. Obviously, stocks of equipment appropriate to different techniques cannot co-exist both in time and space. It should never been drawn in a plane diagram in the first place. Different techniques are not isolated from each other on 'islands'. They succeed each other through time as new discoveries and inventions become operational. Normally, a new technique is *superior* to the one in use and does not have to wait for a change in the rate of profit to be installed.

2

There was a second, independent, appearance of pseudo-production functions after 1960.

The model in *Production of Commodities* . . . is a one-technique system in a self-reproducing state but it does permit of some variations (Sraffa, 1960). One of the ingredients among the inputs exists in two versions or brands. The difference between them is in the time pattern of reproduction, not any physical characteristic. Sraffa did not intend this for a pseudo-production function. His purpose was to refute marginalism by showing that the least conceivable difference alters the whole system. As one or the other brand is eligible, according to the level of the rate of profits, everything is transformed. There is a different pattern of prices, distribution and value of capital. Even the numeraires are different for each brand appears in its own standard commodity. The brand eligible at

---

[6] Ibid., p. 45.

the higher rate of profit may require the higher value of capital, as in the case of a backward switch point on a pseudo-production function.

Samuelson is correct in saying that grammar is awkward. It is hard to describe a map without using the language of moving about on it. Sraffa habitually uses the language of change but, properly speaking, there are no events in his world except the cycle of self-reproduction and the flow of net output to wages and net profits. The second brand was not *introduced* at some date. It had always existed in the specification of the model, but it was mentioned only when a certain point in the argument was reached.

There is no movement from one position to another, merely a comparison of positions corresponding to different levels of the rate of profits at which different brands are eligible. This comparison was an important element in his prelude to the critique of economic theory, clearing the ground for further analysis which, however, Sraffa himself did not supply. Certainly, thought experiments are justified by preparing the ground for an analysis of change, but to identify a comparison of static positions with an event, as Samuelson does, is not a practicable short cut.

Samuelson's (1962)[7] first reaction to Sraffa was to produce a form of pseudo-production function in which, beyond each switch point, a higher rate of interest is associated with a lower ratio of value of capital to output so that backward switching cannot occur. This was countered by the construction of a spate of pseudo-production functions exhibiting switches of all kinds.[8] They are now so elaborate, elegant and beautiful and their designers have become so fond of them that it seems cruel to point out that they are unable to say anything without falling into Samuelson's fallacy.

3

Keynes, at the opposite extreme to Sraffa, discusses only events. In businesses, households, public agencies, etc., each within its own sphere, decisions are taken under the influence of convention, imperfect information and uncertain expectations. Their interaction as they are implemented brings about the movements of the whole economy.

Objection is sometimes raised to the emphasis on expectations as introducing an unduly subjective element into analysis. But if we cannot

[7] 'Parable and Realism in Capital Theory', *The Review of Economic Studies*, Vol. 29.
[8] This began in *Quarterly Journal of Economics*, November 1966 and has been going on ever since.

mention expectations, we cannot say anything at all. Any economic action, say, buying a bus ticket, is made with a view to its future consequences and is influenced by beliefs about what the outcome will be. Expectations are revealed in intentions and intentions are revealed in actions. However, a businessman is not a black box. You can ask him about his intentions. You will not necessarily believe what he says, but you are bound to learn a lot from how he answers.

It is sometimes supposed that the aim of business is to maximize its rate of profit. This is a gross confusion. Investment plans must be guided by views of the possible *rates of return* on alternative schemes of investment, but these are highly problematical. The aims of a business, this year, are concerned with the *flow* of profits this year. The accountants can work out, according to the accepted conventions, what the *rate of profit on capital* has been after the year is over.

Only in Sraffa's intellectual experiment does the rate of profits have an exact meaning, for it is a *postulate* of the system that prices are such as to make the rate of profits uniform over the whole value of capital reckoned at these prices.

A short-period thought experiment can be clear and precise. What is to 'remain the same' can be specified. Within a general frame of institutions, knowledge and habits, the stock of means of production in existence, the capability and training of the labour force, the distribution of wealth, habitual patterns of consumption, business and financial organization are all taken as given; what can change from week to week is the amount and content of expenditure, causing changes in employment and the utilization of resources. New bargains can be made for pay and prices adjusted to them. The quantity of money changes mainly to accommodate these, but it may also exercise an influence of its own through the relation of the supply of credit to requirements.

In real life, the dichotomy between short and long-period aspects of a situation is not so sharp; every week long-period changes, resulting from past decisions, are coming into being — stocks are changing slowly through time while flows may run rapidly to and fro. The underlying historical movements ensure that the economy is not so madly unstable as Keynes was sometimes tempted to suppose. There may even be times when the short and long-period influences are sufficiently in harmony with each other to allow a run of near-steady growth to be enjoyed for a time. But if we are going to bring history into the analysis, we must consider the effects of technical change.

This is the question that we have neglected to discuss for twenty five years.

14

JOSEPH SCHUMPETER

CAPITALISM, SOCIALISM AND DEMOCRACY

PROFESSOR SCHUMPETER takes his stand on a highly original and personal point of view. Most of those who advocate or expect the supersession of capitalism by socialism have a strong sympathy with the idea of socialism and, indeed, call themselves socialists. Professor Schumpeter, as many tart phrases reveal, has little love for socialism, and none at all for socialists. His natural sympathy is all with the heroic age of expanding capitalism. But yet he regards capitalism as doomed and socialism as inevitable. His reasons are set out in Part II of the book, *Can Capitalism Survive?* This forms the central core of his argument. Before considering it, we may glance at the outlying portions of the work.

First comes an essay on Marxism. Professor Schumpeter treats Marx primarily as a great economist: 'It is easy to see why both friends and foes should have misunderstood the nature of his performance in the purely economic field. For the friends, he was so much more than a mere professional theorist that it would have seemed almost blasphemy to them to give too much prominence to this aspect of his work. The foes, who resented his attitudes and the setting of his theoretic argument, found it almost impossible to admit that in some parts of his work he did precisely the kind of thing which they valued so highly when presented by other hands.' He distinguishes between Marx's vision and his analysis. He holds that Marx's analysis is often faulty, but that, in particular in connection with the theory of value and the theory of crises, his vision of the general development of capitalist society is substantially correct, or at least far superior to that of most of his critics. On one major point, however, both analysis and vision fail – the theory that there is an inherent tendency in capitalism to lower the standard of life of the masses. With this, Marx's theory of the cataclysmic end of capitalism falls to the ground.

Next, turn forward to the sections on Socialism and on Democracy.

Can socialism work? Is socialism compatible with democracy? In each case the answer is affirmative. The section on Socialism is somewhat perfunctory, though illuminated with many telling points, such as that one of the important economies of socialism would be the release of numerous first-class brains, now occupied in the business of legal tax evasion, for more productive uses. The section on Democracy is, perhaps, the weakest part of the whole. The reader is left with a baffled feeling that Professor Schumpeter is not really as cynical about democracy as he pretends, and that the main issues have not been discussed. Professor Schumpeter freely succumbs to the temptation to tease and provoke; perhaps this section is aimed mainly at pricking some specifically American bubbles.

Now return to the main argument. Section II is arranged on the plan of a detective story. It opens: 'Can capitalism survive? No. I do not think it can.' But none of the obvious suspects are guilty. We have already seen that Professor Schumpeter does not accept Marx's diagnosis. Nor does he agree with the usual run of contemporary analysis. Monopoly is not a blemish in capitalism, but an essential factor in its development. A competitive system of the textbook type is simply impracticable in a dynamic world. What appears in any given situation as restriction is necessary to maintain the profitability which makes expansion in the long run possible. (In this chapter Professor Schumpeter is at his most brilliant, and his argument blows like a gale through the dreary pedantry of static analysis.) Nor is unemployment the villain of the piece. With the continuous advance of productivity which capitalism brings about, society, can easily afford to keep the unemployed in sufficient comfort to prevent unrest (it must be remembered that Professor Schumpeter is writing on the other side of the Atlantic; in a European setting, perhaps he would not take so airy a view). The spectre of declining investment opportunity is an illegitimate projection of the great slump into long-run prospects. None of these is responsible for the decay of capitalism. The real secret is that capitalism destroys itself, not by its vices, but by its virtues. Its rationalism undermines the authority of the governing class, which capitalism inherited from the feudal age, and without which it cannot control the masses. The rising standard of life and the spread of education create a class of discontented intellectuals who canalize and make articulate the resentment of the masses at the inequality without which capitalism cannot function. Above all, technical development leads to the obsolescence of the entrepreneurial function. With the growth of big business and of experimental science innovation itself is reduced to routine, and the entrepreneur sinks into a bureaucrat. Subsidiary reasons, of which the decay of the family is the most important, undermine his will to survive, and when, in the fullness of time, the system becomes ripe for transformation, his resistance will be negligible, and socialism will come into being without any break in the process of evolution.

The reader is swept along by the freshness, the dash, the impetuosity of Professor Schumpeter's stream of argument. But pause on the brink a moment and look around the contemporary scene. On reflection some rather large elements seem to be missing from the analysis. First, what about USSR? 'It must be remembered that the bolshevik conquest of rule over the most backward of all the great nations was nothing but a fluke'. Perhaps. But in that case the exception seems rather more important than the rule. Who knows what flukes may accompany the end of the present war? And, even if the bolshevik fluke remains unique, there cannot be much doubt that the existence of a socialist Great Power will play at least as important a part in the future development in other countries (even without any deliberate intervention in their affairs) as the more subtle processes of evolution according to the imminent characteristics of capitalism. And then, what about Fascism? Does present-day experience really lead us to expect that capitalism is destined to a quiet and pious death? But, no matter whether it convinces or not, this book is worth the whole parrot-house of contemporary orthodoxies, right, left, or centre.

15

PIERO SRAFFA

PRODUCTION OF COMMODITIES BY MEANS OF COMMODITIES

IT is no wonder that this book[1] took a long time to write. It will not be read quickly. Addicts of pure economic logic who find their craving ill satisfied by the wishy-washy products peddled in contemporary journals have here a double-distilled elixir that they can enjoy, drop by drop, for many a day.

For some, indeed, the logic may be too pure. We plunge immediately into the argument without any preliminary discussion of assumptions and delimitation of topics. Evidently we are in a capitalist economy, but to avoid the ambiguities which have clustered around the word, capital is never mentioned. There is profit, but no enterprises; wages, but no pay-packets; prices, but no markets. Nothing is mentioned but the equations of production and the necessary conditions of exchange.

There is a great deal to be said for this method of exposition (over and above its lapidary style), for every attempt by an author to explain himself in terms of the preconceptions of one reader confuses another. Best leave each to work it out for himself.

To find a clue, let us go back a stage and pick up the argument from Sraffa's Introduction to Ricardo's *Principles*. Postulate that corn is the only commodity consumed by workers and that the corn-wage rate is fixed. Corn is required also as seed, and there is no other commodity or equipment necessary for the production of corn. Then a stock of corn in existence at the beginning of a year has reproduced itself with a surplus at the end of the year. The ratio of the surplus to the stock is the rate of profit. The workers are, so to speak, intermediate goods, like machines, necessary for the process by which corn produces corn.

The corn-profit may be used to employ more workers either to produce

[1] Cambridge University Press, 1960.

Oxford Economic Papers, February 1961.

luxuries, or to carry out investment; or it may rot in the barns. The way it is used cannot affect the rate of profit, which is fixed by technical conditions, and the equilibrium prices of all other products are determined in terms of corn (and so in terms of each other) by their costs of production, including profit at the corn-rate upon the capital (valued in corn) required to produce them.

Can the propositions derived from this model survive the removal of the postulate that only corn is required to produce corn?

The first step — here the present argument begins — is to introduce a variety of wage goods. Let there be a number of distinct commodities each of which is required, in a particular quantity, to be consumed by a worker, just as particular quantities of oil and fuel are required to operate a machine. The commodities are also required to produce each other and themselves. (To set us off on the right tack, wheat, iron, and pigs are mentioned. But they soon become commodities 'a', 'b', . . . , 'k'.) The same argument applies as before. The commodities reproduce themselves with a physical surplus. The condition that the rate of profit is uniform throughout the economy settles their relative prices. The value of the stock of commodities at the beginning of the year and of the surplus after they have been replaced can be expressed in terms of any of the commodities. The value of the real wage (which is fixed in physical composition by technical necessity) is also determined, and the cost of production of any commodities that do not enter into the real wage (subject to the condition that they yield the ruling rate of profit) settles their prices. This merely elaborates the corn-wage model without altering its essence.

The next step takes us much further. Instead of the real wage being fixed by physical necessity, the workers receive a share of the surplus. The author toys with the idea of separating the wage into a part which is necessary and the rest; he rejects it in deference to ordinary usage. He makes this concession with evident reluctance, but readers may welcome it, not only to avoid verbal clumsiness but also because we could hardly imagine that, when the workers had a surplus to spend on beef, their physical need for wheat was unchanged. Wage goods thus cease to be necessary for production in technically fixed proportions. There remain, however, commodities which are necessary as means of production for themselves and each other. (The pigs and wheat presumably drop out, but the iron remains.) They reproduce themselves with the aid of labour and yield a surplus out of which the labour is paid.

We are now launched on the main problem — the effect upon prices of changes in the division of the surplus between wages and profits.

Nothing is said about what determines the division. We are to consider the consequences, not the causes, of changes in the real wage.

It is this, not the austere style, that makes the book difficult. We are concerned with equilibrium prices and a rate of profit uniform throughout the economy, but we are given only half of an equilibrium system to stand on. We need a fence to prevent us plunging off into the abyss. The author suggests as a helpful (but not necessary) provisional assumption that constant returns prevail. I, for one, found that this only made me all the more dizzy. It seems better to assume that changes in the share of wages do not affect the composition of output.

There is a further difficulty. The wage 'changes' only in the sense that the value of x changes as we run our eye up and down a curve. In the year that we are examining, each change has already happened. So long as all commodities reproduce themselves within a year, this is easy to accept; but when long-lived machines come into the picture (in a later chapter) it causes discomfort. Can the equalization of the rate of profit throughout the economy come about except through the equalization of expected profits on new investment in various lines? If the rate of profit has changed during the life-time of machines in existence this year, there is no equality between expected and realized profits in any one line — why should there be equality between realized profits in different lines? Let us add to the protective fence of provisional assumptions that we need not take the word 'change' literally. We are only to compare the effects of having differing rates of profit, with the same technical conditions and the same composition of output. Thus reassured, we can remain on the narrow ledge without vertigo.

When the wage is not given by technical conditions, what do prices mean? A change in the division of the surplus between wages and profits alters relative prices. But we need to know the prices to value the surplus that is to be divided. This was the problem that flummoxed Ricardo.

Sraffa's solution is ingenious and satisfying. He isolates those *basic* commodities which enter directly or indirectly into the production of all commodities and, from the technical equations which show how each enters into the production of the others, he constructs a standard of value in the form of a composite commodity into which each particular item enters, as means of production, in the same proportion as it appears as output.

The beauty of this is that, as the wage reckoned in terms of this standard rises, the prices of some of the commodities composing it (in which wages are a high proportion of cost) rise, and others (in which profits are a high proportion of cost) fall, to just such an extent as to balance each other, and leave the ratio of the value of the surplus to the value of the means of production unchanged. This provides a technically determined ratio of surplus to means of production which is independent of the division of the surplus between wages and profits.

Now, given the n technical equations for n commodities, and the wage rate in terms of the standard, the $n - 1$ prices and the rate of profit are determined. Or, given the n equations and the rate of profit, the wage is determined.

Assuming that wages are paid at the end of the year (no capital is required to finance a wage fund) there is a linear relationship between the share of wages in the surplus and the rate of profit.

This having been established, the standard commodity can be left to look after itself and the argument is conducted in terms of the rate of profit corresponding to zero wages (that is, the ratio of surplus to means of production), and the actual rate of profit, with the wage rate that it entails.

In order to construct the standard commodity it must be possible to find a quorum of basics – commodities that enter directly or indirectly into the production of all commodities. So long as there are necessary wage goods there are bound to be basics, for, via labour, the wage goods enter into all production. But when wages are part of the surplus we have to fall back on an assumption that there is at least one basic commodity. Certainly that is plausible enough, but it is natural to ask what would happen if there were none. Does the whole method stand or fall on this assumption? I think not.

Suppose that technical equations could be divided into two systems without any overlap, in one of which iron enters directly or indirectly into the production of all commodities, and in the other, wood. The two systems of equations belong to the same economy in the sense that the rate of profit and the wage rate are the same in both. Now, when the rate of profit is given, the wage rate in terms of the iron-standard is determined for the iron system and the wage rate in terms of the wood-standard is determined for the wood system. The fact that the wage is uniform determines the price of iron in the wood-standard. The assumption of at least one basic commodity thus appears to be a mere simplification, not a crucial step in the argument.

After exploring the properties of a system in which each productive process takes one year and produces one commodity, we are shown the application of the method to joint products, fixed capital and land, and to the choice of technique when alternative methods are available for producing a single commodity. The argument then ceases as suddenly as it began.

In elaborating the method to deal with complexities such as long-lived machines, many points of great interest are turned up (including a version of the formula for the relation of the value of a machine to its cost which was worked out, presumably, much later, though published earlier, by Kahn and Champernowne),[2] but the main point of dealing with these problems is just to show that it can be done. The essence of the argument remains that which is exhibited with circulating capital only.

The sub-title gives a hint of the purpose for which it has been established — *Prelude to a Critique of Economic Theory*. In the preface, after referring to a draft of the book which he discussed with Keynes in 1928, Sraffa writes:

> As was only natural during such a long period, others have from time to time independently taken up points of view which are similar to one or other of those adopted in this paper and have developed them further or in different directions from those pursued here. It is, however, a peculiar feature of the set of propositions now published that, although they do not enter into any discussion of the marginal theory of value and distribution, they have nevertheless been designed to serve as the basis for a critique of that theory.

The significant word is 'however'. Others have developed input–output systems and process analysis to higher degrees of elaboration than are shown here, but they have not brought them to bear on the foundations of orthodox doctrine.

Can we divine what the critique will be? There are three main propositions which can be derived from the corn-wage model and which have been shown to survive all the necessary modifications that follow from elaborating its assumptions.

The first is that, when we are provided with a set of technical equations for production and a real wage rate which is uniform throughout the economy, there is no room for demand equations in the determination of equilibrium prices. (When we take down our protective fence, and allow that changes in distribution to affect the composition of output, we shall need a fresh set of equations relating them, but that is quite another matter.)

Some might complain that this is only flogging a dead Marshallian

---

[2] See Joan Robinson, *The Accumulation of Capital*, Appendix.

horse (which Sraffa himself helped to kill, even before 1928). But to my mind it emphasizes a point which, both in its scholastic and in its political aspect, is of great importance; in a market economy, either there may be a tendency towards uniformity of wages and the rate of profit in different lines of production, or prices may be governed by supply and demand, but not both. Where supply and demand rule, there is no room for uniform levels of wages and the rate of profit. The Walrasian system makes sense if we interpret it in terms of an artisan economy, where each producer is committed to a particular product, so that his income depends on his output and its price. Each can have a prospective rate of return on investment in his own line, but there is no mechanism to equalize profits between one line and another. In real life, no one expects to see an equalization of the rates of profit obtainable from sugar in Cuba and cocoa in Ghana or can even say what an equal rate of profit would mean.

The intrusion of demand equations into the theory of the wage economy, and the attempt to foist a rate of profit on to the exchange economy, have led to endless confusion; a critique to clear it up is long overdue.

The second proposition is mentioned by Sraffa in his *References to the Literature*. It is the rejection of the claim 'that the price of every commodity, either immediately or ultimately, resolves itself entirely (that is to say, without leaving any commodity residue) into wage, profit, and rent.'

In the corn-wage economy, the production of corn this year requires that there should be a stock of corn already in existence, to provide seed and the subsistence of the workers until the next harvest. Sraffa has removed the assumption of a technically determined physical real wage. This throws great weight upon commodities regarded as means of production, a weight made all the greater by the assumption that capital is not required for a wage fund. *Production of Commodities by Means of Commodities* is his central theme.

It leads to the very striking proposition that there is a technically determined maximum notionally possible rate of profit, which would obtain at zero wages. (It is only notionally possible, for even when the postulate of a precise physically necessary wage has been abandoned, there is still a vague but tough lower limit to possible real wages and so an upper limit to the possible rate of profit.)

The third proposition, if we may indulge in a loose mode of expression that the author carefully avoids, is that the marginal productivity theory of distribution is all bosh.

Sraffa does not deny any sensible arguments that can be expressed in marginal terms. His treatment of diminishing returns from land and of the choice of technique makes room for legitimate uses of the concept of a production function. What he demonstrates decisively (though doubtless the deaf adders will take no notice) is that there is no such thing as a 'quantity of capital' which exists independently of the rate of profit.

It is important to realize that the third proposition does not depend upon the second.

Certainly the proposition that no production, by the methods known today, could take place without some pre-existing commodities, is highly plausible, but it is a matter of fact, not of logic. It does not mean that if prices could be reduced without residue, to wage, profit and rent, then the marginal productivity theory of distribution would be cogent.

Flint mines were dug with antlers picked up in the forest. If this economy was run on capitalist lines, it must have been necessary to advance wages to the men collecting antlers (otherwise they would be self-employed traders). Men dug the pits and shaped the flints. All processes could be reduced to terms of dated inputs of labour. To find the capital required for production (in the sense in which capital is the principal on which profit is the interest) we must know either the wage in terms of axes or the rate of profit.

Certainly, Sraffa is right that in Ricardo's time, or our own, commodities are necessary to produce commodities. But even the neolithic rate of profit was not determined by the 'marginal product of capital.'

Presumably, it will be a little time before the critique to which this is the prelude will be published. We might have some self-criticism meanwhile.

16

GUNNAR MYRDAL

AGAINST THE STREAM [1]

THERE is no doubt that, of all economists alive today, Gunnar Myrdal has made the most important contributions to the subject, but it cannot be said that they have been the most influential, because of the entrenched resistance of the profession to ideas that challenge received orthodoxy. In this volume of collected essays and addresses he records and reflects upon the various phases of a long life's work.

In 1929 Myrdal published *The Political Element in the Development of Economic Theory* in Swedish (a German edition was published in 1932). The English translation, which did not appear until 1935, was reviewed by the *Economist* under the title 'Time Bomb for Welfare Economics'. In that book he showed how the orthodoxy of the day had been evolved in order to glorify the economic system of the day and how the doctrine of 'utility', which logically points to extreme egalitarianism, was twisted into a defence of laisser faire. He found an explanation in 'the need of the economists to protect themselves from their own radical premises from the era of the Enlightenment'. Nowadays they defend themselves by expressing circular arguments in elaborate mathematics. Myrdal believes that this phase will pass and 'that much that is now hailed as most sophisticated theory will in hindsight be seen to have been a temporary aberration into superficiality and irrelevance'.

In 1931, Myrdal published *Monetary Equilibrium*, which drew out from the heritage of Wicksell the conceptions that became known as the Keynesian Revolution (though here Myrdal's patriotism claims too much). The victory of a theory that demanded Government intervention in a slump was assured by the convergence of all interests behind a policy to increase both employment and profits; but on the present problem of

[1] Panther Books, 1973.

stagflation (a term which Myrdal put afloat) economists are divided and policy is confused because any possible solution involves sharp conflicts of interest.

Partly by good luck and partly by enlightened management, the great slump was quickly overcome in Sweden. Gunnar and his wife Alva devoted themselves to problems of social welfare and population. He is a patriot for the achievements of the welfare state in his own country; there is sometimes a hint in his comments on other peoples that if only they would be sensible like the Swedes their problems could easily be solved. In 1938 he began his great study of what was then called the Negro problem in the southern United States. As a citizen of a neutral country he was able to carry on during the war. *The American Dilemma* was published in 1942. It is not primarily a study of the poverty and disenfranchisement of the blacks, though it is a rich source of information on those subjects; it is concerned chiefly with the divided conscience of the whites – the gulf between their actual behaviour and the political tenets that they believe themselves to hold.

Still today: 'The whites continually live in moral confusion. They proclaim ideals that are bluntly disobeyed in their daily life. This is the dilemma'.

This inquiry brought Myrdal to see that the character of economic life depends very much upon what the profession regards as 'non-economic' factors. He tells us that when he first came to the USA in the twenties, it seemed that the 'wind of the future' was institutional economics, in the line of the great Americans, Veblen, Commons and Mitchell. He himself was passionately attached to the 'theoretical' school and played some part in founding the Econometric Society. But when it came to a study of poverty, he realized what was the flaw in traditional teaching – the separation of the problems of production from those of distribution. This

> distinction had been used by economists as a means to escape from the problems of distribution by concentrating on those of production, usually with only a general reservation in regard to distribution, and then thinking about distribution as a simple matter of money incomes. This reflected a bias in economic theory which is still with us, not least in research on underdeveloped countries, implying the view that egalitarian reforms are necessarily costly in terms of economic growth, and very definitely not productive.

To the study of underdevelopment, which has occupied Myrdal for the last twenty years, he brought an acute sense of the hypocrisy, which he politely describes as 'bias', in orthodox opinion.

In the colonial period, the problem of world poverty was simply ignored. Welfare theory and the ideals of egalitarianism applied only at home. The miserable conditions of the mass of the subject peoples was a perfectly acceptable consequence of their natural inferiority. Now there has been a reversal in fashion; diplomatic language is always used and the spokesmen of the capitalist world have a vested interest in optimism, for if 'development' is on its way, popular demand for radical reforms can be held off.

Self-interested optimism is no more helpful than the old attitude of complacent superiority. It would be better to recognize the great burden that history and geography has laid on those countries – harsh climate, overpopulation, a family tradition that favours corruption.

But what is to be done? Myrdal sees problems more clearly than solutions. In spite of pious sentiments about aiding development, the policies of the Western countries have been aimed at inhibiting it:

> It is understandable that business interests in the West would be more willing to invest in an underdeveloped country where the reins were tightly held by an oligarchic regime bent upon preserving the social, economic, and political status quo. It was also natural that they preferred to deal with the rich and powerful there. Indeed they had to. That this, in turn, strengthened these people in their own countries is equally self-evident. They are, however, exactly the groups who raise the resistance to domestic reforms or see to it that they became ineffective or even distorted. The governments in developed countries felt inclined to take into account the interests of their business firms operating in underdeveloped countries. In their aid policies the governments, like business firms, also had to deal with the groups in power.
>   . . . Financial and unilateral aid was, and still is, very firmly awarded to utterly reactionary regimes.

When he turns to American problems he is no less blunt. After Vietnam, the American nation needs to go through 'a catharsis in order to be at peace with itself. . . . To have an "honourable end" to a thoroughly dishonourable war, implying continued backing of an American puppet government in Saigon, is not acceptable'.

A genuine 'war on poverty' would be costly and 'the healing process will take at least a generation even if begun with courage and determination and pursued persistently' and though it would be a good investment in the long run, many vested interests are working to prevent the necessary reforms.

All the same Myrdal's optimism and belief in the power of enlightenment shines through all his argument. In an address to the youth of America, after listing the unprecedented dangers facing every country in 'spaceship earth', he concludes with a warning against defeatism. His faith is in our inherited ideals of justice, liberty, equality and brotherhood. His life's work has been to show where they have failed, in the hope of showing how they might succeed.

17

MARXISM: RELIGION AND SCIENCE

ONE of the most important contributions of Marx to the development of thought was the concept of ideology – the recognition that ideas and beliefs, especially in the sphere of the social sciences, are an expression of economic interests.

As the Soviet *Textbook* puts it:

> Political economy studies, not some transcendental questions detached from life, but very real and living questions which affect the vital interests of men, society, classes. Are the downfall of capitalism and the triumph of the socialist system of economy inevitable; do the interests of capitalism contradict those of society and of the progressive development of mankind; is the working class capitalism's grave-digger and the bearer of the idea of the liberation of society from capitalism – all these and similar questions are answered differently by different economists, depending on which class's interests they voice. That is just why there does not exist one single political economy for all classes of society, but instead several political economies; bourgeois political economy, proletarian political economy, and also the political economy of the intermediate classes; petty-bourgeois political economy.[1]

But Marxism itself is an ideology. Is it not then just as much an expression of interests, and just as little a branch of science as any other?

The *Textbook* faces the dilemma squarely, and hacks it down.

> Is it possible in general for a political economy to exist which is objective, impartial and does not fear the truth? Certainly this is

[1] *Political Economy.* A Textbook issued by the Institute of Economics of the Academy of Sciences of the USSR (English version Lawrence and Wishart, London, 1957), p. xx.

possible. Such an objective political economy can only be the political economy of that class which has no interest in slurring over the contradictions and sore places of capitalism, which has no interest in preserving the capitalist order: the class whose interests merge with the interests of liberating society from capitalist slavery, whose interests coincide with the interests of mankind's progressive development. Such a class is the working class. Therefore an objective and disinterested political economy can only be that which is based on the interests of the working class. This political economy is the political economy of Marxism–Leninism.[2]

This itself could be treated as a scientific hypothesis. We might inquire whether the claim that Marxism is more scientific than other ideologies (on whatever criteria seems reasonable) is borne out by the evidence.

It is not easy to demarcate 'Marxism', for the purpose of such an inquiry, and separate it clearly from 'non-Marxism'. Marx's teachings were only one element in a wide stream of thought – the growing self-consciousness of modern man as a social being, and of man in society as a potential object of scientific investigation – which would in any case have borne many ideas like his in its course. At the same time, Marx's contribution to that stream was so important and has had so great an influence on the habits of thought of his opponents as well as his supporters, that it is as difficult nowadays to find a really pure non-Marxist amongst historians and sociologists as it is to find a flat-earthist amongst geographers.

In economics, however, a purely non-Marxist doctrine was for long incapsulated in the impermeable casing of neo-classical static equilibrium theory. Here the contrast is clear cut, and the comparison, certainly, is highly favourable to Marx. The relevance, the scope, and the penetration of his analysis of the 'laws of motion of capitalism' make the marginalists' scholasticism appear merely frivolous. Indeed, since the capsule was broken open from within by Keynes, there has been the same sort of infiltration of Marxian ideas into economic theory as had already occurred in history. For a discussion of the questions nowadays found to be interesting – growth and stagnation, technical progress and the demand for labour, the balance of sectors in an expading economy – Marxian theory provided a starting point where academic teaching was totally blank.

On the other hand, there are certain deficiencies in the Marxian apparatus, which have often been noticed. The lack of a measure of physical output, to supplement *value* (a unit of labour-time) cripples the

[2] Loc. cit., p. xxi.

analysis of real income; the definition of a key concept – the organic composition of capital – is ambiguous; the treatment of the relation between the level of real wages and the money-wage bargain is unsatisfactory. And so forth.

But any such attempt at evaluation is beside the point. The *Textbook* is not inviting students to make a critical appraisal of the statement that Marxist ideology is scientific. It expects them to believe it. The appeal of ideology is to faith. With faith, science comes to a halt.

It was inevitable that it should be so. A revolutionary movement needs faith; an organized society requires an established orthodoxy. The scientific aspect of Marxism had to give way to the need for a creed.

1

The religious emotions of Communists are described only by those who have become disillusioned, which gives their testimony a tainted air; all the same it provides some evidence. Take Djilas for example:

> For the Yugoslavs, Moscow was not only a political and spiritual centre, but the realization of an abstract ideal – the 'classless society', something that not only made their sacrifice and suffering easy and sweet, but that justified their very existence in their own eyes.[3]

After his first interview with Stalin:

> It was already dusk as we were leaving the Kremlin. . . . The northern lights can be seen at Moscow at that time of year, and everything was violet hued and shimmering – a world of unreality more beautiful than the one in which we had been living.
> Somehow that is how it felt in my soul.[4]

When you come to think of it, there is nothing surprising in a rationalist ideology serving as a religion. Whatever it is in the biological make-up of mankind that, over all recorded ages, has given rise to the need for faith, the combinations that have made religion a political force, the problems of private and public life that religion helps to ease, could not be suddenly abolished by teaching people to believe that God was invented to serve the interests of a ruling class. From the point of view of a rationalist, God never did exist, but religion always has. To abolish God

[3] *Conversations with Stalin*, p. 15.
[4] Ibid., p. 64.

does not make any radical difference. And if it did, mere scepticism could not call up the devotion and heroism to carry through a revolution, or the cohesion and discipline to rebuilt society after it. A rationalist may feel that he gets on all the better without religion. But those of us who take that view have to admit that we are really parasites, drawing nourishment from the effects of faith in others. Without our professing the beliefs of our forebears, our habits of thought and behaviour run in grooves which they wore out.

It is not only that rulers like to have some opium to keep their people tranquil. More than anyone, the leaders of a politial movement require the guidance and support of an accepted doctrine. Power may quickly corrupt, but to take power in the first place mere cunning and ambition have rarely been sufficient; the leader must have the self-confidence that comes from faith.

Self-confidence cuts both ways. 'I must believe in whatever is right' easily slips into 'Whatever I believe in must be right'. Thus all kinds of idiosyncracies, for better or worse, get embodied in the creed. The fact that Mohammed loved a widow had a liberalizing effect on Moslem institutions; the fact that Stalin was a Philistine was disastrous for Soviet art.

Faith brings in its train the persecution of unbelievers. It is evidently part of the social function of religion to inhibit natural kindliness and steel the heart against deviants within a group or aliens without.

Of all the great systems, it could be argued that Christianity, on its public, historical record, is the most bloodstained and oppressive; the most obscurantist; the almost bluntly opposed to the teaching of its founder, and therefore the most hypocritical. But none is innocent. Jains, who literally would not hurt a fly, have been known to knife each other in doctrinal disputes between sects.

It seems that the illusions of Djilas and his like were the consequence of that trick of confusing ideology with truth that the *Textbook* so blatantly displays. Since their faith purported to be rationalist, they did not recognize that it was a religion and were shocked to find that it could produce just those results that, to a rationalist, make religion most repugnant.

2

It was inevitable, and in a certain sense right, that Marxism should have developed into a faith rather than a science. The notion of a scientific revolution is delusory. Action has to be taken much faster than science can work out results. Marx made the first attempt to establish the laws of motion of capitalism. His hypotheses have been confirmed by events at some points and disproved at others. To check, revise, and establish them is a programme for generations.

Moreover, it is not only a matter of time, but of the way the human mind works. The intellect cannot provide the driving power for political action. Science cannot propose any objective except science. The applied scientist has his aims given to him from outside his own discipline – to increase production, to reduce disease, to poison and smash up the world, as the case may be.

The analyst of history may predict that a revolution will occur. He predicts it because he thinks that he can see that the idealism, the interests, and the passions of the oppressed will bring it about, and that the balance of forces is such that it will succeed. As a scientist, his business is to investigate the process and to see if his prediction turns out right. As a human being, if his sympathy is with the oppressed, he is impelled to use his intellectual authority to give them courage and comfort with his prediction of their success. He ceases to be a scientist and becomes a prophet. No one who shares his sympathy with the oppressed can say that he is wrong. But the prophecy is useful because it is believed. It is believed because it is believed to be true, not because it is believed to be useful. Then hypothesis becomes dogma, and science is drowned in theology.

A new faith establishes itself through the appropriateness of the feelings and behaviour that it calls forth to the situation into which it is injected. The details of the intellectual content of its doctrines are rather a matter of luck.

This is a thought that professed Marxists find totally unacceptable. To them, the achievements of the Soviet Union are a proof of the correctness of Marx's theories. This line of argument has worn thin since those achievements have been admitted to be scarred with errors and crimes. To claim the successes for Marxism and blame the rest on a 'cult of personality' that Marxism was powerless to check is analogous to defending the historical record of Christianity by identifying it with the teaching of the Gospels and blaming the rest on original sin.

In any case the argument is based on much too simple a view of the relation between belief and action. After all, the British Empire, in its day, was a resounding success; and though this may have been connected with the influence of Protestant education on character, it could not be claimed to prove the truth of the Anglican version of Christian theology.

The ideology which Marx developed for the industrial working class of the leading capitalist nations has been transplanted and taken root outside the capitalist sphere. There could not but be large discrepancies between the theory and the situation in which it was applied. All the same there were elements in Marxian doctrine that were of priceless value to the Soviet system.

The notion that national patriotism means nothing to the working class encouraged Lenin's policy of defeatism which made the October Revolution possible. The belief that property is the seat of power led to the establishment of thoroughgoing socialism. Marxism cannot claim any particular credit for the development of economic planning. Planning was forced upon the system by the very fact of expropriation. Since there were no capitalists to carry out investment, some other means was necessary to fulfil their function. (Its success has now brought planning into fashion in the capitalist world, and a new ideology is being propagated according to which property is not after all necessary for control.) But Marxism can claim the credit for saving the planners from believing in academic economics. Imagine the present state of Russian industry if they had regarded their task as the 'allocation of given resources between alternative uses' instead of 'the ripening of the productive power of social labour' by investment, exploration, and education.

On the other hand there are important aspects in which Marxian doctrines have been a drawback rather than a help in building socialist states.

To decry national patriotism was useful in 1918, but heavy drafts had to be made upon it later. The discrepancy between theory and practice has led to a kind of emotional confusion about the whole subject, which no doubt contributed to the clumsy handling by Russians of other peoples' national susceptibilities and has even permitted racism to survive in the socialist world.

Marx's concentration upon the industrial working class has turned out unfortunately since the revolutions made under his banner have been in predominantly peasant countries. The Chinese had to pay a heavy price before the doctrine could be altered. The neglect of agriculture in the scriptures is no doubt partly to blame for its poor showing in practice. The failure to allow *value* to natural resources is today being criticized in the Soviet Union as a serious cause of wasteful planning.

Marx's attitude to the population problem left a pernicious legacy to the modern world. (It was certainly necessary for him to attack the reactionary pessimism of Malthus, but he might well have given his blessing to Francis Place.)

The prediction of 'growing misery' for the workers under capitalism is a more doubtful case. It seemed very plausible when it was made, and unemployment gave it a new lease of life in the 1930s but today it has been obviously falsified; to continue proclaiming it in face of experience has contributed to discrediting the Communist Party with the labour movement in the West. But if Marx had correctly foreseen that capitalism was going to douse the class consciousness of the industrial workers with television, washing machines, and a five-day week, the wind would have been completely taken out of his sails. This error, like Jesus' belief that the world was shortly coming to an end, is so central to the whole doctrine that it is hard to see how it could have been put afloat without it.

Here is a point of great difficulty for the theologians. They are torn between denying that real-wage rates have risen in the West, and denying that Marx predicted that they would not. A recent restatement of Marxist doctrines — *Traité d'economie Marxiste*, by Ernest Mandel, temperate, learned, and reasonable as far as the commitment to orthodoxy permits — rejects the fanciful arguments put forward, for instance, by Arzumanian, to explain away the facts. (I have heard it said that, for an American worker, a motor car is part of the *value of labour power*, because he needs to get to the factory from the suburb where he lives.) The author chooses the other way out of the difficulty, and maintains that Marx did not deny that real wages will rise under capitalism[5] On a straightforward reading of the texts, especially the *Communist Manifesto*, this seems to be a distortion of the plain meaning of words. 'You have nothing to lose but the prospect of a suburban home and a motor car' would not have been much of a slogan.

The contention that what Marx really meant was that the *relative* share of wages in the product of industry would fall is backed up by the quotation of a few figures which show a declining share. In this field the figures are notoriously ambiguous because of the difficulties of definition; a case can be made, by judicious selection, as easily one way as the other. But that is beside the point. The point is that if Marx really meant that he expected the rate of exploitation to rise somewhat, but by much less than productivity, so that there would be a marked rise in the level of real wages, he could have said so. To twist what he said to fit the supposed facts destroys his status as a scientist, without doing much to support his credit as a prophet.

3

But the reason why the assertion of the *Textbook*, that Marxism is a scientific ideology, does not hold water is not because of any defects in Marx's theories. It would be easy to argue that the Marxian system of

[5] English Translation, Merlin Press, 1968, Vol. I, pp. 179–83.

ideas (though not unexceptionable) is less unscientific than any other brand of sociology or political economy that has yet been offered. The difficulty does not lie in what is taught but in how it is learned. Ideology demands acceptance. Science demands doubt. A particular proposition may occur in both, but its mode of operation is different in the two contexts.

Many years ago a committee of theologians was set up to pronounce upon doctrines of the Anglican church. They decided that belief in the virgin birth was optional. But one of them, a high dignitary, felt obliged to append a note stating that, *as a Bishop*, he thought it right to state that he did believe in it. Is this not analogous to the statement by a writer on economics that, *as a Marxist*, he believes in the labour theory of value?

It is perfectly legitimate to have schools of thought in a developing subject. A school of thought is distinguished by its method, not by its tenets. Science itself, in a certain sense, is based on faith – on a confident belief that all phenomena will yield to investigation and will turn out to fit into a scheme of natural law. But this faith expresses itself in a programme of work, not in a body of settled conclusions. Professor Popper seems to fall into just the kind of dogmatism that he so admirably exposes in other fields when he denies that history can be scientific.[6] He may turn out to be right. The well-tried method of controlled experiment is not available, and perhaps no adequate substitute will ever be found. In history every important event happens only once and alters all that comes after. Perhaps we can never hope to collect enough examples of any kind of phenomenon to generalize about them. But let us try. Let us see how far we can get. Postulate that history plays itself out through the interaction between the technical conditions of production and the forms in which society is organized, and see how much our postulate explains.

Marx, as a scientist, proclaimed this grand programme, and made an impressive start upon it. But it got very little further. A school of thought flourishes when the followers continuously revise and sift the ideas of the founder, test his hypotheses, correct his errors, reconcile contradictions in his conclusions, and adapt his method to deal with fresh matter. It takes a great genius to set a new subject going; the disciples must admire, even reverence, the master, but they should not defer to him. On the contrary, they must be his closest critics.

Marxism did not develop so. Within the socialist movement, it was too soon embalmed. Revision came to mean the search for slogans to justify a

[6] *The Poverty of Historicism*, Routledge and Kegan Paul, 1957.

change of policy. Only the highest political authorities could pronounce on matters of doctrine, and even they had to be careful to express new thoughts in old forms.

Nor did Marxism benefit from criticism from without. The association with dangerous thoughts frightened off the 'bourgeois' intellectuals, and allowed smart-alec debating points to pass as a sufficient refutation of his ideas. Nowadays in the US even to think about the questions that Marx raised is suspect and a great deal of mental energy goes into finding safe, trivial theorems to elaborate.

It was inevitable that Marxism should develop as a closed doctrine, not a growing science. But now the loss begins to be realized. In a settled society, when the heroic age is over, science is more useful than faith. But a switchover is not at all easy.

The case of the Bishop is instructive. It would be beside the point to believe in the now optional doctrine in the sense in which one believes in scientifically established facts. If a virgin birth happened, it would be one of those things that happen, subject to biological inquiry. It would lose all spiritual significance. He must have meant that he believed in the doctrine, not in the fact. He felt obliged to say so, not for any personal reason; his personal position was perfectly secure, with no fear of Stalinist or McCarthyist persecution. Most likely he felt that for a Bishop to withdraw belief from a point mentioned in the Creed would be an offence to many worthy, simple souls and damaging to the cause to which his life had been devoted.

This dilemma (as well as the habit of caution formed during the period of persecution) is hard to escape in the socialist world. The natural sciences, it seems, have been pretty well freed, but political economy is a delicate matter.

Not long ago, I was teasing a good-natured professor behind the ex-iron curtain. I attacked various points at which it seems to me that Marx's analysis is defective, and he defended them with the stock arguments. At last I said: Do you regard Marx as a superman, or, though a great genius, as a human being? — Of course he was human. — Then he could make mistakes? — Yes. Would you mind mentioning a mistake that he made? — The professor did not actually wink, but he changed the subject.

There is one great advantage, however, of a faith based on scriptures. Each new generation can read for themselves, and rejecting the filtered waters of official teaching, drink from the original source. The Reformation came from reading the Bible. Emancipation will come from the application of the method of Marxian analysis to Marxist ideology.

The process has begun; but it is much impeded by the Cold War. The silly, twisted, and poisonous interpretation of developments in the socialist world that emanates not only from the press, but also from academic quarters, in the so-called free world, give ever-renewed support to the anti-liberal element within the Communist movement. Moreover, the young intellectual, patriotic though critical, is disinclined to speak up when what he says will be taken down and used in evidence against his country. It is we who are largely to blame for smothering him. Perhaps even this essay of mine will do more harm than good.

18

AN OPEN LETTER FROM A KEYNESIAN TO A MARXIST

I MUST warn you that you are going to find this letter very hard to follow. Not, I hope, because it is difficult (I am not going to bother you with algebra, or indifference curves) but because you will find it so extremely shocking that you will be too numb to take it in.

First I would like to make a personal statement. You are very polite, and try not to let me see it, but, as I am a bourgeois·economist, your only possible interest in listening to me is to hear which particular kind of nonsense I am going to talk. Still worse – I am a left-wing Keynesian. Please do not bother to be polite about that, because I know what you think about left-wing Keynesians.

You might almost say I am the archetypal left-wing Keynesian. I was drawing pinkish rather than bluish conclusions from the *General Theory* long before it was published. (I was in the privileged position of being one of a group of friends who worked with Keynes while it was being written.) Thus I was the very first drop that ever got into the jar labelled 'Left-wing Keynesian'. Moreover, I am quite a large percentage of the contents of the jar today, because so much of the rest has seeped out of it meanwhile. Now you know the worst.

But I want you to think about me dialectically. The first principle of the dialectic is that the meaning of a proposition depends on what it denies. Thus the very same proposition has two opposite meanings according to whether you come to it from above or from below. I know roughly from what angle you come to Keynes, and I quite see your point of view. Just use a little dialectic, and try to see mine.

I was a student at a time when vulgar economics was in a particularly vulgar state. There was Great Britain with never less than a million workers unemployed, and there was I with my supervisor teaching me

Part of a pamphlet, *On Rereading Marx*, published by the Students' Bookshop, Cambridge, 1953; also in *Collected Economic Papers*, Vol. IV.

that it is logically impossible to have unemployment, because of Say's Law.

Now comes Keynes and proves that Say's Law is nonsense (so did Marx, of course, but my supervisor never drew my attention to Marx's view on the subject). Moreover (and that is where I am a left-wing Keynesian instead of the other kind), I see at a glance that Keynes is showing that unemployment is going to be a very tough nut to crack, because it is not just an accident — it has a function. In short, Keynes put into my head the very idea of the reserve army of labour that my supervisor had been so careful to keep out of it.

If you have the least little pinch of dialectic in you, you will see that the sentence 'I am a Keynesian' has a totally different meaning, when I say it, from what it would have if you said it (of course you never could).

The thing I am going to say that will make you too numb or too hot (according to temperament) to understand the rest of my letter is this: I understand Marx far and away better than you do. (I shall give you an interesting historical explanation of why this is so in a minute, if you are not completely frozen stiff or boiling over before you get to that bit.)

When I say I understand Marx better than you do, I don't mean to say that I know the text better than you do. If you start throwing quotations at me you will have me baffled in no time. In fact, I refuse to play before you begin.

What I mean is that I have Marx in my bones and you have him in your mouth. To take an example — the idea that constant capital is an embodiment of labour power expended in the past. To you this is something that has to be proved with a lot of Hegelian stuff and nonsense. Whereas I say (though I do not use such pompous terminology): 'Naturally — what else did you think it could be?'

That is why you got me so terribly muddled up. As you kept on proving it, I thought that what you were talking about was something else (I could never make out what) that needed to be proved.

Again, suppose we each want to recall some tricky point in *Capital*, for instance the schema at the end of Volume II. What do you do? You take down the volume and look it up. What do I do? I take the back of an old envelope and work it out.

Now I am going to say something still worse. Suppose that, just as a matter of interest, I do look it up, and I find that the answer on my old envelope is not the one that is actually in the book. What do I do? I check my working, and if I cannot find any error in it, I look for an error in the book. Now I suppose I might as well stop writing, because you think I am stark staring mad. But if you can read on a moment longer I will try to explain.

I was brought up at Cambridge, as I told you, in a period when vulgar economics had reached the very depth of vulgarity. But all the same, inside the twaddle had been preserved a precious heritage – Ricardo's habit of thought.

It isn't a thing you can learn from books. If you wanted to learn to ride a bicycle, would you take a correspondence course on bicycle riding? No. You would borrow an old bicycle, and hop on and fall off and bark your shins and wobble about, and then all of a sudden, Hey presto! you can ride a bicycle. It was just like that being put through the economics course at Cambridge. Also like riding a bicycle, once you can do it, it is second nature.

When I am reading a passage in *Capital* I first have to make out which meaning of c Marx has in mind at that point, whether it is the total stock of embodied labour, or the annual flow of value given up by embodied labour (he does not often help by mentioning which it is – it has to be worked out from the context) and then I am off riding my bicycle, feeling perfectly at home.

A Marxist is quite different. He knows that what Marx says is bound to be right in either case, so why waste his own mental powers on working out whether c is a stock or a flow?

Then I come to a place where Marx says that he means the flow, although it is pretty clear from the context that he ought to mean the stock. Would you credit what I do? I get off my bicycle and put the error right, and then I jump on again and off I go.

Now, suppose I say to a Marxist: 'Look at this bit – does he mean the stock or the flow?' The Marxist says: 'c means constant capital,' and he gives me a little lecture about the philosophical meaning of constant capital. I say: 'Never mind about constant capital, hasn't he mistaken the stock for the flow?' Then the Marxist says: 'How could he make a mistake? Don't you know that he was a genius?' And he gives me a little lecture on Marx's genius. I think to myself: This man may be a Marxist, but he doesn't know much about geniuses. Your plodding mind goes step by step, and has time to be careful and avoids slips. Your genius wears seven-league boots, and goes striding along, leaving a paper-chase of little mistakes behind him (and who cares?). I say: 'Never mind about Marx's genius. *Is* this the stock or is it the flow?' Then the Marxist gets rather huffy and changes the subject. And I think to myself: This man may be a Marxist, but he doesn't know much about riding a bicycle.

The thing that is interesting and curious in all this is that the ideology which hung as a fog round my bicycle when I first got on to it should have been so different from Marx's ideology, and yet my bicycle should be just the same as his, with a few modern improvements and a few modern disimprovements. Here what I am going to say is more in your line, so you can relax for a minute.

Ricardo existed at a particular point when English history was going round a corner so sharply that the progressive and the reactionary positions changed places in a generation. He was just at the corner where the capitalists were about to supersede the old landed aristocracy as the effective ruling class. Ricardo was on the progressive side. His chief preoccupation was to show that landlords were parasites on society. In doing so he was to some extent the champion of the capitalists. They were part of the productive forces as against the parasites. He was pro-capitalist as against the landlords more than he was pro-worker as against capitalists (with the Iron Law of Wages, it was just too bad for the workers, whatever happened).

Ricardo was followed by two able and well-trained pupils – Marx and Marshall. Meanwhile English history had gone right round the corner, and landlords were not any longer the question. Now it was capitalists. Marx turned Ricardo's argument round this way: Capitalists are very much like landlords. And Marshall turned it round the other way: Landlords are very much like capitalists. Just round the corner in English history you see two bicycles of the very same make – one being ridden off to the left and the other to the right.

Marshall did something much more effective than changing the answer. He changed the question. For Ricardo the Theory of Value was a means of studying the distribution of total output between wages, rent and profit, each considered as a whole. This is a big question. Marshall turned the meaning of Value into a little question: Why does an egg cost more than a cup of tea? It may be a small question but it is a very difficult and complicated one. It takes a lot of time and a lot of algebra to work out the theory of it. So it kept all Marshall's pupils preoccupied for fifty years. They had no time to think about the big question, or even to remember that there was a big question, because they had to keep their noses right down to the grindstone, working out the theory of the price of a cup of tea.

Keynes changed the question back again. He started thinking in Ricardo's terms: output as a whole and why worry about a cup of tea? When you are thinking about output as a whole, relative prices come out in the wash — including the relative price of money and labour. The price level comes into the argument, but it comes in as a complication, not as the main point. If you have had some practice on Ricardo's bicycle you do not need to stop and ask yourself what to do in a case like that, you just do it. You assume away the complication till you have got the main problem worked out. So Keynes began by getting money prices out of the way. Marshall's cup of tea dissolved into thin air. But if you cannot use money, what unit of value do you take? A man hour of labour time. It is the most handy and sensible measure of value, so naturally you take it. You do not have to prove anything, you just do it.

Well there you are — we are back on Ricardo's large questions, and we are using Marx's unit of value. What is it that you are complaining about?

Do not for heaven's sake bring Hegel into it. What business has Hegel putting his nose in between me and Ricardo?

19

THE ORGANIC COMPOSITION OF CAPITAL

THE concept of 'the organic composition of capital' is an important element in Marxian analysis; because of its connection with a theory of a falling rate of profit, it has been taken to resemble the neoclassical concept of 'the ratio of capital to labour' and since the latter has been pulverized by Sraffa's critique[1] it is necessary to re-examine the former in the same light.

1

The notation in which Marx set out his formal analysis is very confusing. A flow of production, say per week or per year, in terms of *value* is expressed as $c + v + s$, that is, the *values* of the depletion in the pre-existing stock of means of production, of wages and of surplus. Net output, $v + s$, represents all the man-hours of work performed over the period. (The labour-force is partly engaged on replacing means of production, but this is compensated for by c, the *value* released from the means of production used up.)

At the same time, Marx writes $c + v$ for the stock of capital and c/v for organic composition. Clearly the stock of constant capital is a multiple of c, the depletion of stock, say *per annum*, that has to be made good over the period. Let us write C for the stock of physical means of production in existence at a moment of time. But then what is v, regarded as part of the stock of capital? At one time I believed that 'variable capital' should be treated as a wage fund, represented by V, so that the stock of capital should be written as $C + V$. But now I think that this was a mistake. A

---

[1] *Production of Commodities by Means of Commodities*, Cambridge University Press, 1960.

wage fund is essentially a financial concept – the sums required to pay out wages over the period of turnover of working capital.

In Ricardo's corn model, the turnover period was given by nature – the period from harvest to harvest, which is a year in high latitudes, and the wage fund had a physical existence as a stock of grain, available after the harvest to be paid out week by week until the next harvest. In tropical agriculture and in manufacturing industry, the turnover period of working capital may be shorter than a year or sometimes longer, and it varies for various lines of production and for various techniques; there is no standard turnover period to define the wage fund required for output as a whole. Furthermore, the equipment and stocks required for producing a flow of output of wage goods cannot be distinguished (like corn in a barn) from the rest of the stock of means of production. Thus it seems best to write C for all existing physical capital, including stocks of grain, and to use v only in one sense – the flow of *value* of wage goods being produced.

It is clear that Marx thought of the stock of capital as consisting of two parts; one part was the physical means of production and the other part somehow represented labour employed, organic composition being the ratio between them, but there does not seem to be any way of representing this in his notation as c/v.

An alternative definition of organic composition is 'the ratio of dead to living labour', that is the quantity of labour embodied in the stock of means of production, required for a particular technique, per man employed on current production. Here, as we shall see, we can find a clue to guide us through the mazes of 'capital theory', but it has to be handled with care.

2

A change in methods of production brought about by accumulation and technical improvements is an extremely complex process. It is best to begin by comparing 'islands' each using a different technique, each equipped with the stock of means of production that its technique requires. Since the comparison is a pure intellectual experiment with no pretension to realism we can simplify it as much as we like provided that we introduce no inconsistencies into the picture.

The concept of the *technique* for producing the whole output on an island is basically the same as Sraffa's 'system' of equations depicting all the physical relations between the ingredients in a flow of production and the labour force that operates them. However, we modify the details of Sraffa's picture to suit the requirements of our problem.

Sraffa's system was designed to emphasize the effects of differences in the rate of profit in a single economy, while we are interested in differences between economies that are independent of differences in their rates of profit.

Instead of Sraffa's distinction between basics and non-basics, we depict a physical difference between net (consumable) output and means of production. Net output is measured in 'baskets' made up of commodities in fixed proportions, the same on each island. The labour force on each island consists of the same number of men, working the same hours per day, per week and per year. Each labour force produces a flow of output of baskets while keeping intact the stock of means of production required for the technique that it is operating.

We can compare flows of production growing through time provided that the growth rate is the same on each island, but the most convenient growth rate to take is zero. On each island the whole net output is consumed and the stock of means of production is continually being replaced, item by item. We need not bother about the distinction between equipment, say 'machines', and stocks of materials being used up in the process of production, for the whole stock on each island has existed in its present form from time immemorial; a photograph of it taken on a given day in any year would always look exactly the same. Consumption of workers and of rentiers is of baskets of uniform content so that the distribution of income does not influence the composition of net output.

Now we come to the difficult question. How are we to compare the stocks on different islands, each being composed of entirely different physical items required for different techniques?

Marx was content to treat the stocks as 'dead labour', that is, he measured a stock by the number of man-hours of work performed in the past to produce it, but this is very rough, for a stock of means of production was not produced by labour alone. The flow of net output *per annum* can be represented by its *value*, $v + s$, a number of man-hours of work, but to produce a physical output workers require a pre-existing stock, appropriate to the technique in use, of which a part, c, is used up and replaced during the year. Marx treats c as a quantity of *value*, formerly created and now released, but this year's c could not have been produced without the aid of some earlier pre-existing c.

This conception plays an important part in Sraffa's argument. It means that the cost of investment cannot be reckoned in terms of labour alone. It depends also on the time-pattern in which the work was done and this entails that the value, in any *numéraire*, of a specific physical stock of available inputs varies with the rate of profit.

We cannot get out of this difficulty merely by postulating that the same rate of profit is actually ruling on each island. We do not have any theory of what determines the ruling rate of profit on any island, only, following Sraffa, an account of the relationship, for any specified technique, between the rate of profit and the share of wages in net output. But we can escape the difficulty, for the purpose of an intellectual experiment, by postulating that the time pattern is the same for all techniques.

Divide the labour force into two sectors. In one sector, workers are operating 'machines' to produce a flow of 'baskets'. Here the period of through-put is very short, so that work in progress as part of the stock can be neglected. In the other sector, workers (with the aid of machines) are replacing machines as they wear out. Now suppose that, on each island, the stock, whatever it may be, is completely replaced every ten years. Then C, the stock measured in labour-time, is ten times c, the annual depletion of stock. An island where C is larger has to have a greater proportion of the labour force in the machine-making sector and requires, in a clear sense, a higher capital to labour ratio to operate its technique. By this, or some equivalent set of assumptions, we can justify treating differences in stocks as differences in 'labour embodied' and we can write organic composition as C/L where L is the number of men employed.

In this part of Marx's argument the problem of effective demand (realization of the surplus) does not arise, so that we assume given employment (not necessarily full employment) on each island.

We now present a technique in a modified version of Sraffa's wage-profit diagram. The curves, though with a consistent negative slope, are full of wiggles. This was very important in the capital controversy but in the present context we are not interested in re-switching and all that. We will suppose that on any island, labour-value prices rule, that is to say that the relative prices of items in the basket and in the stock of that island are the same (at any rate of profit) as they would be at a zero rate of profit. Then on each island the wage-profit curve is a straight line.[2] (This is in no way necessary to the logic of the argument; it is introduced merely to simplify exposition.)

A given labour force, L, is providing a flow of work ($v + s$ per man)

[2] Cf. Figure II.

Figure I

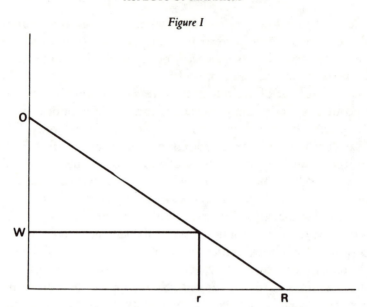

which produces a flow of net output, O/L, while keeping intact the physical stock of means of production represented by C. Net output, in 'baskets', is shown on the vertical axis and the rate of profit on the horizontal axis. The maximum rate of profit, corresponding to the imaginary position of zero wages, is shown by R . K, the value of capital,

Figure II

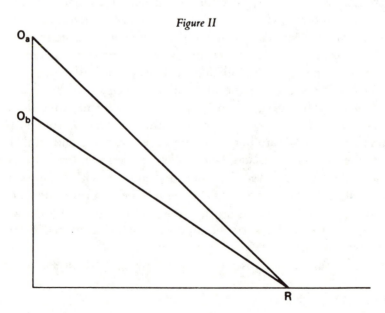

in terms of a unit of output is O/R. (With labour *value* prices for all items of current output, the value of capital is independent of the actual rate of profit.) The capital to labour ratio, K/L, is shown by the slope of the wage-profit curve, OR, and the output to capital ratio, O/K, is shown by R, the maximum rate of profit. Thus, a higher capital to labour ratio is shown by a steeper slope and a lower capital to output ratio by a higher maximum rate of profit. In the diagram, the actual rate of profit is shown as r and the wage as W. The rate of exploitation (s/v) is shown as $O-W/W$.

We are interested in comparing five typical islands. *Beta* is the basis for comparison; on three superior *Alpha* islands, output, O/L, is greater than on *Beta* without requiring a higher capital to output ratio, K/O. There is also an intermediate case, quasi-*Alpha*, on which O/L is greater than on *Beta* but in a smaller proportion than K/L, so that K/O is greater.

On *Alpha I*, net output for the given labour force is greater than on *Beta* while the maximum rate of profit R, is the same. The value of capital, K, is greater on *Alpha I* than on *Beta* in the same proportion as output is greater; thus $O_a/K_a = O_b/K_b$.

The relation of these two techniques to each other is neutral.

On *Alpha II* the technique in operation is capital-saving in comparison with *Beta*. Machines in the investment sector which are used to produce machines are of superior design such that a smaller proportion of the

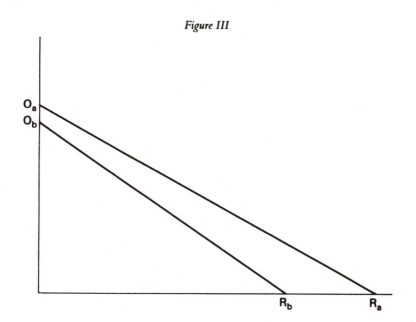

Figure III

labour force is required to keep the stock intact. For this reason, net output (for the labour force as a whole) is higher on *Alpha II* than on *Beta*, even if physical output per man in the consumption sector is identical. Here K_a/O_a is less than K_b/O_b.

Marx regarded capital-using change – a rise in organic composition – as the normal case. This is illustrated by the comparison of *Alpha III* with *Beta*.

The capital to output ratio on *Alpha III* is lower than for *Beta*, although the cost of investment per man employed is greater. $K_a/L > K_b/L$; $K_a/O_a < K_b/O_b$. This appears to correspond to the type of technical development most prevalent in modern large-scale industry.

In all three cases, if we compare the techniques at a given real-wage rate, *Alpha* yields a higher rate of profit than *Beta*.

The intermediate case, quasi-*Alpha*, is shown in *Figure V*. Here higher net output per man, O/L, requires a cost in terms of labour embodied in the stock of capital per man employed higher in a greater proportion. Thus the capital to output ratio in this case is greater than for *Beta*. $K_a/O_a > K_b/O_b$. The maximum rate of profit, R_a, is lower than R_b.

Here there are two ranges of cases. On an island where the wage rate was below the level corresponding to the intersection of the curves (W'

Figure IV

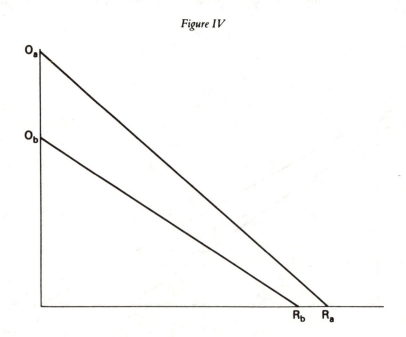

Figure V

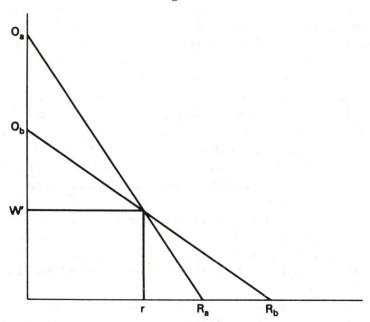

in the diagram) if the *Beta* technique was known, the quasi-*Alpha* technique would not have been installed, but at any higher level of wages, quasi-*Alpha* offers the greater rate of profit.

Over that range, $O_a - W'$ is greater than $O_b - W'$ in a greater proportion than K_a/L is greater than K_b/L. Similarly, if the rate of profit is less than r, quasi-*Alpha* provides the higher wages.

Marx wanted to argue that rising organic composition would cause the rate of profit to fall (though when he was working on Volume III of *Capital* he was evidently very uneasy about this proposition).[3] The above analysis indicates a missing link in his argument which he evidently overlooked.

3

In a recent contribution to the debate,[4] Professor Okishio purports to provide the assumptions which would justify Marx's proposition, but he

---

[3] *Capital*, Vol. III, Ch. 14.
[4] N. Okishio, 'Notes on Technical Progress and Capitalist Society', *Cambridge Economic Journal*, March 1977.

falls into a trap of Marxian terminology. He treats $v + s$ (labour time) as the measure of product and so identifies the capital to output ratio with the capital to labour ratio. A rise in organic composition, by definition, is a rise in the capital to labour ratio. It lowers or raises the capital to output ratio according to the technique which it embodies. Furthermore, a rise in the capital to output ratio does not cause the rate of profit to fall, for a capital-using technique would not be adopted unless it raised profit per man employed at least as much as the cost of investment per man.

Okishio goes on to construct a diagram of the same type as those used above, with output in terms of wage goods on one axis and the rate of profit on the other. He emphasizes the character of a superior technique (*Alpha* compared to *Beta*) but he maintains that Marx's theorem would be correct if technical progress was confined to the type, quasi-*Alpha*, which requires an increase in the capital to output ratio. He noticed, in the diagram, that the quasi-*Alpha* technique has a lower maximum rate of profit than *Beta* but he failed to notice that at any wage above W' (at the level of the intersection of the curves) the rate of profit is higher for quasi-*Alpha* than for *Beta*.

The ratio of the quasi-*Alpha* to the *Beta* wage, at a common rate of profit, is less than the ratio of the outputs. To yield the same profit with a greater K/O the share of profit in the *value* of output (s/v) must be greater. Thus Marx was correct in saying that, if the rate of exploitation (in terms of *value*) was unchanged, a rise in organic composition would lower the rate of profit. But here we are not concerned with *value* but with physical output. In a comparison of quasi-*Alpha* with *Beta*, when the rate of profit is the same, the real-wage rate in terms of output is higher.

There is another inconsistency in Professor Okishio's analysis, besides identifying organic composition with the capital to output ratio. He writes L for the flow of *value* being produced without distinguishing between the number of men and the hours of work that each performs. In order to keep in touch with this argument, we assumed above that hours of work were the same on all islands, so that both L, the number of men employed, and $v + s$ were the same everywhere but it would be much more natural to suppose that hours of work are less on the islands where output per man is greater.

Marx argued that normally a capitalist employer must maintain a rate of real wages sufficient to support life (the *value* of labour power) while the more effort per day he can squeeze out of the workers and their families, the greater the surplus *value* that he extracts. This applies to a one-technique, one-shift system. It is painfully true of situations where unorganized, under-employed workers are being absorbed into a capitalist labour force. But where a strong trade-union movement has been able to claim a share in the fruits of advanced technology, the advantage has been taken partly in reducing the working day and increasing holidays.

Where the technique in use requires heavy investment, multiple shifts make the working day of equipment twice or three times that of the average wage-earner. This has to be taken into account in measuring the capital to labour ratio. It cannot well be represented by lumping L and $v + s$ together.

4

The discussion of the Marxian theory of a falling rate of profit has been heavily impregnated with ideas drawn from neoclassical doctrines, but meanwhile those ideas themselves have been discredited.

In pre-Keynesian theory, 'saving', that is accumulation of financial capital, forces down the rate of interest (identified with the rate of profit) and so induces the use of more capital-using techniques. This concept has not survived the abrogation of Say's Law by Keynes and Kalecki; the concept of 'the marginal productivity of capital' which falls as the 'capital' to labour ratio rises has not survived the 'Cambridge criticism' which draws a clear distinction between financial capital and a stock of man-made means of production.

The neo-neoclassics have shifted their ground and adopted the concept of a pseudo-production function.[5] This can be represented by a series of islands in which each requires a higher capital to output ratio than the last (as in the comparison of quasi-*Alpha* with *Beta*).

A technique with a higher capital to output ratio, K/O, has a lower maximum rate of profit and a smaller share of wages in net output, but since net output is higher, it is not necessary that the rate of profit should be lower.

We can run over the series of techniques assuming the same rate of profit to be ruling on each island (shown as r in the diagram).

With a common rate of profit, the ratio of the wage to output falls as we ascend the series. In the limit, the increment to output is only just sufficient to yield the constant rate of profit on the increment to the cost of

[5] See P. Samuelson, 'Parable and Realism in Capital Theory: The Surrogate Production Function', *Review of Economic Studies*, Vol. 29, 1962, pp. 193–206.

investment, so that the wage rate remains unchanged. Beyond this point, no further 'deepening' of the stock of capital takes place.

This is a version of the neo-neoclassical theorem, that the maximum output obtainable by deepening the stock of capital (raising K/L) is that which requires zero consumption by capitalists.

The explanation is that, on an island where the stock of means of production is greater, the proportion of the labour force required to maintain it is higher. The limit is reached at the point where the increase in net output due to a more capital-using technique is no greater than the output lost by transferring the requisite amount of labour into the investment sector.

We may observe that the lower the rate of profit at which the comparison is made, the higher the maximum value of K/L. This would not

Figure VI

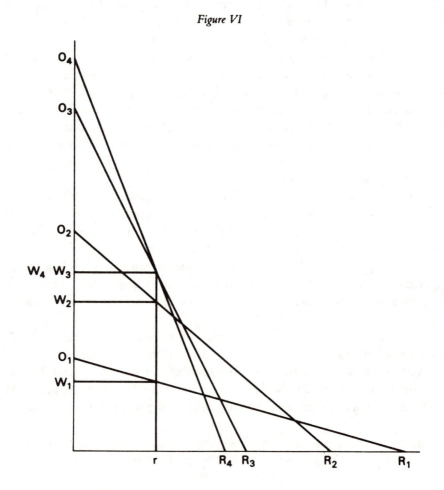

necessarily be true if we had not eliminated reversals and reswitches from the pseudo-production function by assuming labour-value prices to rule on each island. In fact this construction is exactly the same as Professor Samuelson's 'surrogate production function' which was devised to answer the Cambridge critics. Yet Samuelson seemed to believe that his construction was supporting the neoclassical doctrine of a falling marginal productivity of increments of capital applied to labour.

It seems to me to be a great insult to Marx to foist this conception upon him. It is far more honourable to him to admit that his *value* system is not all-inclusive than to try to make out that he was really a neoclassic at heart.

The limitation on the *value* system is precisely that it does *not* provide a unit of physical output. Marx listed among the counter-acting causes that check the tendency for the rate of profit to fall, the fact that technical progress may reduce the cost in terms of labour-time of the physical ingredients in the stock of means of production, thus reducing C while leaving $s + v$ unchanged. (This is our case of *Alpha II*, but without taking account of the increase in O/L.)

He failed to notice the main counteracting cause. A superior technique does not necessarily require a rise in the capital to labour ratio (as Marx admitted) but when it does, it raises the output to capital ratio. Even a quasi-superior technique leaves room for a constant rate of profit with a rise in real wages, or a rise in the rate of profit with constant real wages.

There are many influences that may cause the overall rate of profit to fall as capitalism develops, but rising organic composition has not been shown to be one of them.

5

The foregoing argument is conducted in terms of comparisons of economies each adjusted to its own technique. Marx was actually interested in a historical process of accumulation and technical change going on through time.

This involves the whole of economic theory and most of economic history as well. Our model is too limited to contribute much to it. We have not discussed changes in the labour force and in the types of work required, nor the availability of natural resources, nor problems of the uneven development of national economies. The assumption of rising consumption per head of identical 'baskets' of goods is unnatural, for

technical change is largely devoted to changing the nature of commodities. We have not touched upon the manner in which innovations
are made by profit-seeking firms or the process by which competition
diffuses them. We have not discussed the finance of investment or the conception of technological obsolescence.

All the same, there are three very important generalizations towards
which our argument can be seen to point.

First: if real wages do not rise when productivity is increasing, the rate
of profit, in general, will not be maintained, for there will be insufficient
expenditure to make a market for the greater flow of output (unless
investment happens to increase or thriftiness to fall sufficiently to make up
the deficit in effective demand). This is the paradox of capitalism. Every
individual employer gains by reducing the cost of labour in terms of his
own product but, taken together, they cannot prosper unless real-wage
rates are rising.

Second: when accumulation has been going on for some time with
more or less neutral progress on balance and then the latest eligible techniques take a capital-using form, there will be a gradual decline in employment offered at full-capacity operation of the stock of means of production, unless the flow of gross investment rises sufficiently to equip the
labour force at the same rate as before with the new, more capital-using
plant. This was Ricardo's argument about the introduction of machinery.[6]
It is seen today in dramatic form in Third World countries which are
being invaded by modern capitalism.

Third: when accumulation has been going on for some time with
increasing employment and a moment comes when the reserve army of
long-run unemployment is exhausted, a scarcity of labour develops in the
sense that capitalists want to continue to increase output but cannot get
any more hands. This situation is a strong stimulus to technical change,
but there is no reason to expect the capital to labour ratio to be raised. On
the contrary, in this situation, the motive is all in the direction of saving
labour, that is, raising output per man, and this applies just as much, if not
more, in the production of means of production as in the output of consumable commodities.

These reflections show that when Marxian analysis is disentangled from
its false association with the neoclassical production function, it is seen to
be all the more cogent.

[6] David Ricardo, *Principles*, Third edition, Ch. 23.

20

THE LABOUR THEORY OF VALUE

BEFORE 1956, Ron Meek was a rigid dogmatist. It was his leg that I was pulling in 'An Open Letter from a Keynesian to a Marxist'.[1] He took it very much amiss, and it was still rankling when he was writing the original version of this book, *Studies in the Labor Theory of Value*. His extremely high standard of doctrinal purity was shown by the fact that he treated Oskar Lange and Rudolf Schlesinger (both life-long students of Marx) as hostile critics, along with me. Lange was suggesting that some problems that arise within a market economy can best be treated by orthodox methods, and Schlesinger was pleading to relax the strict quantitative calculation of the 'transformation of *values* into prices' in order to deal with monopoly. These suggestions were dismissed as heretical. I did not intend my *Essay on Marxian Economics* (1942) as a criticism of Marx. I wrote it to alert my bourgeois colleagues to the existence of penetrating and important ideas in *Capital* that they ought not to continue to neglect. In this the book had some success, which it certainly would not have done if it had been written in Marxist terminology, but since I was a bourgeois myself I must have been trying to reconstruct orthodox equilibrium theory. (In fact, that book was the first round in the 'Cambridge criticism' which, with the aid of Piero Sraffa, finally pulverized equilibrium theory twenty years later.)

The year 1956 was one of political shocks (including the riots at Posnan, when both Ron and I happened to be there on a visit with some colleagues). It broke through the crust of dogmatism. Ron became a professor and drifted back towards equilibrium theory, though he continued to work on the pre-Marxian classics (the best part in this book).

[1] See p. 165 above.

A review of *Studies in the Labour Theory of Value*, by Ronald L. Meek, Second edition, 1976, from *Monthly Review*, December 1977.

When he was finally persuaded to prepare a second edition, he found that he regretted the 'defensiveness and didacticism' of his manner of writing, but he did not see much need to change the matter. The present volume is a reprint of the original with a new introduction and postscript by Professor Meek.

VALUE

The labour theory of *value* provides the particular language and set of concepts in which Marxist doctrines are expounded. It is also a shibboleth; to 'be a Marxist', it is necessary to 'believe in' labour *value*. But regarded as a *theory*, what does it assert? For the classics, a theory of value was required to account for the relative prices of commodities; so long as the real wage rate is constant, their theory of 'natural prices' is quite straight-forward, but Marxian *value* is independent of wages. Marxists frequently suggest that it provides a theory of prices, but we all know that the prices of commodities cannot be proportional to their *values* when there are different capital-to-labour ratios in different lines of production. When there is a uniform rate of profit, in a competitive capitalist economy, 'prices of production' rule. Yet somehow *values* 'ultimately', 'basically', or 'in the long run' do determine prices.

We are told that the law of *value* governs the distribution of resources between different lines of production; but surely that could be better discussed in terms of the process of accumulation and the evolution of technology? Sometimes we are told that it is impossible to account for exploitation except in terms of *value*, but why do we need *value* to show that profits can be made in industry by selling commodities for more than they cost to produce, or to explain the power of those who command finance to push around those who do not? For some, *value* theory includes the whole grand sweep of the materialist interpretation of history. But something that means everything means nothing.

We must go back to the first chapter of *Capital* to see what *value* meant to Marx.

'Let us take two commodities, e.g., corn and iron. The proportions in which they are exchangeable, whatever these proportions may be, can always be represented by an equation in which a given quantity of corn is equated to some quantity of iron: e.g. 1 quarter corn = x cwt iron. What does this equation tell us? It tells us that in two different things – in 1 quarter of corn and x cwt of iron, there exists equal quantities of something common to both.' This common something is the property of being products of labour. Here we have it. *Value* is an otherwise indefinable quantity which is put into commodities by the man-hours of labour time required to produce them.

This is not something that one can 'believe in' or 'not believe in'. It is a mental construction that may or may not be useful in analysing reality.

The great advantage of this concept is that it enabled Marx to think quantitatively without being hung up, as Ricardo had been, over the problem of measurement. Along with broad historical and political argument, there are a number of economic 'models' in *Capital*, set out in terms of *values*. The central model, the schema of expanded reproduction, has been absorbed, via Kalecki, into post-Keynesian theory and translated into operational terms.

Some Marxists object to translations. They maintain that a flow of output is a quantity of *value* and cannot be represented in any other way. This is mere dogmatism. Last year's national income is something that actually occurred. It is now part of history, an extremely complex set of events. There are many ways of representing it, none of which is perfectly satisfactory. If we had full information, we could present a flow of industrial production as an input–ouput table of physical goods, making allowance for the wear and tear (but not financial depreciation) of the stock of means of production. We could represent it in terms of flows of money payments and depreciation allowances, or as *value*, that is, the total number of man-hours of work performed over the year $(v + s)$ plus c, the depletion of the pre-existing stock of means of production, valued by the labour-time embodied in it. When prices in terms of money are not exactly proportional to *values*, the share of net profit in proceeds is not exactly equivalent to *surplus value*. In that case, it is the calculation in terms of money that is operational, for the decisions of businessmen who control investment and the distribution of income are influenced by profits, not by *values*.

The concept of *value* enabled Marx to dispense with an exact treatment of relative prices. There are no prices in Volume I of *Capital* and the discussion in Volume III (the transformation problem) is very sketchy. I have always felt that it was a mistake for Marxists to allow themselves to be lured onto the terrain of price theory, where the orthodox economists could score some hits (though their own analysis of prices is far from satisfactory). The Marxists should have said: Do not worry about prices. We will get around to that later. Meanwhile we are interested in the mode of production, the rate of accumulation, and the distribution of income. We have a theory of the share of profit – the rate of exploitation. The *share* of profit is far more important than the *rate* of profit. The *share* of profit is something that actually happens and affects people's lives – the *rate* of profit is a mental calculation.

But Marxists, of course, would never admit that there was any problem that *value* does not solve, and they floundered about proving that prices are proportional to *values*, and that they are not.

The theories that Marx put forward in terms of *value* are the indispensable basis for a treatment of the economics of capitalism, which the orthodox school fails to provide. Many of the Marxian concepts are even more relevant in our own day than they were a hundred years ago. For instance, a *commodity* is something which is produced by employing labour in order to be sold. Marx said that a commodity must have *use value*, otherwise no one would buy it, but nowadays use value becomes less and less essential. Packaging, advertisement, and salesmanship are what generate demand.

The Marxian concept of the nature of an economic system, characterized by the manner in which production is controlled and a surplus extracted from it, is more important than ever, since there are now many systems coexisting in the world and reacting on each other – several types of socialism, and overlapping stages of the development of capitalism, as well as remnants of feudalism in the Third World. The central topic in teaching economics ought to be the nature of productive systems, but this is generally avoided for fear that capitalism would not necessarily always get the best marks.

To interpret history, the interplay of the forces of production and the relations of production is an invaluable clue, even though Marx's predictions of how it was going to work out have not yet been fulfilled.

Marx saw all this in terms of *value*, but the parts of the theory that are most closely bound up with that concept are the least satisfactory. There are some statements that seemed to Marx to contain important truths which now appear only as metaphor. Labour power is sold like a commodity, and, like all commodities, it exchanges for its *value*. The *value* of labour power means a wage rate sufficient to permit the workers to maintain their families at some customary standard of life. But calling it *value* does not explain anything. We know that, in rich countries, the minimum acceptable standard of life is always a little above the average actually obtained, so that the majority are living below it; in poor countries there is no bottom to the level of subsistence; undernourishment makes people grow up smaller (in height and weight) and reduces the length of life. *Value* does not help us here.

Again Marx expresses the rate of exploitation as the division of the working day into the time that a man is producing for himself (creating wage goods) and the time he is working for the capitalist. But a man by himself cannot produce anything. The whole labour force is producing the whole output. We have to go round about to find out total net output and the ratio of net profit to wages, before we can apply the ratio to the division of the working day. The time that a man works for himself is a striking metaphor, not an analytical proposition.

The worst case is the confusion between stock and flow in the concept of *variable capital*. (It was this that I was teasing Ron Meek about in my 'Open Letter'.) Because labour alone produces *value*, Marx maintains that only the part of capital invested in employing labour generates surplus. Constant capital – the stock of physical means of production – passes on to the flow of *value* only the *value* embodied in it in the past. But what is meant by the part of capital that employs labour? Is it a wage fund? The wage *fund* is a financial concept, depending on the turnover periods of particular processes of production. Surely it is the flow of expenditure on the wage *bill* that employs labour and generates surplus (net profit)?

Marx writes the flow of output, say, per annum, in terms of *value* as $c + v + s$ (replacement of means of production used up, wages, and surplus). Here, obviously, v is a year's wage bill. But then Marx writes $(c + v)$ for the stock of capital and $s/(c + v)$ for the rate of profit.

These are all points of exposition that could be cleared up if Marxists would consent to amend the formulae, but there are some cases in which the *value* concept seems to be actually misleading.

Marx suggests that when simple commodity production prevailed, that is when peasants and artisans owned their own means of production, they exchanged the goods that they produced amongst themselves as *values*; this is inconsistent with his own analysis. How can the products of the black-smith and the handloom weaver be treated as *values*? It is true that they are *commodities* designed for exchange, not for self-consumption, but how is the labour-time involved in each to be counted? For an artisan, there is no hard and fast distinction between work-time and leisure; there is no hard and fast distinction between investment and consumption – the working capital of an artisan, which he replenishes from time to time by sales, includes the consumption of his family. Moreover, each kind of work is qualitatively different and is inseparable from the appropriate means of production. Blacksmithing is work at a forge, weaving is work at a loom.

Only employment for wages, as Marx said, is reduced to *abstract labour*, measured in numbers of undifferentiated man-hours.

There is another point at which an argument in terms of *value* is treacherous. The *organic composition of capital* is written as c/v, but means the 'ratio of dead to living labour', that is the *value* of the stock means of production per unit of labour currently employed. (It would be better to write it as C/L.) Marx believed, as was natural in the railway age, that accumulation is associated with continuously rising organic composition (a strong capital-using bias in technical progress). He argued: c/v will rise indefinitely, and s/v, the rate of exploitation, cannot rise indefinitely. Therefore, sooner or later, $s/(c + v)$, which corresponds to the rate of profit on capital, will tend to fall. But this is a *non sequitur*. Organic composition is the capital-to-labour ratio, not the capital-to-output ratio. The very purpose for which capitalists raise organic composition is to raise output per man, not in terms of *value* (which cannot alter) but in terms of physical saleable commodities. As output per head rises, there is room for a rise in either or both the real-wage rate in terms of commodities and the rate of profit on capital – how the rise is distributed between the two depends on the market power of the parties, that is, on the fortunes of the class war. This mistake must be attributed to the habit of thinking in terms of *value*. A rise in organic composition means a fall in the *value* of output $(s + v)$ per unit of capital. So what?

Many devoted Marxists have tried to rescue the argument by mixing it up with a neoclassical production function, which only makes it worse.

The concept of *value* certainly helped Marx to arrive at his interpretation of history, politics, and economics; but we can learn from his ideas without remaining stuck in the groove that led him to them.

PRICES

In his new introduction, Meek reformulates what he believes to be the essence of the labour theory of value in terms of Piero Sraffa's *Production of Commodities by Means of Commodities*, but he does not really throw much light on it. There are no helpful explanations in that book of what it is about. My own view is that it should be understood as follows:[2]

[2] I must insist that this is only my own view. Piero has always stuck close to pure unadulterated Marx and regards my amendments with suspicion. The dogmatists say he 'is not a Marxist', and they have invented a special category – neo-Ricardian – to put him into. It seems that a neo-Ricardian is someone who thinks it worthwhile to take a lot of trouble to express his ideas precisely, while to 'be a Marxist' it is necessary to repeat undigested phrases out of the book.

The equations of production represent a formalized picture of a supposed actual economy, in which actual production is going on – as it were, an x-ray showing its bones. There is a certain labour force being employed and there is a specified flow of materials being continually used up and recreated in the process of production. (Fixed capital is treated separately.) In each period, a certain surplus product emerges, over and above the replacement of materials used up. This is surplus in the sense of net output $(v + s)$ not *surplus value* (s).

Sraffa's equations describe the technique of production in use in terms of an input–output table. (This was a more original concept when it was conceived than it appeared thirty years later when it was published in 1960.) The question is often raised: What about economies of scale? What about demand? In the economy whose picture is being drawn, there is some particular composition of output being produced in some particular proportions; there is no scope for variations in scale. Since there are no unsold goods, there must be just sufficient demand to absorb net output, with the prices and incomes ruling. There is no scope for variations in 'tastes'. The output is being absorbed because it is being produced and it is being produced because it is being absorbed.

Nor is there any variation in technique. The stocks of inputs in the pipelines today were produced in the past by the same processes that are in use today, and the stocks are being restored so as to be available for use in the same processes tomorrow.

Now, by manipulating the equations, we can calculate the labour time directly and indirectly required to produce a unit of each commodity (by the method of subsystems). Here, for the first time, we have an exact statement (within the specifications of the model) of the meaning of *value*. The *value* of any commodity is a number of man-hours only, but labour could not have produced that commodity without a pre-existing stock of appropriate inputs; part of the labour indirectly required to produce the commodity is that which replaces the inputs. However far we go back, in imagination, we should never come to the first man who produced the first output with his bare hands.

To go back is a movement in logical time. In history, of course, if we traced production back, we should soon come to an earlier technique, out of which this one grew, and if we go right back to the hunters catching beavers and deer, the inputs were provided by nature. (Logical time can be traced from left to right on the surface of a blackboard. Historical time moves from the dark past behind it into the unknown future in front.)

Now we come to the point. The technical equations alone cannot explain prices. In the actual economy, some prices are ruling. We may postulate a uniform rate of profit, and when it is given – a rate per cent per period of turnover – we can work out what the prices must be. But this is what they happen to be. They are not determined by the technical conditions.

This is demonstrated by another conceptual calculation. Run the rate of profit through every value from zero to the maximum, with the corresponding share of wages in net output falling from unity to zero, and observe how the pattern of prices behaves. In historical time, of course, it would not be possible to have the same physical composition of output with widely different shares of wages and profits – the capitalists would want to take their share in steel and caviar and the workers in cheese and boots. The calculation is a movement only in logical time.

Now what was the object of this meticulous construction (and of the many elaborations of the simple case which the book contains)? The object was a *Prelude to a critique of economic theory*. It knocks out once and for all the marginal productivity theory of distribution. That theory purported to show how the physical conditions of production determine the 'rewards' of the 'factors of production' in accordance with the contribution that each makes to the output of industry.

Of course, you and I always knew that that theory was nonsense, but however long the Marxists battered at it from the outside they could never knock it down. Now it has been exploded from within.

Piero Sraffa's aim was focused on orthodoxy, but incidentally he has shown the Marxists how to solve the 'transformation problem' and he has answered the old conundrum – does the labour theory of *value* provide a theory of prices? The answer is that normal prices are not, in general, proportional to *values* but, through the rate of profit, they are related to each other in a precise and systematic way. (If the rate of profit is not uniform, prices may be all over the place, as indeed they usually are.)

The next question is: What determines the rate of profit? For all the model tells us, it could be anything.

Some readers have interpreted the calculation of the movement up and down of the rate of profit and the share of wages as a story about the class war. But that is a complete misunderstanding. With a single technique and a given net output, there is little scope for fighting over wages and, anyway, the movement is only the movement of the eye running up and down a curve on the blackboard.

In the actual economy, at the moment when its picture was being taken, the share of wages had already been brought into existence by past history, and in the actual future, in front of the blackboard, it will be influenced by the interplay of technical change, the accumulation of capital, the growth of monopoly, the bargaining power of trade unions, and the benevolent or hostile intervention of the state.

Sraffa's model says very exactly what it can say and nothing more.

On this point, Meek is mistaken. He tries to squeeze out of amendments to the equations an historical process of moving from a precapitalist world where *value* prices ruled into capitalism with a uniform rate of profit. To project the transformation problem into history seems very far fetched. Nothing like that can possibly have happened. Moreover, to present it in terms of Sraffa's model is quite illegitimate. Simple commodity production was not an input–output technology but a set of independent groups of producers each with their own lore and their own equipment. Professor Meek ought to have remembered enough of Ron's Marxism to recognize the difference between different modes of production.

Sraffa's contribution to Marxism is mainly negative, to dispose of the rubbish of orthodox theory. Now it is up to the Marxists to break out of the husk of dogmatism and set about building the political economy of today in the space that he has cleared.

21

MARXISM AND MODERN ECONOMICS

TODAY there are a great number of versions of *what Marx really meant* in the field. It is not easy to say precisely what is 'Marxism' and to separate it clearly from 'non-Marxism'.

> Marx's teachings were only one element in a wide stream of thought — the growing self-consciousness of modern man as a social being, and of man in society as a potential object of scientific investigation — which would in any case have borne many ideas like his in its course. At the same time, Marx's contribution to that stream was so important and has had so great an influence on the habits of thought of his opponents as well as his supporters, that it is as difficult nowadays to find a really pure non-Marxist amongst historians and sociologists as it is to find a flat-earthist amongst geographers.
>
> In economics, however, a purely non-Marxist doctrine was for long incapsulated in the impermeable casing of neo–classical static equilibrium theory. Here the contrast is clear cut, and the comparison, certainly, is highly favourable to Marx. The relevance, the scope, and the penetration of his analysis of the 'laws of motion of capitalism' make the marginalists' scholasticism appear merely frivolous. Indeed, since the capsule was broken open from within by Keynes, there has been the same sort of infiltration of Marxian ideas into economic theory as had already occurred in history. For a discussion of the questions nowadays found to be interesting — growth and stagnation, technical progress and the demand for labour, the balance of sectors in an expanding economy — Marxian theory provides a starting point where academic teaching was totally blank.[1]

But now it is the self-proclaimed Marxists who object to this confluence

[1] This passage is repeated from p. 156 above.

A contribution to the Encounter at Brazilia, 1979.

of ideas. It is dogmatic Marxism which is impervious to reasonable discussion:

> For the project of Grand Theory — to find a total systematized conceptualization of all history and human occasions — is the original heresy of metaphysics against knowledge. . .
>
> It is not only that the attempt to do so, in a 'science' devoid of substance ends up very much like Engel's characterization of the Hegelian inheritance: 'a compilation of words and turns of speech which had no other purpose than to be at hand at the right time where thought and positive knowledge were lacking.' All this is not all. The project itself is misbegotten; it is an exercise of closure, and it stems from a kind of intellectual agoraphobia, an anxiety before the uncertain and the unknown, a yearning for security within the cabin of the Absolute. As such, it reproduces old theological modes of thought, and its constructions are always elaborated from ideological materials. More than this, such total systems have, very generally, been at enmity with reason and censorious of freedom. They seek, not only to dominate all theory — or to expel all other theories as accessories — but also to reproduce themselves within social reality. Since theory is a closure, history must be brought to conform. They seek to lasso process in their categories, bring it down, break its will, and subject to their command.[2]

The capsule of neoclassical theory was broken open from within by two movements of thought which arose in the 1930s from the obvious clash between the textbook doctrine of equilibrium and the facts of experience in the great slump — the revival of the theory of effective demand and the rejection of the concept of the marginal productivity of capital. The two movements turned out to be interconnected though their origins were quite separate. Both were set going by non-dogmatic Marxists: though Keynes got all the limelight, Michal Kalecki's version of the theory of employment was more robust, while Piero Sraffa, who kept his light under a bushel until 1960, was able to understand Ricardo because he had first found out for himself the meaning of the Marxian concept of prices of production. For the sake of a label, I have called this trend 'Modern Economics'. It is both post Keynesian and post neoclassical.

---

[2] E. P. Thompson, *The Poverty of Theory*, p. 303.

1

The main obstacle to good understanding with the Marxists in the English-speaking world is not any point of substance, but a matter of terminology, concepts and style of exposition.

Marx had a powerful intuition of the nature of capitalism, which he backed up with a great deal of factual study. In the formal argument, he found it natural to put ideology into the definitions, which often makes them difficult for us to handle.

We can make out a clear commonsensical account of the process of production and exploitation at the level of the individual capitalist. For Marx a capitalist was a family man, Moneybags, not the corporate entity that we have to deal with. He has a command of finance – purchasing power – with which he sets up plant – fixed capital – that can be kept intact with care and maintenance, along with a source of energy, a revolving fund to supply material inputs and a fund for paying wages. He organises workers to produce a flow of output, pays the lowest wage rates that he can get away with and sells the product at the highest price that competition permits. The flow of receipts in excess of costs provides him with profits out of which he pays his household expenses, adding the rest to his store of financial wealth, which if times continue prosperous will be invested in enlarging his business.

For industry in general, this is put into a formal scheme in terms of $c + v + s$ – depletion of stock, to be replaced, wages and net profits. It is to be observed the c, constant capital, is nothing to do with fixed plant. It represents physical inputs into production such as materials and fuel. There are some difficulties about the time-schemes (stocks and flows) and it is clearly a mistake to treat $s/(c + v)$, the share of net profit in turnover, as though it was the rate of profit on capital. But the main difficulty with the formal model is its lack of articulation. There is no unit for a flow of physical output or for flows of payments. Everything is supposed to be measured in *value* – that is, labour time, though an operational definition of this concept has never been offered.

In a process of production, with given land and fixed equipment, the main input is the work of the employed labour force, along with materials and fuel which one business buys from another and the industrial sector as a whole takes in from primary production. A worker receives his share of the output – his wage – in the form of current purchasing power, while a business receives its share – net profit – in the form of future purchasing power, finance, which can (but need not be) invested to expand productive capacity.

There are many questions to be raised here. For instance, on the physical plane, why does output per man differ so much amongst industries in different countries using the same engineering technique? What causes the difference in real-wage rates between groups of workers with more or less the same productivity?

On the level of flows of payments, how does monopoly power affect the level of profits? On the plane of finance, what are the relations between the own capital of a business and its borrowing?

It is not much use trying to discuss such questions with Marxists. They generally refuse to play.

In his recent writings in *Monthly Review*, Paul Sweezy seems actively to dislike and deplore clear definitions and analytical reasoning, though formerly he was a practitioner himself.

A Marxist believes that what he says is correct because he is a Marxist but he likes to stick to Marx's own often opaque terminology for fear of drifting into heresy unawares.

All questions are to be answered in terms of the 'law of *value*', but *value* has ceased to be a concept and become a shibboleth.

What was meant by *the labour theory of value*? Ricardo was looking for a *theory of value* in order to be able to measure a flow of output independently of its distribution between wages and profits. He did not succeed, to his dying day, in finding an 'invariable standard' of value and Marx did not either. We cannot separate $(v + s)$, the flow of man hours of labour performed per annum into wages and profits, without going round about through flows of money payments.

Marx sometimes wrote as though the separation could be made directly. When the ratio of exploitation (s/v) is, say half he considered that a man is working two thirds of the day for himself, producing his wages and one third for his employer. This, clearly, must be treated as a metaphor not an analytical proposition. The whole labour force is producing the whole flow of industrial output, including replacements of inputs used up, and there is no way of separating out the hours used for producing wage goods from the rest.

If wage goods were produced by a separate integrated industry, we could calculate the ratio of exploitation in physical terms. A part of the output of wage goods is consumed by the workers in that industry and the rest is used by capitalists to employ workers to produce investment goods, to maintain and enlarge productive capacity and provide luxuries to be consumed in their households.

This way of putting the point gives some insight into the process of exploitation. It is the basis of the 'corn model' which Sraffa disinterred

from Ricardo and it is not without relevance to food production in predominantly agricultural economies, but with modern industrial technology the stock of equipment required for an output of wage goods
cannot be isolated from the rest.

The relation of the prices of commodities to their labour *values* involves
the rate of profit on capital. This requires an amendment of the Marxian
formula which dogmatists are generally reluctant to undertake. Marx was
well aware that the physical stock of capital in existence at any moment is
a multiple of c, its annual depletion but he did not provide any symbol for
it. The flow of gross profit per annum may be represented by $(c + s)$
though it is not clear whether c should be taken to represent labour-time
used to produce physical inputs in the past or current labour required to
replace them.

Sraffa's model (1960) cuts through these puzzles.[3] The technique with
which a given labour force produces a given flow of output is represented
by an input–output *system* of equations in physical terms. The economy is
in a self-reproducing state, physical inputs used up being replaced in kind
as production goes on. The flow of net output is then a list of specific
quantities of specified physical commodities.

For any one technique and physical flow of output, Sraffa shows the
relationship between the share of wages in net output and the rate of
profit on capital. For any given share of wages, there is a unique pattern of
prices that yields a determinate rate of profit on the value of capital,
uniform throughout the system.

As is well known, the prices corresponding to a uniform rate of profit
are proportional to labour *values* only in the special case where the capital
to labour ratio (organic composition) is uniform throughout industry.
Once we have found out the prices of production corresponding to a
particular rate of profit, there does not seem to be any point in going
through the transformation problem backwards to find out the labour
values. But it is important to notice that the real wages that workers can
consume depend upon the physical composition of output as well as upon
the ratio of exploitation. In Sraffa's system the wage is a share in net
output, whatever it may be, not a flow of particular consumable commodities.

Since the wage bill is a flow of money payments, when the rate of profit
is known, all prices can be reckoned in money terms, though Sraffa

[3] *Production of Commodities by Means of Commodities*, Cambridge University Press.

himself scorns to do so. Then the ratio of exploitation can be expressed as the ratio of the flow of net profit to the wage bill.

Sraffa does not pretend to offer a thoery of what determines the ratio of exploitation. He shows only the relationship between technical conditions, exploitation and the uniform rate of profit on capital that they make possible.

It is here that the Marxian theory of class war comes into the argument, along with the evolution of a reserve army of long-period unemployment. These are the influences that govern the distribution of a technically given flow of net output between wages and profits. Meanwhile Sraffa has knocked out the neoclassical theory of distribution according to marginal productivity which the Marxist dogmatists, muffled up in labour *values*, were never able to do.

2

Neoclassical dogmatists refuse to recognize what the argument is about. Thorstein Veblen, in a review of a book by J. B. Clark, published in 1907, had exposed the fallacy concealed in the orthodox concept of 'capital'.

> Much is made of the doctrine that the two facts of 'capital' and 'capital goods' are conceptually distinct, though substantially identical. The two terms cover virtually the same facts as would be covered by the terms 'pecuniary capital' and 'industrial equipment.'. . . .
>
> The continuum in which the 'abiding entity' of capital resides is a continuity of ownership, not a physical fact. The continuity, in fact, is of an immaterial nature, a matter of legal rights, of contract, of purchase and sale. Just why this patent state of the case is overlooked, as it somewhat elaborately is, is not easily seen.[4]

When I revived the question after reading Sraffa's *Introduction* to Ricardo's *Principles* (1951) it was not so much overlooked as carefully eliminated by conflating means of production with finance in the concept of 'putty capital' or 'malleable machines'.

Marx always had in mind the dual nature of capital as technical means

[4] 'Professor Clark's Economics', *Quarterly Journal of Economics*, Vol. 22, 1908, reprinted in *The Place of Science in Modern Civilization* and in *A Critique of Economic Theory*, ed. E. K. Hunt and Jesse G. Schwartz, Penguin Modern Economics Readings.

of production and as rights over property which permit businesses to employ labour in such a way as to make profits but his system of measurement in terms of labour-*value* did not permit him to express it clearly. From this arises the confusion over the theory of a long-run tendency to a falling rate of profit.

In terms of the formula for labour *values*, this theory is a mere rigmarole. As accumulation goes on faster than employment is increasing, there is a rise in the ratio of means of production, regarded as embodied labour time, to the labour-*value* of current output; c is rising relatively to $(v + s)$. Then a constant ratio of $s/(c + v)$, which was intended to stand for the rate of profit on capital, requires a rise in s/v, the ratio of exploitation. The argument is that in the long-run there must be a tendency for the rate of profit on capital to fall because $c/(v + s)$ can rise indefinitely as accumulation goes on, but s/v cannot rise indefinitely, for v cannot fall below the subsistence level. This is a non sequeter; v stands for the wage in terms of labour time; technical progress, accompanying the rise in c per man employed, raises output per head of physical wage goods. It is perfectly possible for s/v to rise indefinitely while the standard of life of workers is constant or improving.

Marx laid great emphasis upon the effect of large-scale organisation and technical innovations in raising output per unit of labour, but he did not seem to be able to fit it into his theory of exploitation. Let us compare two technical situations (two Sraffa systems) with the same labour force, producing flows of net output composed of similar items. With a superior technique, Alpha, net output per man in higher than with the other, Beta – more of some items and no less of any. When (with the same money-wage bill) prices in each are such as to yield the same rate of profit in both, then, depending on the nature of the technical difference between them, the value of capital for Alpha may be lower, higher or the same as for Beta.

Marx recognized the possibility of capital-saving innovations – the cheapening of elements in constant capital – but he believed (as a matter of observation) that capital-using innovations are more prevalent. In such a case, when the rate of profit on capital is the same in Alpha as in Beta, the ratio of exploitation (the ratio of net profit to the wage bill) must be higher; the level of real wages in terms of physical commodities is higher in Alpha, though in a smaller proportion than output per head. It may be objected that a continual series of capital-using innovations over a long run, accompanied by a rising ratio of exploitation, would sooner or later reach an impasse. But the greater the bulk of stocks of physical means of production, the greater the scope for capital-saving innovations; it is unlikely that the capital-to-labour ratio would go on rising for ever.

When Marx was working on what became Chapter 14 in Volume III of *Capital*, he was backing away from the theory of an inevitable tendency to a falling rate of profit, mentioning conteracting causes which prevent the tendency from being realized, but he could not quite bring himself to give it up altogether.

Since Volume III was not published in his life-time, we may suppose that he was not sure that it was satisfactorily worked out. Perhaps the long delay in completing *Capital* was mainly due to the difficulty of absorbing a rising tendency of real-wage rates into the argument.

There was another strand in Marx's treatment of technological change – the prediction that the mechanization of production will cause long-run unemployment – recruiting the reserve army of labour whenever its numbers have fallen too low. Before we can discuss this question, we must open up the other half of the anti-neoclassical argument – the theory of effective demand.

There are two layers in Marx's analysis of industrial capitalism. The organic composition of capital, the ratio of exploitation and the rate of profit are all long-period concepts in the sense that they imply that a given stock of physical capital is operated by a particular number of workers, that is, that plant can be utilized only at its designed capacity. Short-period phenomena – booms, slumps and crises – are treated in terms of the problem of the realization of profits. Given plant can be worked more or less intensively according to the state of effective demand.

This aspect of Marxian analysis was brought into a coherent form by Michal Kalecki.[5] Keynes (though he was personally allergic to Marxism) covered much the same ground and the brilliance of his polemic attracted all the attention. Kalecki's version is better able to resist the wave of reaction that is at present sweeping over academic teaching.

The essential core of Kalecki's analysis is simple. In an industrial economy, with given productive capacity, firms set their prices in such a way as to cover costs of production at a standard level of utilization and yield the flow of net profit that, in the light of competitive conditions, is the most that they think it prudent to go for. The overall flow of receipts that are realized by selling output at these prices depends upon the flow of expenditure upon them. In a two-class society in which workers spend

---

[5] See *Selected Essays on the Dynamics of the Capitalist Economy*, 1933–1970, Cambridge University Press, 1972.

their money wages on consumption as they are received, it follows that
the flow of gross profits is equal to the expenditure of capitalists upon
investment and their own consumption.

The instability of a market economy (which Marx described but did not
clearly analyse) is explained by the fact that an increase in expenditure on
investment, from one year to the next, increases the flow of business
profits, which both encourages greater hopes of future profit from
enlarged productive capacity and provides more finance for further
investment. But investment means accumulation of productive capacity;
the expected return on investment (which Keynes misleadingly described
as the marginal efficiency of capital) can be maintained only as long as
investment is accelerating so as to sustain a growth in the flow of gross
profits commensurate with the growth of the stock of capital.

This simple outline of the analysis must be elaborated by introducing
house-building in addition to industrial investment and a budget deficit as
boosters to effective demand, variation in the proportion of household
consumption to income, the relation of home expenditure in one country
to its balance of trade and the effects of continuous inflation. However
much it is complicated, the main core of the argument remains valid – in
an industrial economy, the flow of gross profits primarily depends on the
flow of expenditure on investment.

To combine the analysis of long-run accumulation with short-run
instability we have to descend from the pure air of Sraffa's abstraction to
the fogs of actual history. As investment goes on, the physical specification
of capital goods is continuously changing. Net output (after allowing for
replacements) cannot be demarcated in physical terms; consequently the
concepts of net profit (*surplus value*), the value of capital, the rate of profit
and the ratio of exploitation all involve an allowance for depreciation in
financial terms which is necessarily partly conventional. However, in
broad terms, the Marxian categories as interpreted by Kalecki provide a
language that permits us to discuss the interaction of the short and long-
period elements in the process of capitalist accumulation.

When technical development is markedly capital-using (with rising
organic composition), as Marx believed to be normal, employment per
unit of industrial productive capacity is falling over the long run but this
may be masked by rising expenditure sustaining profits in the economy as
a whole. Perhaps we should regard the high employment in the Western
world for twenty years after the end of the Second World War as a long
boom, helped out by expansionist 'Keynesian' fiscal and monetary policies
when it threatened to flag, while an underlying tendency to long-period

unemployment has come to the surface during, the present phase of stagnation.

This has evidently been exacerbated by another tendency which Marx foresaw, the growing concentration of financial power which strengthens the influence of monopolistic control over prices.

Kalecki establishes a paradoxical relationship between the ratio of exploitation and the rate of profit in a market economy. When some firms attempt to increase their profits by raising profit margins they succeed only at the expense of other firms' profits, unless expenditure is increased simultaneously. Higher prices reduce real wages and reduce employment in producing wage goods, while the overall flow of gross profits remains equal to the flow of capitalists' expenditure.

When technical development and capital accumulation are raising output per head while profit margins are held constant, real wage rates fail to rise and (unless investment and capitalists' consumption are expanding sufficiently) effective demand fails to expand enough to maintain employment and the level of utilization of plant. Trade unions, which insist upon raising money wage rates in step with productivity, are necessary to prevent an advanced economy from falling into stagnation. At the same time, the uneven development of various industries and services means that a rise in money-wage rates that is sufficient to preserve the share of wages in proceeds (to prevent the ratio of exploitation from rising) for the most progressive firms is too much for backward sectors and precipitates inflation.

Once a vicious spiral of rising prices and wages has set in, to check it merely by freezing wage rates cannot be relied upon to prevent profit margins from continuing to rise while the attempt to check it (as is fashionable nowadays) by restricting credit reduces employment and the flow of output so that the remedy is worse than the disease.

The dilemma of modern capitalism, which Marx did not foresee, is that no policy has been found to solve the financial problem of rising prices without making the real problem of unemployment worse. Behind this lies a further dilemma.

Employment, in a market economy, can be maintained only when investment is profitable. To maintain investment requires continuous growth of output and industrial growth involves continuous consumption of exhaustible natural resources.

'Growth' is advertised to the public as a means of overcoming poverty. This is evidently a deception. Obviously a far greater contribution to human welfare could be made by reducing inequality in the distribution of household incomes, overcoming misery at the bottom of the scale and the need to cater to conspicuous consumption at the top.

To keep up his own courage, Marx predicted that the working class 'constantly increasing in numbers and trained, united and organized by the very mechanism of the capitalist process of production' would finally revolt and take over the system for their own benefit. Up to now, it seems that industrial workers are both intimidated by the complexity of the technology that capitalist development produces and reluctant to imperil the rising standard of life that it provides. This is most marked where the introduction of modern technology into the Third World creates a slowly growing class of relatively privileged industrial workers amid a rapidly growing swamp of non-employment but the same principle seems to be at work also in countries where capitalism has been developing for more than a hundred years since Marx predicted its collapse.

Behind this again, lies a worse dilemma. To maintain 'growth' capitalist governments have to foster investment; investment beneficial to their populations is a concession to socialism so that investment in armaments is preferred. But to justify armaments, it is necessary to have enemies. We cannot blame the Cold War only on commercial motives, but they certainly play a part in preventing it from being called off.

These menacing problems must be discussed in a wider historical setting. Mere economic analysis by itself cannot contribute much to solving them nor can looking up quotations in a book.

The difference between a scientiest and a prophet does not lie in what some great man says but in how it is received. The duty of the pupils of a scientist is to test his hypotheses by looking for evidence to refute them, while the duty of the disciples of a prophet is to go on repeating his very words.